After the Gold Rush

The Henley Centre

The Henley Centre for Forecasting, founded in 1974, is Europe's premier research based consulting organisation. It works closely with some of Europe and America's largest companies as well as government departments and the European Commission. *After the Gold Rush* is the first book to be published under its auspices.

After the Gold Rush

The Trouble with Affluence: 'Consumer
Capitalism' and the Way Forward

Stewart Lansley

CENTURY
BUSINESS
BOOKS

First published 1994
© The Henley Centre 1994 all rights reserved

The Henley Centre has asserted its rights under the Copyright,
Designs and Patents Act, 1988, to be identified as the author of this work.

First published in the United Kingdom in 1994
by Century Limited

Random House, 20 Vauxhall Bridge Road, London SW1V 2SA

Random House Australia (Pty) Limited
20 Alfred Street, Milsons Point, Sydney,
New South Wales 2061, Australia

Random House New Zealand Limited
18 Poland Road, Glenfield,
Auckland 10, New Zealand

Random House South Africa (Pty) Limited
PO Box 337, Bergvlei, South Africa

Random House UK Limited Reg. No. 954009

ISBN 0 09 982450 7 ✔

Typeset by SX Composing Limited, Rayleigh, Essex
Printed by Clays Ltd, St Ives plc

Contents

List of Tables and Figures   vi
Introduction   viii
Acknowledgements   xiii
1.   Out of Joint   1

Part One: The Roots of Malaise   7

2.   A 'Leap-Frogging' Culture   13
3.   The Dream Turns Sour   29
4.   Nice Work If You Can Get It   54
5.   Material World   84
6.   The Rise of 'Competitive Individualism'   107
7.   From 'Ethical' to 'Managerial' Politics   141

Part Two: Out of Malaise?   167

8.   Consumerism – Is There A Limit?   173
9.   The Abstinent Consumer?   195
10.   A New Dawn?   223
    Notes   242
    Bibliography   250
    Index   258

List of Tables and Figures

Table 2.1:   The proportion of households with
             consumer goods, 1990   14
Table 2.2:   The proceeds of growth, percentage
             change, 1978-1990   15
Table 2.3:   Necessities in Britain, 1990   25
Table 3.1:   Unemployed persons receiving neither
             unemployment benefit nor social assistance, 1985   35
Table 3.2:   Changes in national income tax rates   36
Table 4.1:   Unemployment record since the war   69
Table 4.2:   Growth rates of capital stock   77
Table 4.3:   Long term changes in employment patterns   80
Table 6.1:   Government spending as percentage of GDP   115
Table 6.2:   Attitudes to taxation, 1987   126
Table 9.1:   Materialists and post-materialists   203
Table 9.2:   Attitudes to living on present income, 1990   212

Figure 2.1: A hierarchy of wants   21
Figure 3.1: The rise in inequality in the 1980s   32
Figure 3.2: Blaming immigrants, 1992   52
Figure 4.1: Male unemployment and non-employment rates
             (aged 25-54), Average, 1980-89   56
Figure 4.2: Real GDP growth per capita   58
Figure 4.3: Economic fears across Europe, 1992   68
Figure 4.4: Long term unemployed as percentage of
             total unemployed   76
Figure 6.1: A typology of values   120
Figure 6.2: The dominance of 'pragmatic self-interest',
             Great Britain, 1992   122

Figure 6.3:   Lack of confidence in institutions, 1981-1990
      (a)Europe as a whole   128
      (b)Britain   129
Figure 6.4:   Decline in involvement in traditional
      community organisations, Britain   131
Figure 6.5:   Personal aspirations in Europe, 1991   134
Figure 6.6:   Priorities in a new job, Europe, 1991   136
Figure 6.7:   Attitudes to private health care, 1992   138
Figure 7.1:   Outward foreign investment as a proportion
      of exports   153
Figure 8.1:   Satisfaction with the life you lead, 1973-90   174
Figure 8.2:   Stress in Europe, 1992   178
Figure 8.3:   The time-money paradox, 1992   180
Figure 8.4:   Comparing growth in GNP and the index
      of economic welfare   190
Figure 9.1:   Competitive individualism and affluence   199
Figure 9.2:   Willingness to pay a premium for
      environmentally sound products, Britain   206
Figure 9.3:   Exploding 'needs and wants'   210
Figure 9.4:   A path to material saturation   211
Figure 9.5:   Consumer awareness, 1992   213

Introduction

As the western world approaches the end of the century it does so at one of the most critical points in its post-war history. Its future is now more uncertain than at any time since the end of the Second World War. Dogged by an unstable global economy, widespread political fatalism and deep-seated public disaffection, few commentators are willing to offer coherent or optimistic forecasts of the next few years let alone the next decade.

The key reason for such uncertainty is that the world's richest societies are facing structural changes from without and within that are making political and economic management much more difficult than it has been in the past. Not since the 1930s have modern societies been faced by such difficult challenges.

This book was commissioned by the Henley Centre to draw on its special brand of analysis to try to make sense of the wider forces now shaping modern developments and to lay out the alternative scenarios for the future. At first sight this might seem like an unusual departure for the Centre. Our business has been to help private and public organisations understand the dynamics of the environment in which they have to operate, and to assist them in translating that understanding into practical action.

The success of the Henley Centre – which this year celebrates its 20th anniversary – lies in its reputation for offering a distinctive service to clients. It has done so by attempting to offer a much fuller picture of the wider forces at work in shaping our economic and social destinies.

It is especially true today that the fortunes of companies, public institutions and individuals depend upon what happens to the 'big picture'. We believe that the particular combination of social, economic and political circumstances in the 1990s is such that the stage is set for fundamental transformations in the way that everything operates, from everyday life to the economic and political relationships between regions of the world.

One source of this dramatic change is the external environment. Since the late 1980s, the global balance has been transformed by the collapse of communism in Eastern Europe, the break up of the Soviet Union, the completion of the single market in the European Community and the rapid economic rise of the countries of the Pacific rim. These momentous, and largely unpredicted, events led many to believe, and hope, that we could be in for a period of relative economic and political calm and the development of a new and more stable world order.

It has not turned out like that. The temptation has been to see the changes on the international stage as the key motors of movement. Yet they have not been operating in isolation. These changes have meshed with other *internal forces* to create a much more unstable and unpredictable climate. Indeed, while the changes that are taking place within societies have been given less attention they are as, if not more important in shaping current trends.

A particular focus of our analysis has been how relationships between individuals and between individuals and institutions have been altering. In retrospect, the period from the end of the last war to the early 1970s has turned out to be a unique one. This has often been said since the 1970s when oil shocks and the ensuing 'stag-flation' made the period that preceded it appear a golden age. However, until now the terms of the analysis have typically been about the problems of economic management. The key to understanding the success of that period and, by contrast, many of the difficulties we face today requires a broader analysis of the social and political as well as the economic factors that created the settlement that we have termed in the book 'welfare capitalism'.

We believe that there are a series of long run and predominantly 'internal' social, political and economic changes that are undermining the traditional bases for understanding, operating in and (for governments) running our modern societies. These are what *After the Gold Rush* concentrates on. Today, the fortunes of everyone are heavily dependent on the 'total system'. Politics, social values, individual expectations and economic relationships have never been hermetically sealed, but their interactions are now even more critical in understanding the evolution of today's more complex societies. This book is our attempt to provide a better understanding of this total system as a means of explaining the roots of the volcanic changes facing modern nations.

Of course, the trends in modern societies have a variety of roots. No single explanation can account for the variety of experiences and complexity of change taking place. What we have attempted to do is concentrate on what we see as the key, and often under explored forces at work.

Our analysis of trends starts by trying to understand what the growth and spread of prosperity had done to contemporary societies. A central thesis of the book relates to the impact of widening affluence on individual and social expectations and behaviour. One of the key problems of the management of modern societies can be traced to the growth of unsustainable demands and expectations. These unmet demands have contributed to economic instability, deepening public disaffection and widening social divisions.

Simultaneously driving and expressing the changes inherent in the growth of affluence has been a phenomenon which we have christened 'competitive individualism'. While greater autonomy and individuality is a wholly beneficial trend, the problem has been that the individualism that has been developing is an essentially intolerant one that has contributed to a loss of social and community cohesion. Unless individualism can evolve to take a more cooperative form, the risk is that the divisions between the winners and losers in the more competitive societies being created will push the fabric of western societies to breaking point.

Let us stress that our concern about 'competitive individualism' and our association of the phenomenon, explained in the book, with an excessive consumerism is not because we condemn the phenomenon outright.

Rather, our concern is with its pervasive nature in contemporary society. To function more effectively our societies need a new pluralism. We need to value a number of 'currencies' other than materialism and material success. Consumerism has a dynamic and constructive role to play in a modern society. But we need additional sources of reward, motivation and symbolic values to those found in the consumer marketplace. To that extent maybe it is to be regretted that we have all become 'customers' and ceased to be passengers, patients, voters and . . . *citizens*.

This singular and dominating market or customer model is not enough to understand, organise, motivate and reward individuals in our societies. It is not just that a singular society of this sort may feel emptier, flat, levelled, spiritually bereft. It is a practical concern we have that there are physical and social limits on the amount of that single currency to go around.

Although this book draws on a great deal of Henley Centre data, ideas and methodology it needs to be stressed that we do not necessarily endorse everything that is contained in it. Nor do we expect our clients to buy the whole thesis. We have commissioned it as one contribution to a better understanding of the character of the societies being created and the options being faced for the future.

We have also commissioned it because the issues raised are ones of vital importance to individuals and organisations and because we believe that they deserve a wider audience than the narrower client base that is usually privy to Henley Centre output. We hope that the analysis offered will add to a debate that is already beginning to emerge and that is desperately needed about how to break the impasse into which modern societies seem to have steered themselves.

Today's governments and institutions, both at national and international level, seem increasingly to be characterised by a lack of imagination. That mood needs to be overturned if modern societies are to find the will and the means to tackle what are in danger of becoming irreversible problems of division and instability.

We do not go on to make detailed predictions of what the rest of the decade and beyond has in store. The future is unknowable, not least because it depends upon the choices and decisions of individuals, organisations and political parties. Instead, the book ends its analysis not with a single view of how western societies will develop but with a series of three scenarios. These are not intended to provide a definitive list but to give an idea of the range of possibilities now facing the world's richest nations. The balance of the options laid out is essentially pessimistic.

Sadly, it has to be said, very recent developments have only served to reinforce our sense of pessimism. The quite legitimate and important debate about the future size and the funding of welfare state expenditures in Europe threatens to become infected by the worst features of competitive individualism. The biggest political idea of the last twelve months coming from any party seems to have been the rediscovery of irredeemably evil people, beyond possibilities of secular salvation. Less dramatically, new categories of social deviant are being invented (smokers, single mothers) to legitimate their exclusion from social support.

Only one of the scenarios – the least likely – could we describe as optimistic. We call the scenario 'optimistic' because it sees continuing increases in levels of overall prosperity along with increasing social cohesion. We see this as the least likely scenario not because the changes in individual and social behaviour needed to bring about a simultaneously dynamic and cohesive world are impossible to conceive. Rather it is because if the conditions can exist in logic and in the imagination, in reality they seem a long way off. Bringing them closer is a challenge that faces all of us that believe a more cohesive, inclusive society to be both desirable as an aspiration for the future and pragmatically necessary if we are able to have a future.

Bob Tyrrell
Chief Executive
The Henley Centre
January 1994

Acknowledgements

As with all books, this is the product of collective effort. My greatest debt is to the Henley Centre which generously provided employment, a base, and, above all, access to their own original surveys, research and ideas.

At the Centre, special thanks are due to Bob Tyrrell and Paul Ormerod for initiating the project, for encouragement throughout, for helpful comments on successive drafts and for many of the ideas in the book. Without them, it would not have appeared. I am also grateful to other colleagues at the Centre: to Steve Barnett and Leon Kreitzman who gave generously of their time to comment on drafts and to discuss many of the book's themes, to Michael Wilmott, Fiona Stewart and Jim Murphy for many helpful discussions and to Ann Tritton for preparing the tables.

Thanks are also due to Jon Shields and Steve Schifferes for invaluable comments on drafts; to Noel Timms who kindly provided the data for figure 6.3; to Peter Taylor-Gooby for helpful comments on chapter 6; to David Gordon and Christina Pantazis for undertaking special analyses of the 'Breadline Britain' data in chapter 2; to Stephen Webb for advice on Chapter 6; to Alan Murie and Ray Forrest for advice on chapter 3; and to Alan Day, Francisco Estela, Alex Hanisch, Ranveig Jacobsson, Jean-Marc Laforest, Derek Reed, Friedrich Roll, Tessa Ryan, Jesper Schunk, Rob Van de Water and Giancarlo Vilella for help with European political and social trends.

Finally, I would like to thank Charles Elliott at Random House for ruthless, but essential, editing! Ultimate responsibility, of course, remains with the author.

Stewart Lansley
September, 1993

1. Out of Joint

Peter: We could get a nice flat in a nice part of London, go to the sunshine whenever we want to, take all the sweat out of life. Enjoy it. Life's too short for all the aggravation.

Polly: That's not what I want.

Peter: Well, what do you want? Working in a factory, living in a two up, two down, a zinc bath on Fridays, egg and chips for tea, living on what we earn?

Polly: A lot of people do it.

Peter: Do you think they want to?

Polly: Look, I know what money does to people. I know what it's like to be rich. It destroys you. It makes you false and useless.

(Nell Dunn)[1]

We do not want to enter the age of abundance, only to find we have lost the values which might teach us how to enjoy it.

(Anthony Crosland)[2]

No decade since the war began with such a strong sense of foreboding as the 1990s. War and recession in Europe. Famine in a third of Africa. Growing and unsustainable migration. A deteriorating global environment. The erosion of political and economic stability throughout the west.

The crisis of the nineties is not confined to the problems of political and economic adjustment in Eastern Europe nor to persistent impoverishment in large parts of the developing world. Despite claims of the final triumph of western liberal capitalism, the democratised west is facing its own deep-seated crises of identity and management. Western values seem increasingly out of tune with the needs of modern societies.

The global recession has been one symptom of the wider malaise, and one compounded by a growing national economic impotence. Another has been a mounting disenchantment with government and with mainstream political parties. Governments everywhere are suffering from tarnished images of incompetence, failure and often corruption. Most world leaders have suffered widespread unpopularity. Europe has entered a period of turbulence and upheaval that has brought political revolution in Italy, the near elimination of the Socialist Party in France, rising neo-Nazism in Germany, and the eclipse of social democracy in Sweden. In the United States, a change of Presidency has done little to satisfy a restive electorate.

These symptoms of disquiet are not confined to growing public disaffection with elected governments and traditional parties. There is a much deeper sense of unease that is reflected in widespread uncertainty, in growing social unrest and lack of purpose, in a declining sense of the common good. Crime and drug addiction seem set on an irreversible upward course. Societies have lost their way and become increasingly difficult to govern. With the steady decline of social democracy and the apparently early failure of the pro-market experiments, political conviction has given way to uncertainty and self-doubt, and ideology to pragmatism as a governing philosophy.

The international institutions established over decades to deal with the growing global interdependence have also been found wanting on the major issues. Invested with so much early hope, the European Community has become riven by discord and doubt. The attempt at greater international co-operation through the European Exchange Rate Mechanism fell foul of the very global instability it was designed to prevent. Summits of world leaders have failed to come up with effective answers to tackle global recession and the return of mass unemployment. The United Nations has proved no match for international crises from Somalia to Bosnia. International attempts at co-operation to tackle environmental deterioration have achieved relatively little and the development policies of the World Bank have contributed to ever deeper divisions between the world's richest and poorest. While international co-operation is ever more vital, it seems increasingly difficult to achieve.

These problems of governance in the world's economically advanced nations have a variety of roots. Some commentators have blamed them on the collapse of the cold war. The demise of communism has, it is argued, swept away the old ideological enemy that was necessary to secure a sense of common purpose in the west. The Soviet ideological and military threat provided a cohesion and gave meaning to western goals and institutions. The removal of this opponent brought an initial euphoria which has slowly given way to a deeper void.

It is true that some contemporary problems have been accentuated by the collapse of communism which was bound to create at least a temporary identity crisis for the western victors. Germany's problems can, in part, be traced to unification. The rising tide of refugees sweeping in from Eastern Europe has added to political and economic pressures stemming from other sources. In the United States, the removal of the old enemy has left a vacuum that is being filled by a deepening concern with formerly neglected domestic politics.

The increasing globalisation of the world economy and the accompanying revolution in technology is another contributory factor. Both have had the effect of intensifying the nature of international competition and weakening the power of the nation state. The rapid economic rise of first, South East Asia, and now, China, is transforming the global economic balance and posing a new challenge to the economic dominance of North America and Europe.

These external pressures are important. They have changed the nature of global competition and of international purpose. But they are not the only forces at work. Changes in the *external* political and economic environment have also been accompanied by major shifts in the *internal* character of modern societies. It is the contention of

3

this book that western upheaval is as much the product of internal as of external trends.

The roots of dislocation lie in the wider impact of the steady move from scarcity to affluence in the developed world. This has transformed individual aspirations, economic management, the nature of politics and the character of government. In general, people in richer societies are more individualistic, self-dependent and competitive and the society itself potentially more divisive and unstable. It is these forces that have been eroding the elements of the post-war blueprint which brought political consensus, economic success and sustained social stability for close on a generation. In this sense, the rise of affluence across post-war western societies has sown the seeds of its own demise. Material progress has brought many benefits but at a price, simultaneously contributing to the mounting problems of political management and to economic and structural instability.

The irony is that greater wealth was seen as the route to creating better societies, the means to greater prosperity for everyone and the solution to poverty and unemployment. Growth has long been the single most important goal of western governments. For three decades after the war, historically high and stable growth brought lower unemployment and rising living standards in most western societies. Absolute poverty fell. More resources became available to build the welfare states that contributed to more equal and socially cohesive societies.

That success, however, proved unsustainable. Rising prosperity has failed to bring many of the social and economic improvements that it once promised, and has become much more unevenly shared than in the earlier period. Rising living standards for the majority have been accompanied by falling or static living standards for a minority. Job opportunities have expanded for some groups but declined for others. Unemployment is universally higher than it was. Economic crises have become more frequent and more difficult to handle.

A central explanation for these contradictions is the growing mismatch between aspirations and social capacity that has accompanied growing affluence. Expectations have risen out of line with economic, social and environmental potential, putting increasing strains on the way societies function. People's

4

interpretation of their own interests has changed as societies have become more affluent. The growing middle core has become more self-dependent and less supportive of state intervention and redistributive welfare. Growing individualism has combined with greater competitiveness to create a new climate of 'competitive individualism' which is neither consistent with economic efficiency nor with social and economic stability. Greater internal competition and declining social protection have enabled today's winners to outbid the losers, contributing to growing and more intractable divisions and to deepening instability.

This is not to claim that the shift from success to failure as affluence has progressed is inevitable. There is no iron law which says that prosperity is automatically associated with social decline. Indeed, although the direction and processes of change are relatively common across societies, their impact has varied. Although most western societies have been facing similar external and internal pressures of economic and social shift, albeit from a variety of institutional backgrounds, different starting points, and at different speeds, some have coped with these forces more easily than others. The changes are therefore incomplete and uneven across countries.

The societies that have proved best able to withstand the pressures at work have been those that have been least infected by the new culture of competitive individualism, that have maintained a sense of the importance of consensual behaviour and that have been best able to keep expectations in line with economic capacity. It is no coincidence that the most successful nations, economically and socially, of the last twenty years have been those which have maintained a better balance between individual and social responsibility, between competition and co-operation, between personal freedom and state planning and intervention.

The first signs of upheaval came in the United States and then Britain. Most of mainland Europe held on for longer as did Japan. Now even the most successful are beginning to show similar symptoms of malaise. Germany and Sweden, for example, that found successful formulas for combining economic vitality and social stability, are now beginning to face the same contradictions suffered by the less successful nations. Even the traditionally frugal Japanese population is showing signs of a lower inclination to accept the sacrifices of the past that contributed to the nation's high investment, its post-war 'economic miracle' and its ability to adjust to the oil crisis of the 1970s.

The book's argument is divided into two parts. Part one looks at the roots of the present crisis – to what extent is western malaise related to the economic, political and social impact of the rise of affluence? Part two considers the prospects for the future. Is it possible to secure another shift in social behaviour and political culture that could enable affluent societies to use the proceeds of prosperity to create more socially stable societies? Or are the forces at work too powerful to resist?

Part One:
The Roots of Malaise

After the war, most western nations adopted a new approach to political and economic management that can best be termed 'welfare capitalism'. Nations emerged from the war with popular demands to create greater fairness. Governments across the political spectrum set out to achieve more harmonious societies, with a much more central role for state intervention. With some exceptions, this period was a time of broad political and social consensus, of economic success and social stability, in which the economic insecurity and instability of the pre-war decade gradually gave way to steady and stable growth and lower unemployment.

The economically developed world moved from the pre-war age of scarcity to the beginnings of the age of affluence, from a society where the majority were struggling to meet every-day basic needs to one where these were taken largely for granted across most, though far from all, groups in society. The success of this period was the product of a special and probably unique set of economic, social and political circumstances. Consensus helped to create an era of the 'politics of inclusion', characterised by a more developed sense of social responsibility and the public good, and the wider goal of full employment which contributed to declining inequality. Although expectations were high, societies had found the means to ensure that they were largely met so that inflation could be kept in check and full employment maintained.

In the first three decades after the war, economic success ushered in by a virtuous circle of rising productivity, wages and investment enabled governments of all political persuasions across Europe to fund the public welfare programmes that in turn contributed to the economic stability and social cohesion of the era. Incomes rose steadily and industry prospered. Mass consumption and mass production moved along hand-in-hand. This was a largely bipartisan era: politicians of Left and Right embraced the changes; private industry was happy to go along with the social reformism of the period since it helped to create the mass demand which was the pre-condition for the long and sustained post-war boom.

A new and successful formula for running societies had apparently been found involving a mixture of Keynesian economics and state welfarism. This was the age of controlled markets in which unsatisfied consumer appetites alongside public redistribution became the twin motors of change. A buoyant level of demand created by rising consumer spending and high public and private investment were the route to full employment. This in turn provided the additional resources for spending on improved social welfare.

This success could not be maintained and gradually gave way to a new era of growing political dissent, of deteriorating economic performance, of rising social instability and political disenchantment. In the process, the welfare capitalism of the post-war era has gradually been evolving into a new model of what we may call 'consumer capitalism'. The new commitments to full employment and social protection that characterised post-war politics and which underpinned the successes of that period have been gradually scaled back.

The last two decades have seen a reversal of many of the earlier gains, with the return of mass unemployment and growing economic and social divisions. The richer nations have continued to get wealthier, albeit at a slower pace, *but* the fruits of that rising wealth have been much more unevenly shared with the rise of a new 'politics of exclusion'. Most societies have lost their former power or commitment to use the gains of growing material wealth in ways that bring benefits to all. The escalator of opportunity has continued upwards for most but has slowed, stopped or even gone into reverse for a minority.

The nature of economic relationships has changed, breaking the former link between economic growth and social justice. Continued growth no longer guarantees low unemployment, and has also been increasingly associated with widening wage differentials. What sense of civic politics and obligations that had existed has faded. Individual aspirations and attitudes have shifted bringing changing economic and social priorities. The state has become a much weaker instrument of redistribution as the former appetite for political change and intervention has waned. These changes have in turn made economic and social management more difficult than it was in the past.

This evolution fits the experience of most of the leading industrial societies, though the process has gone further in some nations than others. Nearly all have suffered slower growth, rising unemployment, more fragmented societies and lower levels of social cohesion, though with varying degrees of intensity. The United States, for example, has always maintained a weaker attachment to welfarism. It has always been much closer to the model of consumer capitalism.

After the war, most of Europe built societies that fitted the description of welfare capitalism. Britain was the first European nation to start to break from that tradition, and has gone furthest along the road from 'welfarism' to 'consumerism'. In more recent years, other countries have started to follow the same path. Few have been able to resist the problems of rising unemployment, slower growth, deepening fragmentation and rising political insecurity. All have faced the wider forces that have brought a more consumerist and individualistic culture. Even those nations that have been able to cope most successfully with the structural forces in play are now facing similar symptoms of shift.

These structural changes have a variety of roots, but they all have a common link in the move from scarcity to affluence, in which the rise of prosperity has contributed to its own undoing. The source of this paradox lies in five interwoven factors – the rise of relative and explosive aspirations, the growing problems of economic management, the rise of a new governing ethos of 'competitive individualism', the spread of consumerism and consumerist values, an erosion of the 'politics of inclusion'. The mechanisms underlying these interlocking factors are outlined in part one.

2. A 'Leap-Frogging' Culture

If everyone stands on tiptoe, no one sees better.

(F. Hirsch)[3]

In past times, the economically and socially fortunate were, as we know, a small minority – characteristically a dominant and ruling handful. They are now a majority . . . They will be called the Contented Majority, the Contented Electoral Majority, or more spaciously, the Culture of Contentment.

(J. K. Galbraith)[4]

No period of modern history has enjoyed such a rapid rate of economic growth as the post-war era. Since the war, average living standards across the nations of the OECD have risen more than threefold.[5] The majority of the population in the world's richest nations enjoy choices and opportunities that were undreamt of by previous generations. Mass scarcity has been replaced by mass affluence. Modern populations are much better fed, clothed, housed and educated.

'Mismatch'

Rising incomes have meant that the consumption horizons that were the preserve of the minority have gradually become more widely available. The consumption patterns of the better off have become the norm rather than the exception. Home ownership, foreign travel, car usage have moved from minority to majority activities. Luxuries enjoyed by the few have become necessities possessed by the many, and have been replaced by new products to satisfy the apparently unlimited appetites of those on the highest incomes. The

13

Table 2.1: The proportion of households with consumer goods, 1990

	Europe	France	Nether-lands	West Germany	Belgium	Italy	GB	Sweden
Fridge	97	99	99	98	95	99	95	95
Television	97	94	98	97	97	98	98	97
Washing machine	85	87	92	90	84	96	78	75
Telephone	84	85	95	89	78	88	85	96
Vacuum cleaner	82	89	98	97	91	55	98	95
Deep-freezer	76	76	81	73	82	87	80	92
Car	69	75	69	69	77	80	63	77
Full-central heating	65	69	78	79	58	65	71	94
Hi-fi system	55	59	90	56	63	37	65	71
Video	41	35	48	42	42	25	58	48
2 or more televisions	38	29	42	32	25	48	55	43
Food processor	36	57	28	49	38	26	31	57
Microwave oven	25	24	19	32	22	6	49	40
Electric dishwasher	22	33	10	31	25	17	12	38
2 or more cars	21	26	11	15	19	35	19	20
Second home	11	12	4	9	9	15	4	16

Source: Reader's Digest, 1991

consumer items listed in table 2.1 were either available to only small minorities or simply did not exist before the Second World War.

This revolution in living standards stands as one of the most significant trends of the post-war era. It has changed the character of modern living, transformed attitudes and recast expectations. Ironically, such a rapid improvement in material well-being might have been expected to bring a moderation in aspirations. In fact, it has done the opposite. Consumer desires have expanded not contracted, creating unsustainable expectations. This in turn has contributed to today's increasingly 'aspirant culture' and the growing problems of instability facing the richest nations.

Many of the contemporary problems of political and social management can be traced, at least in part, to the mismatch between aspirations and economic and social capacity which pervades every aspect of modern living. People want the latest gadget as soon as it appears on the market, wage rises outstrip productivity, public spending is not matched by a willingness to pay. Crimes are rising faster than the capacity of the judicial system. Roads can't cope with the soaring traffic. Many of the world's largest cities are becoming too big to function effectively. The demand for improved health care is becoming more and more difficult to meet.

Table 2.2: The proceeds of growth, percentage change, 1978–1990

	UK	US	Japan	Germany	France
Private consumption	45.7	36.4	54.6	24.7	35.3
Public consumption	16.2	37.2	38.1	19.8	32.4
Gross fixed capital formation	45.8	18.7	82.2	31.9	32.0
GNP	29.0	31.9	65.3	29.7	32.0
Private consumption as % of GNP					
1978	58.0	64.6	61.6	58.9	56.5
1990	65.5	66.8	57.7	56.6	60.4

Source: Author's calculations from OECD, 1991

The poor aspire to the living standards of those on middle incomes. Those on middle incomes lust after the lifestyles of the rich. The more people have been getting the more they seem to want. Societies want more than is available, creating frustration, dissatisfaction and social discontent. The same pressures contributed to the steady rise in individual, corporate and public debt during the 1980s in which whole populations were effectively borrowing from future generations.

Another effect of this trend has been that the reality of material progress seems at odds with people's own perceptions. Despite the objective improvement in material living standards, majorities claim that they do not feel much better off. Large numbers continue to complain of finding it difficult to manage and higher living standards have not been associated with rising satisfaction, a paradox common to all leading economic nations (see figure 8.1). Creating societies in which even the rich feel poor is a recipe for permanent instability.

Part of the explanation for this mismatch lies in the very economic success of the immediate post-war era. Societies and governments got used to the improvements in consumption, welfare and investment that high growth was able to bring. These heightened expectations have not easily been moderated in the slower growth era of the last two decades. On average, the OECD nations grew by 4.7 per cent a year between 1950 and 1973, but by only 2.4 per cent between 1973 and 1987. One consequence has been that the proceeds of growth have been increasingly allocated to improving levels of consumption, though more so in some nations than others as shown in table 2.2. This problem of 'over-consumption' is especially acute in Britain, the United States and France but less so in Japan and Germany.

The 'affluence effect'

The slowdown of growth is only part of the explanation. The emergence of mass affluence has, itself, led to more fundamental changes in the character of aspirations and of social and personal relationships and behaviour. These, as shown in chapter 4, have contributed to the problems of rising inflation and greater economic turbulence that have led to the poorer economic performance of the last two decades.

A key characteristic of prosperity has been the growing importance attached to relativities. We live in performance related societies which affect work, status, leisure, even friendships. Ambitions are increasingly moulded by others, their jobs, wants and achievements, rather than ourselves or our own families. Individuals measure their success in relation to other individuals and groups, communities in relation to other communities, nations in relation to other nations. Living standards are judged not according to those of the past, less in relation to those of others in their own social grouping, and more to those who are better off. The pleasure we get from the jobs we do, the cars we drive, the holidays we take depends less on our intrinsic enjoyment of them than on how they seem to compare with others.

Part of the explanation for this lies in the distinction between absolute and relative needs. Some items we consume bring enjoyment independently of what others have. The more we have, the more pleasure we get. Other possessions we want not necessarily for their intrinsic worth but according to whether other people have them. This is, in essence, economic jargon for what is more widely known as 'keeping up with the Joneses'. It means that our satisfaction depends on how we see our ranking against others.

Even if we are better off today than in the past, we may actually feel worse off if our perceived ranking has fallen or if we have not made as much progress as we hoped. Satisfaction depends as much on closing the gap as on improving our absolute position. Satisfaction often seems to be a matter of exclusivity. A Porsche remains a status symbol because of its rarity. It gives its owner the distinction of superiority. The appeal would disappear if the car were as common as a Ford Escort. Expensive trainers would lose their significance if too many people wore them.

The more the pleasure we derive from consumption depends on comparisons with others, with keeping up with or pulling away from the Joneses, then the more satisfaction is unlikely to improve through time as living standards rise, and the more unrealistic expectations are likely to become. Those enjoying the privilege of modern status symbols would lose satisfaction if the items became more widely available. Those lacking them feel, and are encouraged to feel, that they are missing out. If everybody gets better off at the same rate, with no changes in relative positions, nobody improves their satisfaction. If people switch positions, some gain and some lose.

Although it is doubtful that the 'relativity' hypothesis – that satisfaction from higher consumption depends on improving our relative position – can account for more than a portion of consumer behaviour, it is arguable that it becomes more significant as societies get richer. The principal reason for this 'affluence effect' is that as more people are able to satisfy their basic needs, a rising proportion of consumption is geared to the meeting of symbolic needs, which are more likely to be the subject of relativities. It applies, for example, not merely to the obvious status symbols cited above, but increasingly to other more ordinary aspects of living such as clothing, food and furnishings. This helps to explain several characteristics of consumer societies examined in chapter 5 – the obsession with shopping, the significance of the purchase, and the ephemeral character of fashion.

Status is not only provided by owning. It also applies to giving. In recent years, charity has become an increasingly open activity. We are prepared to give if we are seen to do so. Organisations have seen the advantage of this and have been arranging public events with big names and highly priced entry tickets. The Labour Party raised large sums of money through dinners costing £500 a head. Private donations of this kind would never provide the same opportunity.

The economist, Fred Hirsch, took this argument a step further by distinguishing between 'material goods', the supply of which is essentially unlimited, and 'positional goods', which are either scarce or subject to congestion or crowding through extensive use.[6] Increases in the consumption of material goods for which satisfaction is independent of what others do will bring enhanced pleasure while those of 'positional goods' will be subject to diminishing returns. Hirsch's example of a pure material good was the satisfaction derived by a hungry man from a square meal which is unaffected by the meals other people eat. Positional goods include items like country houses, old masters and remote holiday resorts whose supply is scarce, and goods like foreign holidays and cars where the pleasure from consumption depends critically on how widely available they are.

In general, material goods are more likely to be necessities and positional goods luxuries such that the demand for positional goods rises as societies become more affluent. In less wealthy societies, the priority is for meeting largely physical needs through the increased production of material goods. As societies get richer, the desire for positional goods rises at a faster rate than that of material goods.

The effect of this process is that the early stages of emergence out of scarcity bring gains for individuals and for society as a whole, but that these gains become more limited as societies get richer. In poorer societies, consumption is concentrated on basic material goods. The positional sector is correspondingly uncrowded. As standards rise throughout society, the increasing demand for positional goods will both raise their relative price and force individuals to seek substitutes which absorb resources which could be used for other more pressing material needs.

If only a fixed and small minority of the population can enjoy an exclusive holiday or a rare painting or a country cottage, those enjoying them as well as those competing for them will find they need higher and higher real incomes to retain exclusive access. Consumers need more real income simply to stand still. They are forced to maintain or improve their relative position just to maintain their absolute consumption level. Increments of pleasure will fall while the wider social costs of use will rise. Eventually, consumption will be extended to the point at which these costs begin to outweigh the benefits. Hirsch drew largely pessimistic conclusions from this analysis. He foresaw a world where 'relativities' of all sorts became people's principal concern, a world of endemic inflationary pressures, of growing social conflict and of a hopelessly zero sum game in which one person's increase in welfare was matched by another's decrease in welfare.

As well as helping to explain the paradox that people do not feel better off despite increases in material living standards, this process provides at least a partial explanation of both the 'competitive individualism' and the unsustainable expectations of modern societies. The consumer process comes to resemble a competitive rat race in which the better off are simply racing to keep ahead of the rest who are battling to keep up. The effect of this constant jostling for position has been the emergence of a 'leap-frogging' culture. The consumption process has become an increasingly vicious cycle in which it is difficult for societies to make continuous gains in welfare. It implies that increases in material well-being eventually reach a point of diminishing returns, that this cycle of chasing our tail in search of higher satisfaction from more consumption is ultimately futile. There is a limit to the process by which what the rich have today is passed on to the poor tomorrow. We can't all drive fast cars to work, have country cottages in unspoiled locations, be chief executives of ICI.

Modern societies correspond only too closely to Hirsch's predictions. They have become ever more competitive. It has become even more important to keep ahead of the field with even more people in the race. This situation has been compounded by another factor associated with rising prosperity. How people view their living standard depends on what Gary Runciman has called their 'reference group'.[7] As societies get wealthier, these points of comparison change. In poorer times the pull of imitation is minimised by the more limited nature of people's reference groups and aspirations.

In the pre-war years of austerity, for example, the aspirations of the poor majority were heavily capped, moulded by the relatively modest appetites of their own social grouping. Working class families, then the dominant social grouping, related closely to their own community and class, and were more likely to have accepted their lot. Consumer horizons in the 1930s extended little beyond a weekly visit to the local dance hall, the occasional outing to the cinema and maybe a wireless and eventually a gramophone. This has become much less the case as societies have become more prosperous and more open and visible. People's sights have become less horizontal and more vertical. Today's expectations are upwards not sideways. Poorer groups judge their success much less in relation to their own social grouping than to those who have reached a higher rung.

The effect of this aspirant culture is that the desire for 'conspicuous consumption' has spread from the few to the many. This expression was first coined by Thornstein Veblen in 1899 as a description of the extravagant and ostentatious lifestyles of the small elite of the leisured classes on both sides of the Atlantic.[8] For parts of the twentieth century, it is arguable that such ostentation became a source of embarrassment and diminished as a consequence. As one sociologist described the United States in the early 1950s, 'the crazy millionaire is dead, and a subdued nonconspicuousness seems to be spreading over our styles in leisure and consumption practices'.[9]

As the post-war years passed, the rich gradually made a comeback as a social phenomenon. Curiosity about the lifestyles of the rich and the famous re-emerged. Money increasingly became a measure of status and success, and so had to be flaunted. Conspicuous consumption returned and spread. This has had a major impact on the process of relativities described. While the activities of the rich elite may remain more a matter of curiosity than aspiration, it has been the lifestyles and living standards of the affluent and comfortable middle that have set the pace.

This pattern not only applies within nations. Internationalism, the media and travel have extended horizons beyond national boundaries. This has also created problems of unsustainable expectations among the populations of poorer countries. The protest movements which contributed to the demise of communism in Eastern Europe were, at least in part, a product of the desire for western lifestyles. Rapid economic growth among the Asian dragons and in parts of China is having a similar impact. Migration is the product of the same phenomenon. If the poorest countries cannot achieve the living standards of the richest, their inhabitants will seek to migrate in order to find them.

Growing expectations with rising prosperity is also the product of a change in the character of personal consumption through the steady addition of 'wants' to traditional 'needs'. The idea of an order of needs and wants has come from Abraham Maslow.[10] He distinguished a hierarchy of five – physiological, safety, belonging, love and esteem, self-actualisation – in ascending order of importance. As the physiological needs for food and shelter are met, 'higher' needs begin to emerge. They begin with the desire for safety, order and security, move on to the desire for belonging and love, and then 'self-esteem' through recognition and approval by others, and ending with a final, open-ended motivation for emotional and intellectual fulfilment, for the full use of one's potential.

The hierarchy shown in figure 2.1 is a development of Maslow's to fit contemporary societies. In poorer societies, there is a dominating concern with basic physical or survival needs of food, shelter and clothing. As people become better off, their aspirations shift towards the satisfaction of the social needs of participation and activity. People spend money on travel, on seeing friends, on holidays and entertainment. Higher income leads to a third stage, involving the addition of 'wants' or 'desires' to the satisfaction of 'needs', or a switch from 'survival' to 'having'. People spend more money on housing than is needed to satisfy the biological

Figure 2.1: A hierarchy of wants

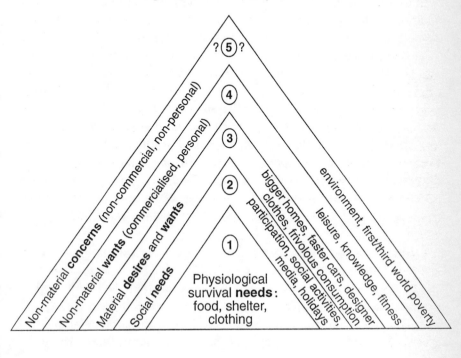

21

requirements for shelter. They buy bigger and faster cars, more expensive clothes.

Spending next shifts to non-material but essentially personal wants such as leisure and fitness activities and the pursuit of knowledge or achievement. This four stage hierarchy fits the pattern of progress towards affluence. The question remains as to whether these wants continue to expand indefinitely, or whether there is a limit to the idea of relativities, that after a certain level, there are diminishing returns to further increases in material well-being. Whether a fifth and final layer of 'non-material concerns', or what some have called 'post-material values' exists, such as a non-personal interest in tackling poverty or improving the environment, and what it means for the function of affluent societies, is an issue returned to in chapter 9.

An 'affluent but discontented majority'

During the 1980s, Peter Glotz, the General Secretary of the German Social Democratic Party (the SPD), described Germany as a 'two-thirds, one-third society', a potent phrase that has become increasingly widely used as a description of today's affluent nations. Glotz was referring to the evolution of post-war Germany from the 'one-third, two-thirds' structure that existed before the war. Others have talked of the growth of an affluent majority or, as Galbraith has put it, of a new 'culture of contentment'.[11]

Rising prosperity has not merely changed lifestyles and aspirations, it has transformed the social structure. Where today's affluent societies differ from the scarce ones of the past is in the growth of a larger middle group. This has led some to talk of a move from yesterday's 'pyramid-shaped' society with a small and privileged minority of the rich, a larger but still small and comfortable middle group and a very large and poor base, to today's 'egg shape' with a small group of the rich and the poor and a much fatter middle.

None of these provide a strictly accurate description of what have become highly complex societies. Nevertheless, they do give a sense of the reality. Most affluent societies have a rich group at the top, a comfortable middle and a poorer group at the bottom, with the actual division varying from society to society. All have moved from a situation of an essentially poor and insecure majority to a relatively affluent and comfortable top and middle. Measured in an absolute sense, living standards have improved dramatically leading to a growing proportion living above what would have been considered a reasonable standard measured at some point in the past.

The contradictions inherent in affluent societies including the rise of discontent among the affluent majority can, in part, be traced to the fact that this objective improvement has not been matched by changes in people's subjective assessment of their situation. This is because the standard against which people judge their living conditions has also moved. How affluent and content people feel depends as much on how they see their relative position as on their objective position. The more their expectations rise in relation to actual improvements in material well-being the less affluent they are likely to feel and the less satisfied they are likely to be. Although they are more than three times as well off as their grandparents' generation, many and probably most of today's top half would not see themselves as part of an 'affluent majority'.

Whether such an affluent majority exists depends, of course, on where the line is drawn. Neither a pure absolute nor a pure relative standard are very useful for making a distinction. A strict absolute approach would allow for no changes in lifestyle through time, while a pure relative approach suggests societies continue to stand still with material progress unless there is a change in the distribution of income. An alternative, and ultimately more objective, approach is to measure affluence in relation to the hierarchy of wants shown in figure 2.1. *Indeed, the definition in this book of an affluent society is one in which a clear majority has been able to satisfy their physical and social needs and is able to enjoy at least some material and non-material wants.*

This definition embraces an element of both the absolute and relative approaches. The poor are those unable to satisfy their essentially absolute physical and social needs, though defined in relation to contemporary standards. The affluent are all those above this level and able to enjoy some essentially relative wants. This distinction could, of course, be refined to subdivide the affluent between the comfortable and the rich.

Simple observation would suggest that the world's richest nations have all satisfied this affluence criterion. Consumerism has reached the point where a clear majority lead more than comfortable lives with a wide range of choice over their spending patterns, and have good housing conditions, an interesting and varied diet, access to a wide range of modern consumer durables and gadgets, and the ability to engage in commercialised leisure pursuits and opportunities. Societies may crave still higher material standards, but this does not mean that they have not yet reached the status of affluent.

Tentative evidence from Britain for this view comes from a survey commissioned by London Weekend Television in 1990 for the documentary series *Breadline Britain*. This asked the sample which of a list of items covering diet, housing, clothing, social and leisure activities and consumer durables they thought 'were necessary, which no-one should have to go without, and which everyone should be able to afford'. This was an update of a similar survey carried out in 1983. The sample selected thirty-two items out of a list of forty-four as being 'necessities' in contemporary Britain. The complete list of items chosen (necessities are those identified by more than 50 per cent of the sample) is shown in table 2.3. Many are items which would not have been identified as necessities in the past such as a telephone and an annual week's holiday away.

The survey also asked interviewees whether they had the items, and if not, whether it was because they 'did not want them' or 'could not afford them'. Table 2.3 confirms that clear majorities have each of the necessities (column 2). Clear majorities also have five of the twelve 'non-necessities'. If those not having the good because of taste – that is, because they don't want the item rather than because they can't afford it – are included (column 3) the majorities are much larger. Indeed, large majorities either have or don't want *each* of the non-necessities. The survey also found that 71 per cent of adults in the sample either had *all* the adult necessities or didn't want them, while 63 per cent of children had, or didn't want, *all* the child necessities. This evidence shows that a clear majority, more than two-thirds of households in Britain, live above the *minimum* living standard determined by a majority of society, while slightly less than a third live below it.

This analysis provides evidence of a public consensus around the idea of a hierarchy of wants. Items defined as physical and social *needs* in figure 2.1 such as essential housing and diet and basic social

Table 2.3: Necessities in Britain, 1990

Necessities	Proportion saying items are necessary	Proportion having the item	Proportion having the item or not wanting it
A damp-free home	98	95	97
An inside toilet (not shared with another household)	97	98	99
Heating to warm living areas of the house if it's cold	97	96	96
Beds for everyone in the household	95	97	98
Bath, not shared with another household	95	98	99
A decent state of decoration in the home	92	81	83
Refrigerator	92	97	98
Warm waterproof coat	91	91	95
Three meals a day for children	90	96	100
Two meals a day (for adults)	90	94	98
Insurance	88	83	86
Fresh fruit	88	88	93
Toys for children eg dolls or models	84	95	97
Separate bedrooms for every child over 10 of different sexes	82	84	89
Carpets in living rooms and bedrooms in the home	78	96	97
Meat or fish or vegetarian equivalent every other day	77	90	95
Celebrations on special occasions such as Christmas	74	91	95
Two pairs of all-weather shoes	74	90	95
Washing machine	73	87	93
Presents for friends or family once a year	69	89	93
Out of school activities, eg sports, orchestra, Scouts	69	64	82
Regular savings of £10 a month for 'rainy days' or retirement	68	60	66
Hobby or leisure activity	67	76	91
New, not secondhand, clothes	65	89	94
A roast joint or vegetarian equivalent once a week	64	84	93
Leisure equipment for children eg sports equipment or bicycle	61	87	92
A television	58	97	98
Telephone	56	87	92
An annual week's holiday away, not with relatives	54	65	78
A 'best outfit' for special occasions	54	85	90
An outing for children once a week	53	76	84
Children's friends round for tea/snack fortnightly	52	72	88
Non-necessities			
A dressing gown	42	84	98
A night out fortnightly	42	62	84
Fares to visit friends in other parts of the country four times a year	39	48	76
Special lessons such as music, dance or sport	39	47	74
Friends/family for a meal monthly	37	68	87
A car	26	63	80
Pack of cigarettes every other day	18	37	93
Restaurant meal monthly	17	42	75
Holidays abroad annually	17	38	66
A video	13	66	87
A home computer	5	24	82
A dishwasher	4	17	81

Source: The Breadline Britain *Survey, 1990*

activities receive much higher votes than items such as regular restaurant visits, foreign holidays and home computers which could be defined as *desires* and *wants* rather than *needs*. It also tallies broadly with the 'two-thirds, one-third' description. According to the survey, 29 per cent of adults lacked one or more necessities because they could not afford them, 20 per cent lacked three or more, while a tenth lacked five or more. Most of these would fall below a basic standard defined by the first two categories of the needs' hierarchy, though where the actual poverty line is drawn remains a matter of judgment. The survey authors, for example, defined the poor as those lacking three or more of these items, this being the level where statistical tests showed a clear break between the living standards of those above and below this level.[12]

Whether the 71 per cent who either have or don't want all the necessities could be defined as an 'affluent majority' is also a matter of judgment, though they are clearly living above both past and contemporary measures of a minimum standard. This group could, of course, be further subdivided. Indeed the survey found that 27 per cent of households had or didn't want the complete bundle of adult items including the 'non-essentials', 46 per cent had either them all or all bar one, while 56 per cent had them all or all bar one or two. Fifty-seven per cent had or didn't want all the non-necessities.

This distinction between the rich, the comfortable and the poor would conform to most people's views of reality. Although these groups are not homogeneous in lifestyles and attitudes, they have some broad common characteristics that broadly correspond to their ability to be able to satisfy different elements of the hierarchy of wants portrayed in figure 2.1. The affluent majority would all enjoy fully consumerist lifestyles, and housing of a high standard. All will have fully satisfied their physical and social needs and be able to enjoy a choice of material and non-material wants. The middle 'comfortable' group would have more restricted choices than the rich, though all will have moved beyond the first two rungs of the hierarchy of needs.

The 'poor minority', in contrast, are largely, though not always entirely, excluded from modern consumerist lifestyles. They will, typically, live in poorer housing, have fewer consumer goods, enjoy poorer access to leisure pursuits and holidays, and face much more limited choices. Their lives are duller, more constrained and often racked by insecurity and debt. They have made only limited progress through the hierarchy of wants, and many would still struggle to enjoy an adequate satisfaction of even basic physical and social needs. This group is also far from homogeneous. It would include pensioners and disabled people heavily or entirely dependent on state support, a large proportion of single parent families, most of the long term unemployed, those who would like to but can't work, and many of the growing numbers of the low paid.

The precise nature of these social patterns clearly varies between affluent societies, with some characterised by higher levels of equality, social cohesion and social mobility than others. Those with the strongest safety nets and lowest unemployment have smaller groups of the poor and rich than others, less inequality between the groups, and a larger group in the middle. Nevertheless, the direction of change since the war has been common with all societies moving from the relatively impoverished to the affluent majorities of today.

The mood of these groups has a critical influence on the functioning of modern societies. Galbraith has described the majority as 'contented', a comfortable, complacent, short-termish and selfish majority with no serious commitment to the poorer minority.[13] What is more likely is that this group has a fluctuating mood. Bad times bring discontent and worry, better times bring greater contentment but not always enough to bring material satisfaction and generosity. They may well have felt contented during the more economically secure climate of the late 1980s, but the arrival of the global recession at the beginning of the 1990s has had a major impact on attitudes, bringing a new sense of insecurity about jobs, incomes, housing and living standards. It is a trend that is being reinforced by the changing pattern of work, the decline of the lifetime job and the rise of the short-term contract. What is emerging is less a culture of contentment than a 'culture of insecurity', and one that is likely to outlive the recession.

The recession showed just how vulnerable some of those in the privileged and comfortable majority are to the economic buffetings of the latter part of the twentieth century. The soaring unemployment in these years was much less partisan in its choice of victim, hitting some highly paid professionals and managers as well as the more traditional low paid and manual groups. Equally, the poor minority should not be seen as a single block, forever trapped and unable to escape their lot. What little evidence exists about income and social mobility suggests some, if limited, movement out of and into poverty over time, and so some crossover between these broader groups, though predominantly at the margins, and leaving most of the poor locked for long periods at the bottom.

The impact of affluence on aspirations is critical to an understanding of the dynamics of modern societies. Prosperity has brought greatly improved living standards, but left widespread dissatisfaction. Appetites have been fanned, encouraging a leap-frogging culture and intensified competition. In the process, the successful have used their competitive strength to secure a rising share of the proceeds of growth. As a result, the spread of affluence has also been associated with growing divisions as the winners have successfully outbid the losers.

3. The Dream Turns Sour

If boys and girls do not obtain jobs when they leave school, they fear society has no need for them. If they feel that, they do not see any reason why they should take part in that society, and comply with its rules.

(William Whitelaw)[14]

Ricky: There's no jobs round here where you can get the money to buy them things, so what are you going to do for your money?

Tiggy: There's shops and that like, burglaring shops and that, some day I've done a house now and then, and I've been really desperate, break into cars see what I can get hold of, things like that. Whatever will bring money to me I'll do it.

Ricky: Get a hundred pounds for a video, all sorts of things. A generator, you can get a hundred pounds for a generator . . . the council vans, there's loads of council vans round here all the time, all sorts of things, just where you can get a bit of money.

Jane Corbin (Reporter): And is this a way of life for most young people on this estate?

Ricky: The majority I'd say.

(BBC, *Panorama*)[15]

29

The first half of the post-war era that brought the beginnings of the transition from scarcity to affluence was characterised by the *sharing of success*. It was a time when the building of socially cohesive societies became a central political objective, to be achieved through the extension of social and economic rights. For a while, this new approach to politics was successful, bringing rises in opportunities and living standards across the board. Gradually, that sense of political purpose has waned giving way to less cohesive and more conflictual societies and a deepening polarisation of success and opportunity.

'A rising tide lifts all boats'

Far from bringing greater social stability, rising prosperity over the last decade and a half has brought growing unrest, greater unease and more disharmony. This period has seen a continuing rise in serious and violent crime, soaring drug abuse and growing social unrest. There has been serious rioting in the United States, Britain and parts of the European mainland, and mounting hostility and violence against immigrant and refugee communities, not merely in Germany but across Europe. The world's most affluent societies have become increasingly fitful and volatile, engulfed by a deep sense of unease unique in the post-war era.

Throughout many affluent societies, continuing rises in public spending have failed to prevent rising relative poverty and a growing crisis in many public services. Begging among the young, the old and the ill occurs in all major British and American cities, and is growing on mainland Europe. Young men and women selling their bodies for the price of a meal or a fix is no longer confined to the urban heartlands of the United States and Britain. Homelessness is on a rising trend throughout much of Europe.[16]

Despite huge spending on health care, the United States has some of the highest child mortality rates in the developed world. In some areas, they approach those of third world countries. Forty million American workers cannot afford health insurance and are ineligible for the medicaid benefits paid to the very poorest. Once almost eliminated, TB has re-emerged in the United States. A disease of poverty, its root causes are homelessness, drug-abuse, Aids and a disintegrating health care system. Its rebirth says much about the social collapse of American cities over the last decade. The disease has also started to rise in several parts of urban Europe, again largely a product of rising poverty. Some experts have even predicted the need for new isolation hospitals like those that existed before the Second World War.

This is not how it was foreseen by the social planners. The post-war years seemed to bring solutions to the pre-war problems of unemployment, social division and widespread poverty. Keynesian economic management and social planning were the twin agents of the new era of *welfare capitalism* which was to deliver both more buoyant economies and a greater sense of social justice for almost a generation. Managed growth was seen as the main mechanism of human progress, the means to a more civilised society. As Anthony Crosland, one of the most influential theorists of post-war social democracy put it,

> Such primary poverty as remains will disappear within a decade, given our present rate of economic growth . . . the aspirations relating to the economic consequences of capitalism itself have been transformed.[17]

This optimism was echoed elsewhere. As John F Kennedy declared a few years later, 'a rising tide lifts all boats'. It has long been assumed that higher levels of wealth would bring solutions to the problems of scarcity – poverty, inequality, instability, unemployment. In the United States, it was widely believed that poverty would gradually disappear with the advent of full employment and rising incomes. Even with the 'rediscovery of poverty' in the 1960s, there remained a cherished belief in the capacity of expanded government programmes to tackle poverty.

In 1964, the American liberal economist, Leon Keyserling, was able to claim that 'more jobs and massive government spending would eliminate poverty in 10 years' while a year later, the President of the American Economic Association spoke of the 'threshold of the golden age'.[18] Yet, far from entry into the golden age, the United States was on the edge of an era of rising poverty and steadily deepening inequality.

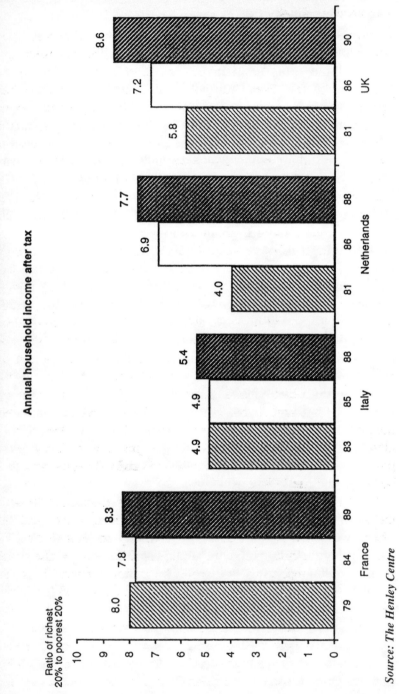

Figure 3.1: The rise in inequality in the 1980s

Annual household income after tax

Ratio of richest 20% to poorest 20%

Source: The Henley Centre

The growing divide

During the long post-war boom, the distribution of income in most richer countries remained remarkably stable. The gap between the rich and the poor fell between the end of the 1930s and the beginning of the 1950s – largely as a result of the sharp fall in unemployment – but then all groups shared roughly equally in rising prosperity until the mid to late-1970s. Since then the gap has been widening. The proportion of the population of the European Community falling below a poverty line defined as 50 per cent of average disposable income rose from 38.6 million in 1975 to 43.9 million in 1985 and to 50 million in 1990, an increase from 12.8 to 15.5 per cent over the fifteen years.[19] This increase has been a product of the rising inequality shown in figure 3.1.

In Britain, the Government's official figures show that from 1979 to 1990/91, the poorest tenth of households suffered a cut of 14 per cent in real incomes, while they rose by 36 per cent on average.[20] It is often assumed that increasing inequality in Britain has been the product of Thatcherism. Although the trend towards a more divided society was fuelled by some aspects of Conservative policy during the 1980s, such as the de-indexing of benefits to average earnings, the movement can be traced to the mid-1970s. Moreover, similar, if weaker, trends have been experienced in other major nations, and for broadly similar reasons. In the United States, the real incomes of the poorest fifth fell by 10 per cent between 1977 and 1989, while the incomes of the top fifth rose by 28 per cent.[21] This growing polarisation pre-dated the election of Ronald Reagan, and in fact began in the late 1960s.

The trend in Europe has been more mixed. Figure 3.1 shows that income inequality rose sharply in the Netherlands over the 1980s. There were also smaller rises in inequality in France and Italy, though the rise in Italy may be understated because of the problem of the under reporting of income by higher earners. In western Germany, the share received by the poorest tenth also fell from 3.3 per cent in 1980 to 2.9 per cent by 1989.

Three main factors account for the deteriorating position of the poor minority. First has been the steady rise in unemployment, an issue dealt with in chapter 4. The second has been the changing political climate and a diminishing commitment to the post-war goal of social cohesion. Rising unemployment, slower economic growth and declining public generosity have put increasing strain on social protection systems throughout Europe. This changing climate has led to both a fall in the relative levels of some state benefits and a reduction in the progressivity of taxation.

In Britain, the Conservative governments of the eighties ended the previous policy of increasing pensions and other benefits in line with earnings. Over the 1980s most benefits rose only in line with prices, and some fell in real terms. Those dependent on social security were thus prevented from sharing in the proceeds of growth. Germany, France, Belgium and Ireland also allowed the value of benefits for the elderly to fall in relation to general living standards.[22] Several countries also allowed the real value of their minimum wage schemes to fall.

The pressure to restrict benefits is well illustrated by the case of the Netherlands. Ruled by governments of the moderate Left during the 1970s, the country emerged with one of the most generous systems of income maintenance in Europe, and a low level of inequality. Unemployment benefit replaced 80 per cent of income for six months, and 75 per cent for the next two years. Faced with a serious public sector deficit, a new Centre-Right government in 1982 cut benefit levels and public sector pay and allowed unemployment to rise, contributing to the substantial rise in inequality over the decade.

Belgium followed a similar pattern with a change of government in 1981 bringing attempts to cut the high level of social spending and public sector deficit by de-indexing benefits. In Italy from 1983 to 1987, the Socialist-led coalition government of Bettino Craxi faced similar pressures and in 1986, a referendum voted against the maintenance of the full *scala mobile* system of wage indexation. Similar cuts in benefits were introduced in West Germany and Denmark during the 1980s.[23]

Although some of these cuts have been fairly modest, at least to date, the two groups most heavily affected have been the unemployed and the young. Under pressure from the rising costs of unemployment and concern about the possible work disincentives of relatively generous benefits, most European governments have introduced some reductions in unemployment benefits leading to a growing gap in income between those in and out of work. These changes have included the de-indexation of benefits to wider living

Table 3.1: Unemployed persons receiving neither unemployment benefit nor social assistance, 1985

	Total unemployed %	Unemployed under 25 %
Belgium	17	22
Denmark	26	39
Ireland	32	40
Netherlands	40	41
Germany	42	50
France	60	67
Luxembourg	79	–
Italy	83	86
Greece	96	–

Source: Commission of the European Community, 1991(a), p 10

standards, shorter periods of payment, and restrictions on eligibility, including tests of willingness to work and train.

During the 1980s, these changes led to an increase in the number of claimants excluded from benefit altogether, especially among the young (table 3.1). Between 1981 and 1989, the proportion of the unemployed in Britain receiving unemployment benefit fell from 40 to 20 per cent. Most unemployed young people between the age of sixteen and eighteen are not entitled to benefit at all, one of the reasons for the steady rise in homelessness and begging in recent years. In Spain, income maintenance programmes are considered to be inferior to programmes of re-insertion into work, with the result that large numbers are ineligible for benefit. In France, young people under twenty-five are excluded from the *Revenue Minimum d'Insertion* because of the priority they receive in vocational training programmes.

During the 1990s, this trend towards less generous social security systems is likely to gather pace as most European governments are being forced to consider further reforms of their benefit systems. In the early 1990s, Germany agreed a package which included a freeze on social security benefits, pay restraint for public sector workers and lower student grants. Sweden imposed cuts in pensions, sick pay and housing subsidies. Similar cuts were being made or considered in Spain, Italy, Britain, Denmark, the Netherlands and Belgium. Some of these cuts ended the post-war tradition that, at the very least, benefits should be protected in real terms.

Table 3.2: Changes in national income tax rates

Country	1975 Tax Rates lowest	1975 Tax Rates highest	1985 Tax Rates lowest	1985 Tax Rates highest	1990* Tax Rates lowest	1990* Tax Rates highest	Changes in top marginal rates
Australia	20	65	30	60	24	49	−16
Belgium	17	60	24	72	24	60	0
Britain	35	83	30	60	25	40	−43
Canada	9	47	6	34	17	29	−18
Denmark	50	73	50	73	50	68	− 5
France	5	60	5	65	5	50	−10
Germany	22	56	22	56	19	53	− 3
Ireland	26	77	35	65	35	58	−19
Italy	10	72	18	65	11	56	−16
Japan	10	75	10.5	70	10	50	−25
Netherlands	20	71	16	72	40	70	− 1
New Zealand	19.5	57	20	66	24	33	−24
Sweden	32	85	35	80	30	50	−35
United States	14	70	11	50	15	28	−42
Average	21	68	22	63	24	50	−18

*1990 Tax rates are proposed or already legislated

Source: Heclo, 1991, p 211

Another characteristic of growing prosperity has been the declining progressivity of tax systems, the result of cuts in direct taxation on the rich and an increasing emphasis on indirect taxation. Table 3.2 shows that for the fourteen countries shown, the highest rate of income tax fell by 18 points from an average of 68 in 1975 to 50 per cent in 1990, while the lowest rate rose from 20 to 24 per cent. While the most substantial shifts occurred in Britain, the United States and Japan, there were also large reductions in the top rates elsewhere.

The reduced commitment to redistribution is only in part a response to economic crisis. It is also the result of a shift in political ideology. Underlying the rise of neo-conservatism during the 1980s was a belief that greater inequality may be the inevitable price of economic success. On both sides of the Atlantic, and increasingly in continental Europe, high levels of social protection financed by high taxation have been seen as creating a dependency culture, undermining personal initiative and killing the incentives considered central to competitive vitality. Lower spending and taxation, the argument runs, might limit the degree of redistribution in the short term, but by generating a more competitive climate, it would stimulate growth and so make the poor actually better off as the benefits of a more buoyant economy 'trickled down' to the poorest. The promised trickle down effect, however, has proved elusive. There is no evidence that lower benefits for the poor and higher rewards for the rich have stimulated economic performance. Despite this, it is doubtful if there will be a return to the more progressive tax and benefit systems of the past.

Third, the trend towards greater inequality has been reinforced by rapid technological change. As argued in chapter 4, this has led to a shift in the skill requirements of industry, an upheaval in employment opportunities and a rise in long term unemployment among those with redundant skills. It is this which underlies the rise of those out of work for more than a year in Europe from less than a fifth in 1975 to more than a half in 1993. It has also contributed to a rise in wage differentials between those with and without competitive skills. Differentials have risen most in those countries such as Britain which have gone furthest in weakening employment rights and minimum wage provision, policies of deregulation aimed at creating a more flexible labour market and greater competitiveness. For these two reasons, wage differentials are now greater in Britain than for more than a century. Between 1981 and 1988, the lowest paid tenth of manual workers saw a real increase in their pay of around 8 per cent compared with a rise of a third for the highest paid non-manual workers.

Similar factors have been at work in other countries, though the trend on the European mainland has been moderated by their more generous employment protection policies. In France, for example, the ratio of the average salaries of the top and bottom tenth of salary recipients widened from 3.09 to 3.30 between 1984 and 1989, less than in Britain.[24] A similar widening in wage inequalities also occurred in the United States over the 1980s. More than a half of the 32.5 million Americans living below the official poverty line lived in households with at least one worker – the highest proportion in the post-war era.[25]

The rise of an 'excluded' minority

This fundamental change in the pattern of opportunities – expanding choices for some and contracting choices for others – has conspired to create what some have described as a new 'underclass' and others 'the excluded', a small but significant sub-group of the poor increasingly unable to participate in mainstream society. The idea of an underclass is nothing new. Societies throughout history have been divided in a hierarchical way by income and by living standards with a variety of different terms used to describe those at the bottom.

In the post-war era, the arrival of affluence gave rise to the hope of creating more socially cohesive and mobile societies in which even those at the bottom were given reasonable opportunities for economic and social participation. For a while, it seemed as if the problem of groups or sub-cultures of excluded and alienated individuals had been largely solved. With the breakdown of the post-war boom, the phenomenon has re-emerged.

The underclass has been described as 'permanently dependent, without hope, demoralised. It is the stratum of society with neither an economic nor a psychological stake in that society.'[26] According to another report, the issue is 'the willingness of more secure sections of the population to recognise any collective obligations towards those who are less secure and who are therefore at risk of social exclusion'.[27] The scale of the problem is more difficult to identify, and varies in size between nations. It is especially acute in the United States, probably growing in Britain, and has begun to emerge in parts of mainland Europe.

One British study has defined the underclass as people permanently removed from the labour market, excluding those not of working age, those who retire early, students and people with long term illnesses.[28] This group increased in size from 1.96 million (4.2 per cent of the population) in 1979 to 4.6 million (9.9 per cent) in 1986 (though the extent of the trend may have been exaggerated by the fact that 1986 was a peak year for unemployment in the 1980s). Using a narrower definition, Ralph Dahrendorf has arrived at a figure of around 5 per cent in Britain and some European nations.[29]

On the European continent, other phrases such as the 'excluded', the 'marginalised' and the 'peripheral' are used to describe the same phenomenon of those finding it increasingly difficult to compete effectively within a more privatised social and economic environment. The problem of 'social exclusion' has become an increasing part of the political vocabulary in several European countries in recent years. The problem is least severe in those countries such as Sweden, Switzerland and Austria which have, at least until recently, been able to maintain generous support mechanisms and low unemployment.

Despite agreement on the emergence of this new group or sub-culture, its roots are a matter of heated controversy. Commentators on the Right have attributed it to a decline in conventional values such as the work ethic and a respect for authority. Others, mainly on the Left, have blamed it on economic and structural change. In the United States, one of the most outspoken writers on the subject, Charles Murray, views the underclass as the product of social, moral and cultural deficiencies – a lack of commitment to the work ethic, aberrant and anti-social behaviour and criminality – a problem which he attributes to the emergence of a dependency culture arising from excessive state support.

Murray's book, *Losing Ground*,[30] revived longstanding theories of the 'undeserving poor' and provided an intellectual rationale for the Reagan rhetoric about the failed war on poverty. By undermining self-reliance and destroying work incentives, Murray argued, generous welfare benefits were self-defeating. They fuelled poverty by encouraging young women to become pregnant outside marriage with the young fathers refusing to marry the mothers of their babies.

Murray's thesis had a popular resonance and proved highly influential. Backed by euphoric and influential reviews, the book eased the way for the subsequent budget cuts in education, housing and other welfare programmes. If poverty was the product of idleness and sexual promiscuity, its solution lay in penalising the poor, not in generous provision. As a federal official told Congress in January, 1985, 'poverty has been institutionalised by the Government's anti-poverty programmes and there is no point in throwing more money at it'.[31]

It wasn't long before such anti-welfare rhetoric crossed the Atlantic. In 1989, Murray wrote in *The Sunday Times*, 'a monster is being created in our midst' with 'active social outcasts, wedded to an anti-social system', an underclass which is 'contaminating the life of entire neighbourhoods'. As in the United States, this thesis of welfare-generated poverty dovetailed neatly with official thinking and provided further reasons for doubting the wisdom of redistributive welfare programmes.

The alternative explanation blames the problem on growing structural inequality and on the emergence of more polarised employment opportunities. Modern labour markets are increasingly characterised by distinctive groups, a 'core' group of well educated, stable and adaptable workers able to get secure, well paid jobs, and a 'peripheral' group of poorly educated and inexperienced workers with a history of low-paying, insecure jobs with poor conditions and few prospects, or of intermittent or permanent unemployment. In the 1950s and 1960s, manufacturing industry required a large body of unskilled labour for mainly routine, repetitive tasks. Those leaving school with no or minimal qualifications were not particularly disadvantaged in the labour market and were still able to get relatively secure manual work.

Those days have largely gone. There are fewer and fewer jobs requiring no skills and qualifications. Those that do exist have become increasingly badly paid and insecure. As production has become more complex, industry needs a smaller but a more highly educated and adaptable workforce. Those without basic educational qualifications and skills find it more difficult to get on the employment ladder, while those with relevant qualifications and skills are at a premium. This divergence has been compounded by the fact that job losses have been concentrated in industries with the lowest entry requirements while job growth has been in areas requiring higher levels of skill and attainment. In addition, modern economies seem to be able to function effectively, in the sense of delivering improved living standards to the most affluent two-thirds, at higher levels of unemployment.

The scale of the problem varies between nations according to differences in the penetration of new technology and the qualifications and skills of the workforce. The proportion of the male population over twenty which has not progressed beyond secondary education varies from 19 per cent in Germany and 48 per cent in the UK to 72 per cent in Italy and 87 per cent in Portugal.

In the European Community, the unemployment rate among under-25-year-olds is double the average. Access to secure, well paid jobs has become more and more closely related to the level of education. In the United States the average pay of someone with no more than a high school education fell in real terms by 12 per cent between 1973 and 1987. If you were black and without a college education, your average earnings fell over the same period by 44 per cent. The fall in the wages of those who dropped out of high school was even greater. Between 1980 and 1990, the gap between the earnings of a male college and high school graduate nearly doubled.[32]

The problem is compounded by the fact that long term unemployment is associated with diminished chances of re-entering the workforce. Even in periods of rapid employment growth, it is difficult for the long term unemployed to be re-integrated into the employed labour force. In 1987, more than a half of those under twenty-five who were unemployed in the European Community had never worked.[33] It is this phenomenon that lies at the heart of the problem of the underclass – a group who remain permanently unemployed or at best move between unemployment and insecure low paid work. The underclass would not exist if the unemployed and peripheral workers were only a temporary phenomenon.

Isolation

In the United States the problem is heavily concentrated in certain inner city areas and among racial minorities. In 1987, an influential book by the liberal sociologist, William J Wilson, *The Truly Disadvantaged*, documented the sharp deterioration, in both absolute and relative terms, in the conditions of blacks living in inner city ghettoes.

According to Wilson, this was almost entirely the result of the growing vulnerability of urban minorities to structural economic change. Racial discrimination had contributed to the decline, but its underlying cause lay in deepening economic divisions. Between 1970 and 1984, all the major northern cities in the United States – from New York and Boston to Philadelphia and St Louis – experienced dramatic job losses in the very industries to which urban minorities had the greatest access, while substantial job gains occurred in sectors which were mainly beyond their reach.

The result of this collapse in the demand for unskilled labour has been an explosion of joblessness and low pay especially among young blacks and an increasing concentration of the poor. Longitudinal studies in the States have also provided evidence of the existence of *long term* poverty.

Although most people who become poor at some point in their lives experience poverty for only one or two years, a substantial minority remain in poverty for a very long time. Indeed these long term poor constitute about 60 per cent of those in poverty at any given point in time and are in a poverty spell that will last eight or more years.[34]

As another study found, 'The average poor black child today appears to be in the midst of a poverty spell which will last for almost two decades.'[35]

The growing polarisation of the urban poor has been compounded by the exit of the black middle class professionals and the stable working class from urban ghettoes to higher income neighbourhoods and the suburbs over the last twenty years. This shift, according to Wilson, has created a sense of 'social isolation' in which the very poor are increasingly quarantined from the people, job networks, role models, institutions and other connections that might help them escape poverty. Most large American cities are now heavily segregated between the inner city and the suburb by crime, by race, by income and by the quality of life. The isolation and segregation that have gone along with it have been reinforced in turn by at best, external indifference, and at worst, intolerance.

This is especially true of the capital city where the black/white divide is almost as clear cut as in South Africa. For middle class Americans living in pleasant suburbs, inner city areas might just as well be part of the Third World; children in East Harlem or South Chicago exert no greater call on the conscience than those in Bolivia or Ethiopia. They are part of 'another America'.[36]

One effect of this trend has been the emergence of pockets of under-development in the heart of the world's richest nation. The UN has ranked the United States as sixth in the world on a measure of human development based on people's life expectancy, educational level and purchasing power.[37] It comes behind Japan, Canada, Norway, Switzerland and Sweden. On the basis of racial groups, however, American whites head the world league table, while African-Americans are 30th, just ahead of Trinidad and the

Bahamas, while Hispanics are 34th, behind Korea and Uruguay. America's middle class has been moving to the suburbs and to the new towns created on the edge of declining cities with their smart housing estates, golf courses, restaurants and riding schools. The areas left behind resemble a Third World economy with widespread poverty, drug abuse, endemic crime and little prospect of improvement.

Similar patterns of ghettoisation are emerging in parts of Europe, where there is much talk of 'new poverty' or the 'poverty of the fourth world'. As one study of nine European countries concluded, 'There are signs in all countries we studied of a small but growing minority of young people who are becoming totally excluded from the mainstream of society.'[38] The European Commission has come to similar conclusions,

> There is considerable risk of two different societies developing within the Member States, one of them active, well-paid, well-protected socially and with an employment-conditioned structure; the other poor, deprived of rights and devalued by inactivity.[39]

Europe is beginning to see the emergence of a core group of under-educated and under-trained youngsters who not only face unemployment but who have virtually no experience of employment. Increasing numbers of these are turning to vandalism, petty and more serious crime, to drugs and drug dealing and sometimes prostitution. In the United States, this has contributed to the development of a thriving and lucrative criminal economy that co-exists with the traditional economy. It is one heavily dependent on drug trading, and Europe is no longer that far behind.

During the 1980s, the number of drug related offences increased threefold in Britain and fourfold in France. In Italy, the quantity of cocaine seized by the authorities rose from fifty-three kilos in 1980 to 800 kilos in 1990. One report has claimed that in the 1980s there were 5,000 minors in Naples working for the Camorra as heroin dealers.[40] A survey by the Henley Centre in 1992 showed that the two most overwhelming concerns in Europe from a list of sixteen were drugs and crime.

As in the United States, the underclass in France is heavily associated with racial minorities, especially the North African settlers who have been living in France for a generation. These groups are heavily concentrated in France's impoverished suburbs, or *banlieue*. They typically suffer from higher rates of unemployment and lower wages when in work. They mostly live in the huge public housing complexes built on the edge of the big cities in the 1960s to house immigrant workers for local factories. Val-Fourré, in Mantes la Jolie, and the biggest in the Paris region, is typical of poor French suburbs. More than half the families are foreign, and more than half live on state support.

These large estates have become increasingly volatile. In 1990, the Lyons suburb of Vaulx-en-Velin erupted in several days of sporadic rioting, sparked by the death of a young man, apparently knocked off a motorbike by a police car. This was a particular blow to the authorities who had just spent £5 million on amenities for the neighbourhood, and had held it up as an urban renewal success story. Similar riots occurred in Val-Fourré in May and June 1991, and in Paris and Lyons in 1992 and 1993. Small scale incidents are commonplace. Such problems have also helped to fuel the rising success of the far Right anti-immigration National Front which has been actively exploiting the insecurity in some of these areas.

The growth of this excluded and disaffected minority has been compounded by the failure of European welfare systems to adjust to the growing problem of long term unemployment. Typically, benefits for the long term unemployed are low and incomplete, a problem aggravated by the weakening of even the patchy safety nets that were in place. It has also been aggravated by declining access to housing since the 1980s and rising homelessness, the product of both falling income for some groups of the young and the steady shift in policy away from state towards market provision. This is also a pan-European problem, though it is more serious in some countries than others. In Germany since 1989, there has been 'an explosive rise in the numbers of emergency shelters, cheap hostels and other forms of emergency accommodation with very limited facilities'.[41] According to some non-governmental estimates, the numbers of people in these hostels or entirely homeless now number almost one million.

In southern Europe, with its less developed welfare systems, the problem is being fuelled by the steady erosion of the role of the extended family. The family has long played an important, protective role in Spain, Portugal, Italy and southern France with their strong Catholic traditions, providing support and accommodation for young people for longer than in northern Europe. While the family still plays a role of support in these countries, its effectiveness has been declining with social change and the erosion of the traditional close-knit community. Studies have shown how the combination of growing pressure by the state to reassert the caring role of the family has coincided with the family's declining *economic* ability to care, creating increasingly 'stressed' families and contributing to their long term decline.[42]

The problem of 'exclusion' is also becoming increasingly geographically concentrated. Growing unemployment has combined with changing housing demand to reshape the urban environment, a process encouraged by a combination of inner city gentrification and suburbanisation. The result has been a growing polarisation in living conditions and opportunities leading to isolation and ghettoisation of the kind that occurred earlier in the United States. The problem is not as serious as in the United States, but it is heading that way. Broadly speaking, in Britain, the middle classes have been abandoning the inner city to escape what they perceive as more insecure and crime ridden communities in search of the safer and better schooled suburbs. On the mainland of Europe, a similar but reverse process of polarisation has been occurring with the better off colonising the more desirable inner city areas of some major cities while the poor have been isolated in peripheral estates.

These bleak and often brutal estates on the edge of mainland Europe's biggest cities – Rome, Milan, Paris, Lyons, Hamburg, Barcelona – and also on the edge of Liverpool and Glasgow in Britain – are increasingly the homes of the very poorest, suffering high rates of welfare dependency, insecurity and patchy public and social services. Many of these increasingly isolated communities have become places of endemic vandalism and crime, rising levels of school absenteeism and teenage pregnancy, and growing levels of drug addiction.

The sense of abandonment is also heightened by an awareness of the surrounding affluence from which these isolated communities are excluded. One study by the European Commission has spoken of the emergence of two circles of urban disadvantage – a circle of excluded people 'living in chronic poverty and extreme isolation in the central districts and the outskirts of big cities' and a 'second circle, which is approximately as large as the first in numbers, composed of those who are in a precarious position . . . and just as likely to end up marginalised'.[43] As the report concluded

> . . . all cities are concerned about these cracks appearing in their fabric and growing deeper by the day, as the economic and social distance increases between the winners and losers in the city, between the borough on the winning side (high tech production areas, for example) and the loser (dormitory suburbs and mono-functional areas, for example).[44]

'Riots waiting to happen'

How far the rise of inequality and of a new group of the 'excluded' can be said to lie behind the simultaneous rise in both social unrest and crime is a matter of controversy. Although most commentators accept a link, they remain split between those citing a growing culture of lawlessness and those blaming the drain of jobs, services and hopes. It is impossible to prove these assertions either way, though what is clear is that they are related. Economic and social decay is a breeding ground for slipping values.

The Los Angeles riots in 1992, which left fifty dead, were an expression of anger that lies at the heart of many American cities. Violent crime has increased nearly threefold across America since the 1950s and 1960s, has risen even more sharply in the inner cities, and much more sharply among the young. It has created communities that are stalked by fear. In 1991, there were 24,000 murders in the United States, a rate of ten per every 10,000 citizens, eight times the European rate.

Between 1985 and 1990, the number of teenage killings doubled. Murder is now the most common cause of death among young black men and is the third most common cause of death among all young men. *Boyz'n the Hood*, John Singleton's film of black gang rivalry in South Central Los Angeles starts with a mind-blowing statistic: that one in every twenty-one young black males in the city will die at the hands of another young black. Over the last ten years, there have been three main trends in the rising murder rate – a trend towards younger killers, the spreading of killings from the rotten core of the giant metropolises to the newly rotting core of medium-sized and smaller cities, and the increasing links with drugs and gangs. Drug dealing is an epidemic in these areas. It brings easy money, and equally important, power.

Another reason for rising crime has been the erosion of many of the former controls that kept anti-social behaviour in check. As Wilson points out '. . . unlike the present period, inner city communities prior to 1960 exhibited the features of social organisation – including a sense of community, positive neighbourhood identification and explicit norms and sanctions against aberrant behaviour'.[45] One reason for the change has been the collapse of the 'social buffer' – the removal of the higher-income groups which provided both mainstream role models and some institutional stability that 'could cushion the effect of uneven economic growth . . . [and which has] made it more difficult to sustain the basic institutions of the inner city, including churches, stores, schools, recreational facilities etc, in the face of prolonged joblessness.'[46]

While the problem of social unrest is less serious in Europe, the gap may be closing. In Britain, crime and civic disorder have been escalating. Recorded crime during the 1980s rose at twice the annual rate of the previous thirty years. Car-jacking has crossed the Atlantic as has drug-related violence. Youthful disorder has become commonplace from the inner city through to smaller suburban areas. Car theft, vandalism and arson are more and more common and spreading to rural areas that have previously been largely immune. In 1991 and 1992, violent confrontations broke out in dozens of deprived estates in widely differing areas of Britain. Each of these incidents followed a similar pattern – the outbreak of violence by large groups of young people, mostly teenagers, involving the use of petrol bombs, arson and looting.

Unlike the riots in 1981 and 1985 in Brixton, Handsworth, Toxteth, St Pauls and Tottenham which had revolved around race, these confrontations took place on mainly white estates. Clearly, as unemployment has risen and spread, the disaffected black youth of the early 1980s have been joined by their white counterparts.

Criminologist Jock Young of Middlesex University described the 1992 riots as 'the politics of despair; the collective bargaining of the dispossessed'.

Young's view is not original. As Lord Scarman noted in his report on the 1981 riots, unemployment, poor housing, and an education system that has not adjusted to meet young people's needs provide 'a set of conditions which create a disposition towards violent protest'. A similar theme was taken up by Sir Peter Imbert, the then Commissioner of the Metropolitan Police, in 1992, 'The growth of crime is a fundamental concern which, in part, I attribute to the marginalisation of our society. The notion that there is a link between crime and social deprivation is compelling.'

Other evidence supports the economic link. Studies have shown a correlation between crime levels and deprivation. Home Office research has shown that crime growth is closely related to economic growth. Crime falls when consumer spending rises and picks up when it falters.[47] Although the Home Office did not draw the conclusion, the corollary of this finding is that even in periods of growth, crime will still rise with increasing inequality. Another analysis of fifty empirical studies of the relationship between crime, deprivation and inequality concluded that 'income inequality is strongly related to criminal activity – with the exception of homicide'.[48]

Another review concluded, 'It is not absolute poverty, but poverty experienced as unfair . . . that creates discontent; and discontent where there is no *political* solution leads to crime.'[49] A study in 1993 of 1,400 young people on probation, commissioned by the Association of Chief Officers of Probation, concluded that there is a 'real link between poverty and crime'.[50] It found that young offenders were 'invariably poor, often destitute . . . and often complete outsiders'. Almost two-thirds were unemployed; only 10 per cent had an income of over £100 a week, and 72 per cent were in poverty according to measures used by the European Commission.

Similar concerns are being expressed across Europe where there have also been sharp rises in crime and disorder. In a confidential report of the OECD to a meeting of finance ministers in May 1992, concern was expressed about the impact of rising unemployment and instability on crime, violence, drug abuse and racial, religious and political intolerance. Other researchers have found a common link. A study of crime in Ireland has found evidence of the 'role of social deprivation in the lives of young people for whom crime has become not only a source of income but also, in the absence of other opportunities, a "lifestyle"'.[51]

Another report for the European Commission has argued that two factors provide the missing link between delinquency and unemployment, 'Where unemployment has given rise to a negative approach to work, a feeling of "what's the use?", and where it has cut the tie with standards which encourage the acquisition of material satisfaction by lawful means, delinquency takes hold.'[52] Drawing on evidence from France, the same report went on to argue that the influence of the surrounding environment, of poor housing conditions, weak parental control, poor school results and lack of qualifications, drags young people into a trail that leads to delinquency and petty crime which the French academic, F Dubet calls 'la galère'. This trail is as much about the need for sociability, for grouping together as a natural tendency to criminality.

In today's new ideology of individualism and individual responsibility, the economic and social explanation is often rejected in favour of one that blames a lack of self-discipline and deteriorating personal values. This explanation is not without some force. There is evidence of a breakdown of the social values and commitment that used to bind families and society together even in deprived areas. Partly this is a problem associated with the breakdown of the traditional family and the growing number of single parent families. Many of the estates characterised by social unrest and high levels of crime also have a large proportion of children being brought up with absent fathers. But this problem cannot be seen in isolation from wider social and economic forces.

Though surveys of the unemployed young show a continuing commitment to the work ethic and apparently mainstream values on several issues from crime to the family, in the explosive atmosphere of these decaying estates, these attitudes are under increasing strain. Schools have lost much of their former authority and teenagers often opt out at an increasingly early age. Social workers and teachers regularly point to the problems arising from a rejection of authority and the lack of example and controlling influence that arises from the widespread absence of fathers. Combined with the absence of jobs, it is only too easy for young teenage boys growing up on these estates to adopt older criminals as their role models. Break-ins for goods like car radios and videos are a daily ritual, and the offenders mostly young. Some have become involved in larger scale, organised crime such as ram-raiding which offers both big money and excitement.

While social changes have brought growing independence for a majority, they have not brought similar benefits to these ghettoised minorities. The process of empowerment has been very partial in its impact. The poor have become less powerful and, with declining job opportunities, have less control over their lives. The idea of self-reliance has a pretty restricted meaning to the poorly educated and inexperienced young.

Some commentators have asked why riots and crime occur today when they did not in the pre-war depression. The answer can be found in two key differences between the periods. First, there was little youth unemployment in the 1930s. At the beginning of 1993, nearly one million under-25-year-olds were out of work in Britain. Second is the fact that mass consumerism was unknown in the earlier period. When no one had a car, a video or a foreign holiday, when aspirations were confined to a visit to the local dance and cinema, there were few grounds for envy. Today's youth have been born into a different culture. As shown in chapter 5, the spread of affluence has fostered new expectations, and new consumerist goals which are out of reach of the poor minority. And today, denial of the new trappings of consumerism means a denial of full citizenship.

For many youngsters crime has become a matter of survival in this new society that appears to cater only for the winners. Left to fend for themselves, the losers are not encouraged to have any investment in the basic structures of wider society. The result has been a growing lack of community cohesion and a declining sense of social commitment. It is a trend compounded by the deep-rooted sense of bitterness and alienation felt by many of the young unemployed in a society where their peers who do have jobs are able to indulge in the requirements of an increasingly materialistic society. One study of growing marginality among the young in Europe expressed fear that

the social cement is crumbling at the edges and that these

processes of marginality may have dangerous and destructive consequences for the social fabric as a whole [unless] alternative forms of inclusion [are found] for young people who are bombarded with ever proliferating needs and aspirations, yet have deteriorating means of fulfilling them.[53]

The rise of the far Right

Another feature of a deeply unsettled Europe has been the rise of racist violence and the rebirth of extreme-Right politics. Such violence has taken particularly extreme forms in France and Germany but has also spread to countries, such as Italy and Denmark, with a tradition of more stable race relations. Xenophobia is now a pan-European phenomenon.

The resurgence of neo-Nazism in Germany came to a head in the summers of 1992 and 1993 with persistent violence against refugees and asylum seekers in dozens of towns. Similar, if less frequent, incidents had been occurring for two years, and the problem is far from confined to the east. In the first seven months of 1992 alone, there were 970 acts of violence leaving 700 people injured and ten dead according to Ernst Uhrlau, head of Hamburg's counter-intelligence service. Mr Uhrlau also warned 'There is a '68 movement from the right that could change German society more fundamentally than the left-wing student movement was ever able to do.'

The growth of racist attacks has been accompanied by the political rise of extreme groups on the Right. Recent years have seen the revival of parties like Jean-Marie le Pen's National Front in France, the Freedom party in Austria, the Vlaams Blok party in Belgium and the Republicans in Germany. Partly, the rise of the Right reflects genuine difficulties in accommodating the huge increase in immigration – nearly 500,000 in Germany in 1992 – from Eastern Europe and north Africa, a problem compounded by the onset of the recession.

It is also reflected in growing political fragmentation and a decline in support for mainstream parties, though other parties on the Left such as the Greens have also been beneficiaries of this change. But it is also a symptom of a deeper sense of unease over unemployment

Figure 3.2: Blaming immigrants, 1992

Europeans who Agree that immigration causes (%) ...		Highest National Figure		Lowest National Figure	
higher unemployment	61	Germany	74	Spain	46
a more interesting and enjoyable society	19	UK	21	Netherlands	14
higher crime rates	54	Germany	69	Spain	28
a stronger economy	11	Germany	17	UK	6

Source: The Henley Centre, Frontiers Survey, 1992

and social stability sweeping across the continent. Research by the Henley Centre has shown a deepening mood of pessimism about the future with more and more people throughout Europe fearful of still greater social and political instability.

This sense of unrest can be linked to wider social and economic problems. It reflects a growing sense of economic vulnerability, especially a growing fear of unemployment, a wider concern about the quality of life, of work and of community, and a growing loss of confidence in established political mechanisms. Such anxiety has contributed to the rise of political extremism and the rise of xenophobia. While most countries contain a small hard core opposed in principle to immigration, figure 3.2 shows just how ready others are to pin the blame for growing social ills on other ethnic groups. No less than 61 per cent of Europeans think that immigration causes higher unemployment while 54 per cent think it adds to crime.

At the heart of this growing antagonism is another failure of the politics of affluence. Affluence offers the means to create the greater cohesion that could accommodate the inevitable demand for migration. Instead, the rising insecurity associated with widening divisions has created a mood of insularity and a hostility towards minorities that has become an additional source of instability. While none of the new Right parties has a serious prospect of governmental power, their growing support has influenced the political agenda, forcing most European governments, and especially Germany and France, to take a much more hardline stance on immigration and asylum.

As the more co-operative cultural climate of the immediate post-war era has been replaced by a new and dominating ethos of competitive individualism, it has brought a greater emphasis on the importance of winning, on the encouragement and rewarding of success and the condemnation and punishment of failure. It is this change which underlies the growth of new divisions and greater insecurity, contributing to the increasingly unsettled and restive climate that now hangs over modern societies.

4. Nice Work If You Can Get It

A society which allows it to be assumed that unemployment will stay around 3 million, or anywhere near it, for the indefinite future, takes risks with its stability.

(Michael Heseltine)[54]

Rising unemployment and the recession have been the price that we've had to pay to get inflation down . . . That is a price well worth paying.

(Norman Lamont)[55]

We have to do something. We cannot live with 3 million unemployed in every major country . . . It seems to us that the world lacks leadership, lacks long term vision.

(Jacques Delors)[56]

After the war, the pursuit of full employment became, for the first time, a central goal of political management. Sir William Beveridge's 1944 White Paper, *Full Employment in a Free Society*, argued that the state should extend its responsibilities from traditional areas like defence and policing to employment. This break with the past and with the market ushered in a new orthodoxy that was to dominate western policy for nearly thirty years.

This commitment arose out of a widespread desire to avoid the mass unemployment of the inter-war years, a new interest in social and economic planning and a new concern with creating fairer and more stable societies. During the 1950s the goal was pursued with unexpected success as unemployment sank to historically low levels. This approach to economic management was underpinned by political commitment. The jobs issue became a central ingredient of political performance, pursued with equal vigour by governing parties of diverse political persuasions.

The principal requirement for the creation of full employment is a favourable political and social environment. This existed after the war, but has largely gone today. The roots of rising unemployment over the last twenty years lie as much in a changing political and social culture as in economic factors. The commitment of government to full employment has gradually waned, while electorates have been willing to tolerate much higher levels than in the past. At the same time economic and industrial change has made it more difficult to achieve. Both these factors can be related, in turn, to rising prosperity.

The return of mass unemployment

After the war, a new set of counter-cyclical measures were used to moderate the business cycle. Since the early 1970s, such economic management has proved more difficult. The more recent recessions – one in each of the last three decades – have been more serious than earlier post-war downturns. There is now less economic stability than was achieved in the immediate post-war era. Governments have continued to try to follow counter-cyclical strategies, but there is much less faith in their ability to get it right.

This greater instability can be traced to the changes in the character of societies as they have moved from scarcity to affluence. Prosperity has brought escalating and competitive expectations which have led to heavier demands on productive capacity, and growing inflationary pressures. Economic upheaval has become more commonplace leading to a change in economic orthodoxy which has contributed to a steady rise in unemployment.

Since the early 1970s, the dole queues have failed to disappear with an upturn, settling at higher levels at comparable points of the cycle. Economic recovery no longer necessarily means lower unemployment. In 1992 there were 13 million people unemployed in the countries of the European Community, equivalent to 10.1 per cent of the labour force. This compares with 4.1 per cent in 1975 and 2.1 per cent in 1965. The most serious problem has been a rise in long term unemployment. Between 1980 and 1989, the proportion of the unemployed out of work for more than a year in Europe rose

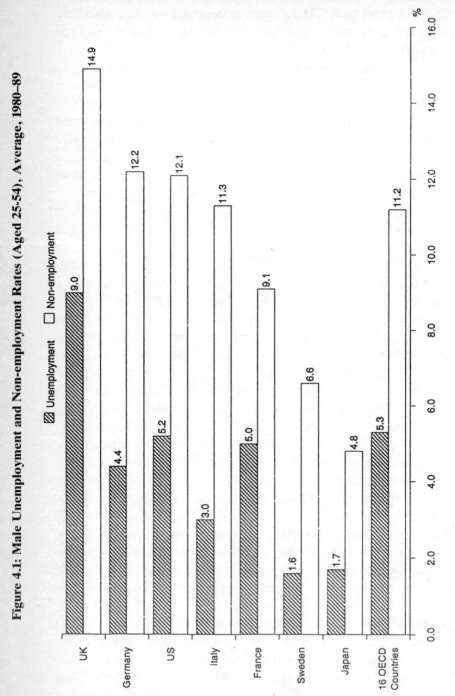

Figure 4.1: Male Unemployment and Non-employment Rates (Aged 25-54), Average, 1980–89

Source: OECD, 1992 (a), Chapter 2

56

from 31.5 per cent to 52.8 per cent.[57] Most projections suggest that western unemployment is set to continue at historically high levels for most of the 1990s, even with economic recovery.

The growth in the numbers of unemployed – those available and actively looking for work – is only part of the picture. Recent years have brought another problem – an increase in the numbers who have no jobs and who have given up the search for employment. The past decade has seen a steady fall in the male labour-force participation rate as many have shifted from being 'unemployed' to 'economically inactive'. These two groups combined represent the 'non-employed'.

Figure 4.1 shows the significance of the rise of 'disguised unemployment'. On average, the non-employed rate for 25-54-year-old males over the 1980s for a group of sixteen leading countries stood at 11.2 per cent compared with an unemployment rate of 5.3 per cent. The differential for younger and older adults was much higher. In Britain, the UK unemployment rate halved between 1986 and 1990, but the non-employment rate fell by just 0.5 of a percentage point. This occurred because large numbers of the unemployed simply shifted between 'different states of joblessness', to, for example, early retirement or sickness and disability benefit. The number of men claiming this benefit rose by 6 per cent between 1980 and 1986, but by 25 per cent between 1986 and 1990, adding more than 200,000 new claimants.[58]

The post-war period brought a conjunction of factors that contributed to sustained full employment. There was both a supportive and consensual political climate and a sympathetic 'public philosophy'. Keynesianism and its belief in state intervention had proved its merits during the Second World War, and fitted the temper of the times. Governments were confident in their use of fiscal policy to manipulate the level of demand. They were helped too by the boom created by the Marshall Plan aid programme, post-war reconstruction and a technological base on which new investment created rather than displaced jobs. While boosts of demand were associated with spurts of inflation, these were modest and were regarded as an acceptable price of maintaining full employment.

Today, the consensus and the confidence has gone. Keynesian fine-tuning is less effective. Full employment increasingly seems a

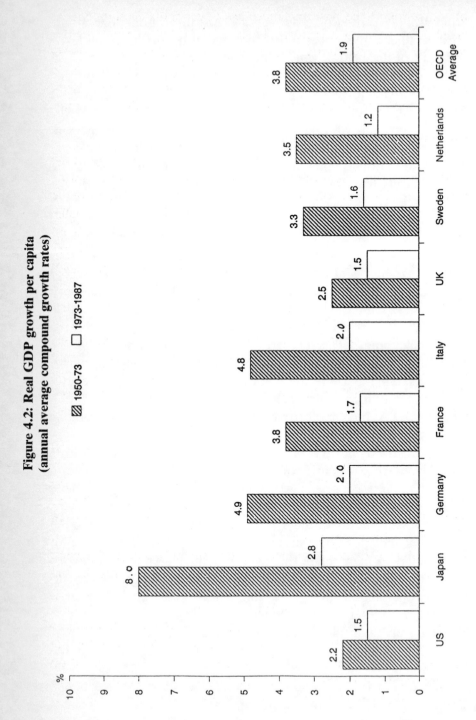

Figure 4.2: Real GDP growth per capita (annual average compound growth rates)

⬚ 1950-73 ☐ 1973-1987

phenomenon of the past and there are few serious economic ideas around for securing its return. There are two key reasons for this reversal, both related to spreading affluence. First, a change in social behaviour which has been reflected in rising inflation, a changing approach to economic policy and lower economic growth. Second, the birth of a much more unsympathetic political climate.

Changing social behaviour

The long post-war boom finally began to peter out at the end of the 1960s. The earliest signs of trouble came in the United States during this decade. The first consumer society and the richest country in the world, it was the first to display the symptoms of the unsustainable appetites which were to prove the downfall of the post-war boom. The swelling costs of the Vietnam war together with the budgetary implications of Lyndon Johnson's 'Great Society' programmes led to a rising fiscal deficit, an increasingly overheated American economy and new inflationary pressures.

In 1971, the dollar was devalued and the fixed exchange rate policy effectively abandoned. With it, these inflationary pressures were passed on to Europe via a much more unstable international financial system. The problems of the dollar were also linked to the oil price shock of 1973 when the oil producers' cartel, OPEC, hiked oil prices fourfold. This increase was, at least in part, the product of the new and less co-operative international climate and the free-for-all atmosphere created by the freeing of exchange rates and speculative capital movements.

It was these inflationary pressures which eventually led to changing economic policies, slower growth and higher unemployment. From 1950 to 1973, consumer prices rose by an average of 4.1 per cent a year in the sixteen leading OECD nations. From 1973 to 1979 they averaged 9.5 per cent.[59] This in turn created the conditions for the deflationary strategies which brought the lower growth rates shown in figure 4.2.

Economic problems cannot simply be laid at the door of these external shocks. The ground had already been prepared. In essence, the problem lies in the breakdown of the conditions underpinning post-war stability. The post-war boom seemed to have opened up the possibility of persistently rising prosperity. Expectations were encouraged, especially by the growth of mass consumerism, and not easily suppressed. Industry wanted higher profits, consumers higher living standards, employees higher wages and governments more spending, power and influence.

The problems of the US economy in the 1960s and the tougher policies of OPEC can be traced to these same trends. Inflation was the product of these contradictory and unsustainable demands. In many countries, wages consistently rose more quickly than productivity, reflecting the reluctance of workers to accept rises in living standards consistent with economic performance. Governments were under pressure to improve public services but without compensatory increases in taxation. As a result, most of Europe moved during the 1970s from a position of budget surplus to deficit. These pressures contributed to rising inflation, falling profits and sluggish investment, and the fracturing of the economic conditions that underpinned the post-war boom.

In the 1960s and 1970s, several countries attempted to tackle these growing inflationary pressures with a variety of incomes policies aimed at moderating wage increases. These measures were an attempt to recreate the social conditions of the earlier period by slowing down the rate of increase of real wages and restoring profitability. It was hoped that this would allow a return to the former situation of relative economic equilibrium.

The policies can be viewed as an attempt to persuade the majority – those with jobs – to make sacrifices on behalf of the minority – those without jobs. The attempts were more successful in some countries than others. Indeed, variations in economic performance during this period can be linked to the willingness of electorates to accommodate themselves to the changing circumstances. The management of demand was to prove a less important factor in determining economic success than the nature of social values and relationships and, hence, wider institutional structures.

It is no coincidence that countries such as Germany, Japan and Sweden were able to cope most successfully with the external shocks of the early 1970s. In Britain, attempts to seek such an accommodation were relatively unsuccessful. Attempts at an incomes policy began in the 1960s with voluntary pay norms that were heavily breached. The experience was repeated in the 1970s with a variety of voluntary and statutory schemes that brought some temporary success. They proved difficult to sustain, however, and ultimately failed. They have not been repeated.

Elsewhere there were similar attempts to reach an accommodation with unions and employers over wage rises, some of which ended in similar failure. They were much more successful in those countries, especially in Scandinavia, with a longer tradition of collaborative bargaining and successful state intervention in labour markets. Germany too, with its more consensual and co-operative industrial and political climate, proved better able to share the proceeds of economic growth through largely successful negotiation. Both American and Japanese workers also seem to have had a better appreciation of the trade-off between wages and job security than elsewhere. Partly as a result, these countries have had a much less serious problem of unemployment, at least until recent years.

These growing inflationary pressures had a dramatic effect on the capacity of political management. Inflation itself brought new economic problems of adjustment including greater uncertainty, changing relative prices and fluctuating markets which probably contributed to slower growth. The main impact, however, was on managing the economy. The old economic levers seemed to lose their power. It was no longer possible to cure unemployment by the expansion of demand, since this simply compounded the growing problem of inflation. The Keynesian orthodoxy began to crumble.

It was into this growing void that the New Right economists were able to step. The apparent weakening of the old economic rules gradually gave rise to a new set of assumptions about the way economies function, and to a second reason for the slowing of growth. This was the emergence of a new economic philosophy geared to tackling the problem of inflation. Gradually, Keynesianism was replaced with a new doctrine of monetarism involving a tighter control of the money supply as the new key to low inflation and economic stability.

For the monetarists, demand management had contributed to the onset of inflation. The essential difference between Keynesians and monetarists is that for the former, extra demand generates more output, while for the latter, extra demand over and above an equilibrium level is simply eaten up by more inflation. For pure monetarists, expanding demand can have no permanent impact on the level of economic activity and hence jobs. This is determined solely by 'supply-side' factors such as the quality of management and labour and overall industrial efficiency and competitiveness. Creating excess demand simply bids up prices and wages and is therefore self-defeating. The solution to inflation was to squeeze out excess demand through tight control of the money supply which would reduce wages and prices, not output. If it affected output too, this would be the fault of structural rigidities such as excessive trade union pressure or too generous welfare benefits.

As tackling inflation became the new priority, monetarism gradually became the new orthodoxy. Ironically, the first serious attempt at imposing monetary discipline came during the mid-1970s under a Labour Government. The next came during the Presidency of Jimmy Carter in 1979. Meanwhile, most other countries continued to try and reflate their way out of the 1970s downturn with quasi-Keynesian measures. In 1979/80 a second oil price bombshell by OPEC plunged the world economy into another recession. This new crisis accelerated the move to monetary discipline as cutting inflation became the overriding goal.

Most countries soon fell into line. Following Britain and the United States, governments of the Centre-Right came to power in Belgium, Denmark, the Netherlands and West Germany during the early 1980s. Faced with large fiscal deficits caused by high levels of public spending, they set about reversing the failed reflationary strategies of the 1970s. France's Socialist Government elected in 1981 was virtually alone in attempting to buck the trend with a full-blooded reflationary programme of public spending and redistribution that had to be ruthlessly reversed after only two years. It was replaced by an austerity programme that led, as elsewhere, to spiralling unemployment.

The move to monetary discipline across western nations amounted to a highly deflationary strategy. Control of the money supply required a tighter fiscal policy and smaller budget deficits to prevent pressure on monetary growth. The effect of tighter monetary and fiscal policy during the 1980s was certainly lower inflation, but at the price of higher interest rates, lower growth and investment and higher unemployment. The monetarists had always hoped that the demand squeeze would lead to only a temporary cut in output and to longer term stability and success. In the event, the effect has been a much more permanent shift, with the broadly expansionist policies of the 1950s and 1960s replaced by a much more contractionary stance, leading to the lower growth rates of the last fifteen years.

Higher growth created by higher levels of demand would, in theory, lead to lower unemployment. The problem is that higher growth rates are proving difficult to deliver. Strong growth throughout the OECD region led to sharp falls in unemployment in the second half of the 1980s. In Britain between 1986 and 1989, growth averaged nearly 4 per cent, and unemployment fell sharply from a peak of 3.3 million in 1986 to 1.7 million in 1990. But the 'demand-led' and 'debt-financed' growth rates of this period proved unsustainable.

In Britain, the high growth at the end of the 1980s was the product of the artificially created 'Lawson boom' which fuelled inflation and led to a serious external deficit. This triggered the deflationary policies which caused unemployment to rise again. These constraints have led some economists to argue that the growth rates required to bring unemployment down quickly from current levels are largely unsustainable, especially if led by high consumer spending. Certainly, modest growth rates are not sufficient to secure low unemployment. From 1979 to 1990, Britain grew at an average of some 2 per cent a year, yet unemployment increased by around half a million, or by as much as 1.5 million if measured in a consistent way. This trend was partly the product of rising labour supply from demographic changes. Yet, even though labour supply will grow more slowly in the 1990s, most economists now accept that the annual rate of growth would need to be at least 2.5 per cent a year simply to prevent unemployment rising further.

There are several reasons why growth may not do as much to reduce unemployment as in the past. The first is that, although growth creates new jobs, an increasing proportion of these are part-time and low paid. Many are also filled by new entrants to the labour market, rather than the registered unemployed. More people want to work now than in the past, especially women. To reduce unemployment, growth needs to sustain a rate of job creation that is capable of providing employment for those recorded as inactive who wish to work as well as for those, mainly men, officially recognised as unemployed.

Parts of the European Community, especially the Mediterranean countries, not only have a relatively high rate of unemployment, they also have a low rate of employment. The percentage of people of working age in the Community who are actually in work averages around 60 per cent in Community countries, but around 70 per cent in the US, Japan and the rest of Western Europe. This helps to explain why even high rates of job creation have had a limited impact on the long term unemployed.

The second factor has been an increasing tendency for management and unions, particularly in Britain, to opt for fewer workers at higher rates of pay. This is a classic example of the politics of exclusion in which those in work have attempted to secure a higher share of the national cake for themselves. Bargaining has often given priority to wages over jobs, a deal that suits both employers and unions.

High real wage increases have contributed to higher rates of unemployment than would otherwise have occurred. This has continued to happen in the middle of recession. In the year to July 1992, the average tax-paying employee in Britain needed an increase of only 2.5 per cent to preserve his or her living standard, yet got an increase of 6 per cent.[60] In September 1992, with the British car industry taking a heavy battering from the recession, Ford management offered the unions the choice between deferring an already agreed 5 per cent wage increase for six months, or the possibility of up to 1,500 redundancies. The unions insisted on the wage increase. Even in the more restrained bargaining climate of 1993, ICI began paying 14.5 per cent productivity-linked pay rises to most of its 20,000 hourly-paid workers, while simultaneously announcing more than 10,000 job cuts over the next year. The story of East Germany since unification has also been one of a rapid catching up of wages to match those of the west rather than one of protecting jobs. In the spring of 1993, the East German engineering industry went on strike to secure an already agreed 26 per cent pay rise which the employers were resisting.

Third, in the recession of the early 1980s, employment growth in services provided a cushion, partially offsetting job losses in manufacturing. A decade on, these losses were more broadly based in services and manufacturing than in earlier downturns, with a particularly strong shake-out of jobs in the wholesale and retail trade, and even in traditionally less cyclically sensitive sectors such as finance and business services. The overall unemployment rate for service workers has also risen more sharply than in the past in all countries except Canada. As the OECD has concluded, 'while workers in manufacturing and construction continue to face a higher risk of unemployment than in services, the recent recession has had a deeper and broader impact on the service sector than in previous recessions.'[61] For this reason, rising joblessness has been affecting white-collar and professional groups as well as those traditionally vulnerable.

It is also unlikely that the 1990s will see a repeat of the experience of the second half of the 1980s, with a service-led economic recovery. In Britain, for example, the 'Lawson boom' was rooted in growth in construction, financial services and retailing. The second half of the 1980s saw a huge growth in office building to house the vastly expanded and newly deregulated financial services sector. The collapse of the Lawson bubble hit these sectors especially badly, and the 1990s is unlikely to bring similar expansion.

Even if there is a return to substantial growth in retailing and other services, its job-creating potential is likely to be much more limited. Rising unemployment in the opening years of the 1990s was not merely the result of the global recession. It was also partly structural, the product of a new efficiency drive, and one facilitated by new information technology. The recession of the early 1990s was accompanied by substantial business re-organisation aimed at survival in an increasingly competitive environment. This has meant that those laid off are less likely to be taken back on than in the past. According to the US Bureau of Labour Statistics, for example, only 15 per cent of those laid off between the beginning of the US recession in July 1990 and June 1992 expected to be recalled to their old job compared with an average of 44 per cent in past turndowns.[62] Some of America's biggest corporations including IBM, General Motors and General Electric announced huge lay-offs during the recession and continued to do so during the mild recovery of 1993. These changes, variously called 'de-layering', 'downsizing' and 'shrinking' are the product of a new approach to management aimed at maintaining and expanding output with smaller workforces at all levels.

Similar job-shedding strategies have been taking place in Europe, as the service sector attempts to improve its competitiveness in increasingly demanding markets. In Britain, many large service companies such as British Telecom, Tesco and the high street banks have been shedding jobs not just in response to the recession but in order to raise productivity. The risk is that, during the 1990s, the higher productivity required to maintain profitability is likely to be achieved more by staff cuts than by job-creating investment. A similar pressure to raise productivity by shedding staff is likely to prevail in the public sector, with a growing need to control public spending faced by all governments.

A changing political climate

In the 1920s and 1930s mass unemployment brought the issue to the centre of the political and social agenda. In 1929, Ramsey MacDonald won the general election on the theme 'The paramount issue: the need to relieve our nation of the scourge of unemployment'. It gave birth to a new theory about the way economies function that dominated economic management for thirty years. Despite steadily rising unemployment from the 1970s, it was not until 1993 that it re-emerged as a source of concern.

A central tenet of the New Right doctrines of the 1980s was the inability of government to do much about unemployment. One of its leading theorists, Sir Keith Joseph, told the Bow Group in 1978, 'Full employment is not in the gift of government. It should not be promised and it cannot be provided.' Gradually this view slipped into political and popular orthodoxy, giving rise to a new sense of inevitability about higher unemployment. Governments abandoned the responsibility they once took very seriously, and electorates seemed happy to follow. The 1980s was a decade when economic impotence became an acceptable philosophy. A report in the *New York Times* in 1986, for example, noted that

> For more than two years, the nation's unemployment has hovered around 7 per cent, a level long considered intolerably high and far above the 4 per cent target set by Federal Law ... Yet for all the lost production and individual stress associated with having 8.33 million Americans jobless – a 7 per cent unemployment rate seems to have become acceptable to the public.[63]

As another US writer put it, 'The changing character of the post-war economy, the attrition of the organized labor force and the values that have been generated by a temporary triumphant corporate economy have enfeebled the once strong sense of social justice and solidarity that in an earlier time would have reacted strongly to this condition.'[64]

This growth of political apathy was encouraged by the emergence of an affluent majority. Before the war, unemployment was not a problem of a small minority. During the post-war era, unemployment became a low risk for most of the population. From the mid-1970s, mounting unemployment was largely confined to narrow social groups, especially the unskilled and poorly educated. The majority could afford to be complacent as they seemed immune from the threat that was afflicting others. After the war, full employment was in everybody's interest because it contributed to social cohesion and growth. Until recently, that became much less the case. For the most part, the better off majority have been able to achieve a steady rise in living standards without the benefit of the low unemployment of the past.

There also remains a clear polarisation of attitudes between those in and out of work. Several studies have revealed that the employed take a fairly hostile attitude to the unemployed, often blaming them for their own fate. The British Social Attitudes Survey, for example, has shown that 40 per cent believe that 'most unemployed people could find a job if they really wanted one', while 30 per cent felt that 'most people on the dole are fiddling in one way or another'. In contrast, among the unemployed, there is more blame of the general economic situation and government policies.[65]

The effect has been a steady rise in the level of unemployment at which public and hence political concern is triggered. Not so long ago unemployment of a million would have been enough to bring a government down. Today, the comparable figure is well above 3 million. The threshold at which unemployment triggers a response depends on a crucial factor – the point at which the majority perceive themselves to be seriously at risk, either directly, or indirectly because of a rise in social instability.

As unemployment rose above 10 per cent in many countries during the recession of 1992 and 1993, concern began to rise with it. The principal reason was a growing sense of unease amongst the affluent majority about their own vulnerability to unemployment.

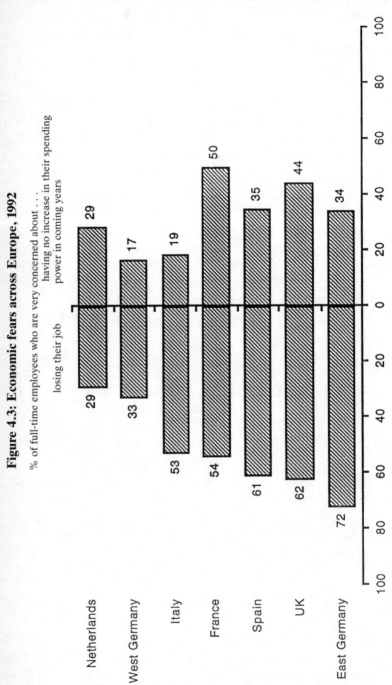

Figure 4.3: Economic fears across Europe, 1992

% of full-time employees who are very concerned about . . .
losing their job / having no increase in their spending power in coming years

Country	losing their job	having no increase in spending power
Netherlands	29	29
West Germany	33	17
Italy	53	19
France	54	50
Spain	61	35
UK	62	44
East Germany	72	34

Source: The Henley Centre, Frontiers Survey, 1992

Table 4.1: Unemployment Record Since the War

Persistently Low Unemployment	Standardised Unemployment Rates (per cent of total labour force)			
	1950-73	**1974-79**	**1980-88**	**1992**
Austria	2.6	1.6	3.1	4.0
Japan	1.6	1.9	2.5	2.2
Norway	1.9	1.8	2.5	6.2
Sweden	1.8	1.9	2.2	5.0
Switzerland	0.0	0.3	0.6	3.0
Medium Unemployment				
Finland	1.7	4.6	5.1	12.7
Germany	2.6	3.6	5.6	7.6
USA	5.9	6.8	7.5	7.4
High Unemployment				
Belgium	2.9	5.4	11.3	9.3
Denmark	2.6	4.9	8.9	11.0
France	2.0	4.5	9.0	10.3
Italy	5.7	6.1	10.1	11.0
Netherlands	2.2	5.9	8.6	5.6
UK	2.8	4.9	10.0	10.1

Source: Maddison, 1982, table C.6; OECD, 1992(b)

Although the principal victims of the recession remained the traditional low skilled, and those working in manufacturing, white collar workers, middle managers and professionals were no longer immune. The reversal of the service boom dented the confidence, and complacency, of the 1980s. In 1992, there were 50,000 business failures in the UK and 45,000 in France. As figure 4.3 shows, economic fears escalated in Europe, with the proportion frightened of losing their job rising to over 50 per cent in the UK, France, Italy and Spain.

This growing anxiety slowly translated itself into a change in the political climate. Unemployment began to get a much higher profile, and emerged as a priority at international summits in 1992 and 1993 of both the G7 and European Community leaders. Jacques Delors talked of the need for a 'jobs crusade' and proposals were prepared on labour market reforms, fiscal incentives and improved training schemes. Overtures were made to Japan and European countries to boost their flagging economies, and to reduce interest rates, but there was more talk than action. The conviction remained that full employment is a phenomenon of the past, that modern societies have lost the capacity to create it.

During the 1980s, table 4.1 shows that this view was at odds with the evidence. Mass unemployment was not a universal problem, and the actual experience of unemployment has been diverse. By the beginning of the 1990s, there was less room for optimism, as even some of those countries with a record of very low unemployment found themselves with sharply rising levels.

Is there an alternative?

Five countries – Norway, Austria, Switzerland, Japan and Sweden - succeeded in preventing sharp rises in unemployment during the 1980s, while also maintaining relatively low rates of inflation. Their policies all had at least two features in common. The first was a commitment to full employment firmly rooted in economic and political systems. This commitment was backed by highly interventionist economic and labour market strategies, amounting to a rejection of the 'hands-off' policies being pursued elsewhere. The second common feature was the existence of a form of co-operative relations between unions and employers involving some degree of agreed wage restraint.

Thus the key to low unemployment in the 1980s was a combination of continued political commitment and a supportive public philosophy. All of these countries were able to resist the broadly deflationary measures adopted elsewhere, though some with the aid of special circumstances. Norway, for example, enjoyed the vital cushion of huge reserves of North Sea oil and gas. Switzerland's record was, at least in part, a product of its strict control of migrant labour and restrictions on female participation in the job market.

Austria pursued a broadly Keynesian strategy with high public employment which succeeded in preventing inflation because of successful co-operation between government, workforce and management including a strong dose of voluntary price and wage restraint. It too was assisted by a heavily restrictive immigration policy. Sweden sustained low unemployment through a combination of a largely unique and successful labour market strategy and a policy of large-scale public employment. In 1987, more than 30 per cent of employed Swedes worked for the government, compared with 21 per cent in the UK and only 15 per cent in the US.

Japan retained a form of Keynesian 'deficit-financing' along with extensive state involvement in private industry and a publicly co-ordinated private labour market strategy. The Japanese model is one in which a powerful and centralised government apparatus devises and imposes a coherent industrial strategy on a weakly organised working population. Discounting the special circumstances of Switzerland, four nations – Norway, Austria, Sweden and Japan – can be viewed as succeeding in maintaining a successful contract between the government, business and employees on the distribution of growing wealth which proved the key to economic stability, full employment and manageable inflation. In each of these countries, consensus and co-operation were largely sustained throughout the 1980s, preventing any one sector from making excessive demands.

Three of the European star performers, Norway, Sweden and Austria, are examples of what has been called 'social corporatism' in which a powerful and well organised workforce has been willing and able to strike deals with other social groups, including the aim of full employment as a national priority. As one study has concluded,

> Not only is such a priority accepted by the other social groups, but labour organisations in return honour their own side of the bargain and accept the sacrifices required to achieve its employment objective. Norway, Sweden and Austria are not the only countries which might be classified under the heading social corporatism. Both Denmark and Finland are often classified under this heading . . . However, in neither is the working class as powerful, nor does it display the same internal coherence and unity of purpose. This may help to explain, perhaps, why full employment has not been such a priority in Denmark and Finland, and why these countries have such high unemployment rates.[66]

Although all these countries were able to buck the international trend throughout the 1980s, the 1990s brought unprecedented increases in unemployment in Norway, Austria and Sweden. Swedish unemployment rose from less than 2 per cent for most of

71

the 1980s to 6 per cent by 1993. Sweden's long success had been a product of two key factors – a steady expansion of public sector employment at the price of higher taxes, and a solidaristic system of wage bargaining which prevented excessive wage demands by the better off. By the 1990s, both were under strain. During the 1980s, other policies had to be galvanised to fight unemployment – demand was kept high, industry was propped up by several devaluations, and inflation began to rise. In May 1991 there were attempts to peg the krona to the ecu, effectively accepting that squeezing inflation had to take precedence over full employment.

In 1991, the Swedish Social Democrats lost the general election to a Centre-Right coalition for only the third time in fifty years. Growing impatience with high taxation finally led to the electorate voting in a government committed to cutting back the public sector. Against a background of deepening recession, the product of tighter economic measures to rein in a debt-financed boom, full employment had to give.

The United States has a more middle record. The major difference between the US and Europe has been the former's relatively free labour market. There is minimal employment protection, a much less generous social security system and what minimum wage schemes exist guarantee only very low wages. Partly as a result, the US has achieved a much higher rate of job creation than Europe, though most of these jobs have been low paid, part-time and insecure. Since 1970, the real wages of the lowest paid tenth have fallen by almost a third. The United States has lower unemployment than the European average, but a free labour market has not created anything like full employment, and has contributed to the serious problem of the underclass discussed in chapter 3.

The maintenance of full or near-full employment has depended on a combination of factors – strong political commitment, a co-operative culture especially in wage bargaining, a large public sector and a clear sense of public will and social consensus. Such conditions prevailed after the war, have persisted in a handful of countries but have gradually been eroded elsewhere. The key reason for this has been the rise of excessive and competitive economic demands which could not be met, and which could not be held in check. Full employment became increasingly difficult to achieve using the traditional and previously successful tools of economic management, and these for the most part, have not been replaced by alternative measures.

Today, most of the developed world is facing a serious policy vacuum. The experience of the last two decades has convinced most economists that demand expansion alone is not the answer to unemployment. Monetarism has also proved no match for the elusive goal of full employment and low inflation. As the limitations of the two alternatives to macro-economic management have become apparent, the distinction between the monetarists and the Keynesians has become more blurred. Keynesians have been forced to acknowledge the importance of monetary influences and of wages in determining employment levels. Monetarists have accepted the dangers of too sharp a contraction of demand in causing unemployment. Despite this growing consensus, there still remains no effective economic strategy for eliminating mass unemployment. The solution will depend, above all, on the development of an alternative political and social strategy and a change in social behaviour which is as yet as elusive as the economic. The possibilities are discussed in chapters 9 and 10.

New technology and unemployment

Another key factor affecting employment opportunities has been the industrial and technological revolution of the last twenty years. While it is not possible to be conclusive about the impact of this process on the overall *level* of unemployment, it has been a major source of the rise in long-term unemployment and in the more fragmented work opportunities of recent years. As in past periods of dramatic change, there has been a failure to ensure that the potential benefits and accompanying costs have been more evenly borne.

Viewed from a long-term perspective technological change has had a largely benign influence on economic development. Technical progress has been a central cause of the vast improvements in living standards enjoyed in developed economies over the last two centuries. Industrial innovations in cotton and iron at the turn of the eighteenth century, the development of the railways in the 1820s, the invention of electricity, chemicals and the internal combustion engine in the 1880s, and the development of electronics and aerospace in the 1930s all contributed to this upward trend in material well-being. Today's developed nations are going through an equally significant, and certainly more rapid period of transformation with the advent first, of computerised production processes in the 1960s, and then, from the 1970s on, the development of information technology.

In today's technological revolution, some industries have experienced big job losses. These have been concentrated among workers with newly redundant skills, the low paid and the least adaptable and skilled. Computerised technology has transformed the production process in manufacturing. In many assembly line processes such as printing and publishing and cars, the workers who used to add and fix components have been replaced by machines doing the same job more efficiently, accurately and quickly.

To date, these job losses have been at least partially offset by the creation of new jobs elsewhere such as in information technology, in electronics and in services. The main sources of these new jobs have been increased domestic demand due to the higher real incomes resulting from reduced costs and prices, higher investment in plant and machinery, and the increased foreign demand resulting from increased price and non-price competitiveness.[67]

A study of the introduction of microelectronics in UK factories found that half the firms introducing new technology did not report *direct* decreases in employment as a result. Taking the whole sample, the study found a total net loss of jobs as a direct result of the introduction of microelectronic production methods of 40–50,000 jobs per year between 1983 and 1987, but that after allowance for the *indirect* effects on employment within the same firms, the impact on job numbers was reversed.[68] Most of the jobs lost in the recession of the early 1980s were the product of plant closures rather than automation. Another study has come to a broadly similar conclusion:

> ... far from causing the big decline in manufacturing employment, microelectronic-based sectors have been the main source of what little employment growth has occurred in the last few years in manufacturing. The decline of employment in the other sectors of UK manufacturing has, however, been massive. It was primarily the result of a

process of restructuring, rationalisation and plant closures in response to international competitive pressures and depressed levels of demand for 'older products'.[69]

The future impact of continuing technical change is more difficult to predict. After a slow start, the impact of information technology in services began to bite in the early 1990s. Many of the big job shake outs then announced by some of the world's biggest companies – IBM, General Motors, BMW, British Telecom – were as much the product of structural as cyclical change. 'Lean production' to cut costs is now the battle-cry in Europe, the US and Japan. Faced with ever tougher competition, firms have started to exploit the potential of the operating methods made possible by electronic data processing, word processing and automated communications and filing systems, leading to big lay-offs among white collar staff, from routine office workers to middle and senior managers. Since many central functions from data analysis to ordering and stock control can take place anywhere, many service companies are following the lead of manufacturing in the eighties and relocating such peripheral functions in cheaper centres abroad, especially in the expanding economies of the Pacific Rim.

The full potential of information technology has yet to be realised, especially as the level of investment in new systems remains relatively low. The revolution can therefore only gather pace during the 1990s, matching the upheaval in manufacturing during the 1980s. The effect on jobs is more difficult to predict. In some sectors, including banking, potential job losses through improved efficiency from automation have been offset by extra demand for banking services. Efficiency improvements will have the effect of creating jobs elsewhere, especially in areas like telecommunications, and in areas of expanding demand such as advisory services, education, training, health care, travel and security. Initial job losses will therefore be at least partially offset, though with a lag, through such job creation.

Nevertheless, these changes are likely to mean greater job insecurity, continuing de-skilling and big shifts in wage differentials. Technological advance has, for example, been a major factor in the sharp increase in the level of long term unemployment shown in figure 4.4. Around a third of the European unemployed have been

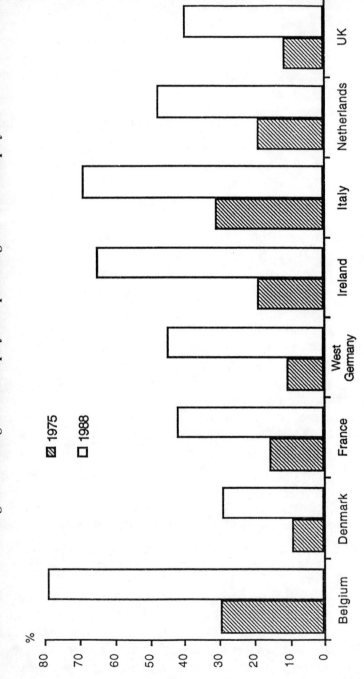

Figure 4.4: Long term unemployed as percentage of total unemployed

1975
1988

Source: Commission of the European Community (1991)

Table 4.2: Growth rates of capital stock (average annual percentages)

	Business					
	1960-73	**1973-79**	**1979-89**	**1979**	**1983**	**1989**
USA	3.7	3.7	3.5	4.3	2.8	3.5
Europe	5.2	3.8	2.9	3.6	2.6	3.4
Japan	12.4	6.6	7.3	6.6	6.5	9.4
	Manufacturing					
	1960-73	**1973-79**	**1979-89**	**1979**	**1983**	**1989**
USA	4.0	3.9	2.3	4.1	1.3	2.1
Europe	5.1	2.4	1.3	2.1	0.8	2.0
Japan	12.4	5.4	6.3	4.9	5.4	7.6

Source: Glyn, 1992, p 86

out of work for more than two years. The problem is that those losing their jobs through the introduction of automation have been those with the least transferable skills, and the least able to compete for the new jobs being created. Job losses arising from new technology have been concentrated among unskilled and semi-skilled production workers, while job gains have been concentrated among the skilled – computer operators, technicians, craftsmen and engineers with electronic and electro-mechanical skills. Many of the new jobs, especially in the service sector, have also been part-time and many have gone to new entrants to the workforce, especially women.

It is also arguable that it has been too little rather than too much investment in new technology that has compounded the problem of unemployment. Despite a problem of short term dislocation, technical progress has a strong medium term job creating potential. As one study has shown, 'the industries at the core of the new microelectronics technology were almost the only UK manufacturing subsectors to show increased employment from 1981–1985'.[70] As the same study concluded, however, the scope for improving employment levels in manufacturing is now extremely limited. It is in services that hopes of reducing unemployment now lie. To date, that potential has not been fully exploited, in Britain or in many other countries. Low increases in productivity and low efficiency have the effect of reducing competitiveness, forcing economies to run at levels of demand insufficient to be able to reduce unemployment.

Over the 1980s, the total capital stock per employee expanded more slowly than during the 1960s and 1970s across the industrialised world, and more slowly in Europe and the USA than in Japan (table 4.2). The consequence has been a limit to the extent to which new techniques and processes can be absorbed into a country's productive potential. 'The legacy has been a severe capital shortage in the 1990s; the capital stock is too small to generate full employment in the European economy.'[71]

This view is supported by another study which showed that the growth rate required in Britain from the mid-1980s to maintain manufacturing employment at mid-1980s levels would require levels of investment of around ten times the historical average investment growth of just above 1 per cent a year. Similar, though less severe, problems were found to confront other European countries, with relatively high output and investment growth rates required to maintain employment. This contrasted sharply with the United States and Japan where no evidence of capital shortfall in manufacturing was found.

> The overall conclusion is that a capital constraint to growth could well occur in the UK in the medium term (late eighties and early nineties), but could be overcome by a combination of higher capital productivity associated with new technology and of higher levels of investment in manufacturing.[72]

There is no evidence that this constraint has been overcome or that the higher rates of investment and productivity required have been achieved.

The most important brake on the introduction of new systems has been a shortage of skilled workers. 'Shortages of engineering staff with microelectronics expertise are the most commonly reported obstacle to companies using the technology.'[73] Economies with the most highly educated and skilled labour forces have been best placed to exploit the potential of new technology. The high unemployment of the 1980s has coincided with the problem of an acute shortage of the key skills needed to implement new technology efficiently.

One effect of these low levels of capital and human investment has been a slowing down in the rate of increase of productivity. After 1973 when unemployment started to rise, productivity growth in most western nations began to falter. During the second half of the 1980s, productivity rates recovered but not to the levels of the 1950s and 1960s. One way of achieving the higher growth rates necessary to reduce unemployment without hitting the constraints of a growing trade deficit and rising inflation would be through higher productivity growth and so, higher competitiveness. Unemployment in the UK and elsewhere is more closely related to a loss of competitiveness arising from inadequate productivity growth than the direct job losses associated with rapid productivity change.

This problem of deteriorating investment and productivity growth is more closely related to social and cultural than economic factors. The most successful post-war economies including Japan and Germany have been those able to sustain high investment and low consumption ratios. Part of the secret of the rapid economic take-off of the countries of the Pacific Rim lies in their cultures of restraint. Ironically, rising prosperity has coincided with a growing domination of short term considerations in many nations.

Affluence has created impatient societies which have contributed to the inflationary and low profit era of recent times. Wages have often outstripped productivity growth leading to lower profits and investment, while the demand for rising private consumption has restricted the scope for public investment. Boardrooms in some countries have been more concerned with share prices and dividend levels than long term growth. Even countries like Germany and Japan seem to be succumbing to similar pressures for giving priority to short term material living standards. It remains to be seen whether the newly developing economies of South East Asia and parts of China can sustain the cultural climate that helped to bring early economic success.

Survival in the increasingly competitive climate of the 1990s will depend on a reversal of the trends of recent decades. Firms will face growing pressure from reduced trade barriers and from the newly industrialising nations. Improved productivity can be achieved by a further shedding of labour or by higher levels of investment in labour-saving technology. In essence, the speeding up of the process of technical change through higher capital and skill investment would increase productivity and improve growth prospects. By improving competitiveness, it would open up the possibility of reducing unemployment by removing one of the obstacles to sustained higher growth. Higher investment, however, will depend on developing a more restrained political and social environment.

Industrial change and the new division of labour

The industrial revolution of the last twenty years has not merely affected employment opportunities. It has transformed the structure and division of the labour force. The history of all societies over the last 200 years has been one of first a shift in employment from the farm to the factory, and then an equally dramatic shift from the factory to the office and the shop. The rise of manufacturing reached its peak in the immediate post-war period and has been in decline ever since. Table 4.3 shows that since 1950, the proportion employed in industry in the OECD has fallen from 36 per cent to 30 per cent while the proportion working in services has risen from 39 to 64 per cent.

Table 4.3: Long term changes in employment patterns (percentages)

OECD average

	Agriculture	Industry	Services
1870	49	27	24
1900	38	31	31
1950	25	36	39
1980	7	34	59
1987	6	30	64

Source: Maddison, 1989, p 20

'De-industrialisation' has been the combined result of changing demand as incomes have risen, and of mechanisation and other technical and organisational trends that have allowed greater productivity first in agriculture, then in manufacturing, and now increasingly in services. It has been further fuelled by the rise of new industrial nations which have used their advantage of lower labour costs to increase their share of world manufacturing output. Jobs have been shifting around the world. These changes are far from complete, as both the intensification of international competition and the effects of the technological revolution have yet to run their course.

De-industrialisation has transformed the character of work, leading to a large-scale loss of jobs among predominantly unskilled and semi-skilled workers and widening wage differentials. It has led to a larger 'peripheral' workforce of part-time and insecure workers alongside a new elite and privileged group of skilled, secure and well-paid professionals. It has also led to an increase in the number of women entering the labour force, mainly in routine white-collar or lower professional jobs, and mainly part-time and sometimes temporary.

While these shifts have been common throughout the industrialised world, the precise impact has depended on the institutional and political framework within which de-industrialisation has occurred, and in particular on three key factors – industrial competitiveness, wage flexibility in labour markets, and the significance of public sector employment. De-industrialisation has proceeded more slowly in the most competitive nations such as Germany and Japan. Germany still has a relatively high proportion of its workforce in manufacturing, though it too is beginning to experience the problems of transition that began earlier elsewhere.

There have been three broad approaches to coping with these changes. First, some countries have set out to try and minimise the disruption and maximise the benefits. These countries would include those defined earlier as examples of 'social corporatism' including Sweden, Norway and Austria. These have attempted to cushion the impact through a combination of public investment in training and a willingness to provide public sector jobs. In these countries, de-industrialisation did not, at least initially, lead to rising unemployment but the birth of a new service sector concentrated in relatively well-paid and secure welfare state jobs. The malign impact of these changes can be mitigated with electorates willing to accept the higher taxes necessary to fund a higher level of public sector employment. In some countries, this has proved an effective way of sharing the costs of change, though the Swedish experience is that it may not prove a durable option.

The predominantly free market approach of the United States lies at the other extreme. Here, the decline of manufacturing has led to the creation of some unemployment and a much larger low-paid service sector both because of a lack of wage regulation and a low level of employment in welfare services. Indeed, the United States has suffered a lower rise in unemployment than elsewhere because it has created a large number of new jobs in predominantly low-paid and low-quality work such as bartenders, waiters, janitors, guards, domestic cleaners, fast-food sellers and clerical workers. In the United States, large numbers of people subsist on unstable or marginal forms of employment.

Other countries such as Britain have adopted an essentially middle way. They seem to have ended up with the worst of both worlds – a sharp rise in unemployment and growing numbers in low paid and insecure work. This trend has been encouraged by attempts to deregulate the labour market through, for example, the weakening of trade union power, cuts in unemployment benefits and employment rights, and the dismantling of minimum wage regulations.

What is emerging in 'post-industrial societies' is a much more complex pattern of employment and division of labour. In the immediate post-war era, industrial workforces could be divided into four main groups: a small number of mostly short-term unemployed; a large body of full-time skilled and unskilled, mostly male, workers; a small middle class of professionals and administrators; and a small well-paid elite of managers and owners. The divisions that existed were for the most part ones of earnings and skill rather than security.

That structure has been and is still being transformed by first, a rise in the level of both long and recurrent short-term unemployment, and second by the emergence of a much larger peripheral group of insecure, often part-time and mainly low paid workers. Today's labour market can be segmented into five main groups: the long-term unemployed; the short-term unemployed; the periphery; the unskilled core; the skilled core. Many of the short-term unemployed are between jobs and not all are especially disadvantaged by one or more short spells of unemployment. Indeed modern economies have brought a more fluid experience of work, with more frequent job and career changes than in the past. But many are also the most vulnerable to periodic unemployment, living on the fringes of the labour market and moving in and out of low paid, insecure work in the peripheral sector. Indeed, workers who experience unemployment frequently have irregular and discontinuous patterns of employment thereafter.[74]

These trends are likely to continue, even accelerate. Job markets are likely to become more polarised and fragmented, with elite groups of workers with special and highly rewarded skills, and increasing numbers with continually redundant experience. The future of work is likely to remain uncertain and insecure for large numbers of the population including some professional groups. The effect on inequality will be the harsher, the more measures of protection for the victims of industrial change are weakened or dismantled.

Some commentators, such as the American sociologist Daniel Bell, have viewed the move towards 'post-industrialism' as heralding the transition to a largely better future in which increasing numbers of the working class would come to achieve the benefits of the middle class with greater prosperity, more leisure and greater democracy at work.[75] There is much truth in this. A higher proportion of society now enjoy new advantages and roles, greater flexibility and more rewarding work. More women have had the chance of work, though for the most part routine and low paid. Nevertheless, the dreams of the 'post-industrial utopians' of the birth of a new industrial order of wider opportunities, more choice and less inequality for all are far from being realised.

5. Material World

Some boys kiss me, some boys hug me
I think they're OK
If they don't give me proper credit
I just walk away

They can beg and they can plead
But they can't see the light, that's right
'Cause the boy with the cold hard cash
Is always Mister Right

'Cause we're living in a material world
And I am a material girl
You know that we are living in a material world
And I am a material girl

('Material Girl', Madonna)[76]

This superdevelopment, which consists in an *excessive* availability of every kind of material goods for the benefit of certain social groups, easily makes people slaves of 'possession' and of immediate gratification, with no other horizon than the multiplication or continual replacement of the things already owned with others still better. This is the so-called civilisation of 'consumption' or 'consumerism' which involves so much 'throwing-away' and 'waste'. An object already owned but now superseded by something better is discarded, with no thought of its possible lasting value in itself, nor of some other human being who is poorer.

(Pope John Paul II)[77]

During the 1980s the process of evolution from *welfare capitalism* to *consumer capitalism*, which had begun in the 1960s, accelerated. The decade of the 1980s was in many ways an iconoclastic period that completed the transition from the moderation favoured by the Pope to the 'material world' symbolised by Madonna. To some it represented the end of a monotonous and unexciting past; to others, it epitomised the growing problem of 'over-consumption', an era of spending that fed the boom years of the late 1980s but ended abruptly in the most serious recession since the 1930s.

The coming of the consumer society

Consumerism and affluence have gone hand in hand. The 'consumer society' arrived first in the United States during the 1920s and 1930s with the emergence of branded goods and packaged, processed foods, and when the automobile assumed its place at the heart of American culture. The 'democratisation of consumption' became the driving force of economic policy. Although the march of consumerism stalled during the Great Depression and the Second World War, it resumed in earnest after the war.

Consumerism did not spread from North American borders until well into the 1950s. After the war, spending in most of Western Europe was concentrated on a minimal range of basic items. The post-war years were ones of austerity. Consumption for most was largely a matter of 'existence'. Discretionary spending was limited. The television sets, vacuum cleaners and refrigerators which were becoming commonplace in the United States were only available to a small minority of Europeans. Many services such as launderettes and 'take-away' food shops did not exist. In the early 1950s some goods, especially foodstuffs, remained rationed, while others such as tinned fruit were virtually unobtainable. The range of products available even for those with some surplus spending were very limited. Only the rich were able to enjoy an indulgent lifestyle.

Gradually this began to change as real incomes started to rise above the level needed to meet basic physical and social needs. New technology led to the creation of new materials from man-made fabrics to plastics, and wholly new products like deep freezers, washing machines and convenience foods. Rising productivity, meanwhile, fed the process of rising real wages. The mass production techniques pioneered by Henry Ford spread to Europe bringing lower prices for some goods like cars and household appliances.

In Britain in 1957, Harold Macmillan spelled out the spirit of the times by declaring, accurately, that 'most of our people have never had it so good'. Basic wants were being widely met, consumption horizons were expanding. Discretionary spending became the norm rather than the exception. Hundreds of thousands poured every year into the Ideal Home Exhibition and the Motor Show. Supermarkets and self-service stores began to appear. The boutique made its debut in the late 1950s, first in Kings Road and then Carnaby Street, and by the end of the 1960s had spread to all provincial high streets. Designers like Mary Quant and Terence Conran became household names, Biba opened its first store in Kensington in 1964 and Habitat followed a few months later. Similar changes were at work on the continent. Europe was starting to catch up with American lifestyles.

Advertising, already well entrenched in the United States, became the new growth industry in Europe. There was an increasing emphasis on marketing and packaging. The birth of commercial television, first in Britain in 1955 and slightly later on the continent, brought advertisements to a mass public. Consumerism was given another upward twist in the 1960s with the emergence of a relatively affluent and fashion conscious youth market. Teenage culture was born and with it the equating of lifestyle with consumerism. Young people throughout the emerging affluent nations of the west were looking for a new image and identity and found it in fashionable and distinctive dress. Clothing became a new code, a badge, a means of self and group expression.

During this period the nature of consumer motivation changed. Aspirations became larger, as desires were moulded by what others had. Imitation was beginning to become the dominant determinant of consumer behaviour.

While the rise of affluence proved the means to mass and imitative consumerism, it also contributed to the rise of a youthful rebellious culture. Ironically, the protest movements of the 1960s were only made possible by the liberating impact of growing prosperity. The protesters were the children of affluence. By the mid-1960s, portions of a youth culture centred on pop music, adventurous dress and having fun took on a more rebellious anti-materialistic and anti-paternalistic colouration.

Anti-materialism was always a minority pre-occupation, however, and was oversold by its champions. It soon lost its appeal in the very different atmosphere of retrenchment that was ushered in by recession in the 1970s. Youth, that had been sold an ideal of liberation and self-fulfilment, discovered that these ends depended on jobs and the very productionism that they had been implicitly attacking. Unemployment forced a recognition that anti-materialism and protest was a luxury that depended on material security. Young people fell into line first, as student rebellions and radical politics fizzled out, and they were followed by other groups and interests, including after much conflict, the trade unions.

If the consumer society was born in the 1960s, it was during the 1980s that it came of age. As the 1970s closed, a new ideology, cleverly subverting but also stealing the clothes of sixties' utopianism, emerged. Thatcherism and its 'do your own thing' philosophy and anti-bureaucratic mission was pure 1960s in every respect but one. The movements of the earlier decade were about liberation for spiritual fulfilment, with material possessions playing a supporting role. The new liberation was for unashamedly material ends.

Repressed consumerist aspirations finally found expression and wider legitimation in the new icons of the decade – the 'money-moving and making' professions, the get-rich-quick attitudes, the yuppies. Working in the City, on Wall Street and in the burgeoning professional openings in European capitals for undreamt of salaries and pretending to adhere to the philosophies of the past was proving impossible. So it was necessary to admit that there was nothing else in life. There was no such thing as 'society', only our 'material selves'. Consumerism and the new 'ideology of pleasure' had become more than legitimate, even for sections of the Left where it was espoused by the Socialist Party in Italy, the Eurocommunists in Britain and the 'la Movida' movement in Spain. By the end of the decade, there was little else to galvanise the individual, the community or the nation. Millions had and were finding new fulfilment through consumerism.

The evolution from welfare to consumer capitalism that had begun in the 1960s thus gathered pace during this decade. As incomes continued to rise, more and more people were able to expand their consumption horizons. Aspirations spread from a small and better-off elite to the whole population. Everybody wanted to be part of the act. The process dovetailed neatly with the changing political ideology and the rise and then the ascendancy of the New Right. Consumerism and individualism were the spirit of the age during the 1980s as improvements in personal consumption were given an increasing priority as both the motor of growth and for the economic gains of the decade (see figure 2.2).

Nations of shoppers

Mature consumerism has been reflected in increasing commercialisation. Shopping has become a family and individual experience in itself. With the aid of the car and the credit card, the family expedition to the giant superstore has become as popular as the day trip to the seaside. In Britain, coach companies run day trips to the newly opening shopping malls. Shopping is one of Britain's most important leisure activities with, according to our data, 2.5 hours per week spent on 'inessential' shopping and another 2.5 hours on 'essentials'. Americans go to shopping centres on average once a week – more often than they go to places of worship. American teenagers spend more time in malls than anywhere besides school or home.[78] Henley Centre surveys show that a half of all Italians and Spaniards view shopping as a leisure activity. As Arthur Miller has put it,

> Years ago a person, he was unhappy, didn't know what to do with himself – he'd go to church, start a revolution – something. Today you're unhappy? Can't figure it out? What is the salvation? Go shopping![79]

Shops are open for longer. As Edwina Curry said in the Commons debate on Sunday opening, 'My constituents want to shop.' In Britain, newspapers and magazines carry mini-catalogues with seductive titles – *Discoveries*, *The Leading Edge*, *Innovation*. An explosion in mail order catalogues offers 'the world's most extraordinary shopping experience', 'accessories for the Jet Age', 'setting the pace for life', the latest advances in designer living to be bought from the comfort of the armchair through the 'mail order hotlines'. In the United States, ads account for a third of mail – 14 billion mail-order catalogues and 38 billion other assorted ads are sent through the post each year.[80]

The telephone and television have become increasingly important means of marketing with the growing use of computerised information systems. Interactive videotex systems are the latest additions to a range of forms of 'distant selling' or 'home shopping'. In most countries, this latest development of mail-order trading currently occupies a small, but expanding, share of the retail market. While telemarketing has been around for some time, especially in the United States, 'television shopping' is a much more recent development, with some countries having specific spots, programmes and entire TV channels devoted to selling. In the United States, jewellery accounts for 50 per cent of such television sales. In 1993, Sky Television launched QVC – Quality, Value and Convenience – Britain's first 24-hour shopping channel. Video-shopping has been expanding in Germany and Norway and has gone furthest in France where it is likely to represent 25 per cent of retail sales by 1995.[81]

The market is also encroaching on more and more areas of life – artistic expression, television scheduling, sport, film distribution, public services. Bottled water of innumerable varieties has started to displace tap water. In Britain, more and more conventional and 'alternative' health care is being bought, with a third of professionals and 14 per cent of the entire population now covered by private medical insurance, a figure we at the Henley Centre predict will rise to 20 per cent by the turn of the century. Domestic activities from home decorating to gardening have increasingly become part of the commercial process, with new service industries offering landscaped gardens, designer bathrooms and personal financial advice. Security services for the home, the office and the high street are big business.

Consumer society is not just about buying things. It is also about things to do. Leisure was once a largely individualised and self-creating pastime. Free time is now soaked up by an explosion of commercialised leisure facilities, and many of our weekends are dedicated to theme parks, leisure centres and shopping. 'Once leisure used to mean free time, a liberated realm, an escape from work and economic responsibility. Today, there's nothing free about it – commerce has invaded pleasure with a vengeance.'[82] Wherever people now congregate – at air terminals, museums, galleries, leisure centres – they are confronted by retail opportunities: sports equipment, gifts, postcards, books, posters. In a highly effective and successful search for ways of maximising turnover, the retail, design and marketing businesses have not been slow to see the potential of what is known in the trade as the 'retail-leisure mix'.

Commercialisation has gone furthest in the United States. 'We live in what may be the most consumer-oriented society in history ... Once a purely utilitarian chore, shopping has been elevated to the status of a national passion.'[83] In 1990, US corporations spent $130 billion on advertising, the equivalent of $6 a week for every man, woman and child in the United States, according to the *Wall Street Journal*. That's 50 per cent more per capita than is spent in any other nation. Supermarkets carry shopping trolleys fitted with TV monitors that advertise the branded products for the aisle you're strolling down. The 1980s saw the birth of a new series of 'Born to Shop' guides. Shopping for some has become an addiction, giving rise to self-help groups like Debtors Anonymous and Shopaholics Limited. As one commentator put it,

> The shop 'til you drop syndrome seemed particularly active during the 1980s, a decade popularly represented as one long spending spree. In the 5 years between 1983 and 1987, Americans purchased 51 million microwaves, 44 million washers and dryers, 85 million color televisions, 36 million refrigerators and freezers, 48 million VCRs and 23 million cordless telephones – all for an adult population of only 180 million.[84]

Today, three-quarters of single-family homes in the United States have at least two bathrooms, two-thirds have air-conditioning, microwaves and dryers, and almost a half have dishwashers. The average household owns two cars. Over 80 per cent of households have VCRs. The European home still has some way to go to match its US counterpart. Nearly 70 per cent of European households have cars, and a fifth two or more, 65 per cent have full central heating, a quarter have microwaves and 41 per cent have videos (table 2.1). In 1950, Japan was further behind the United States than Europe, but rapidly closed the gap. In the 1980s, even traditionally frugal Japan was caught in the addiction. Frivolous items like gold-wrapped sushi and mink coats for dogs appeared on the market. By the end of the decade, the government was urging loyal Japanese to buy more in order to reduce their internationally resented trade surplus.

The manipulated or sovereign consumer?

Consumerism is a dominant force behind the transformation of modern societies. There is much less agreement as to whether this is for better or worse. On the Right, modern consumerism is viewed as wholly beneficial, a product of the virtue of market forces and a more independent and discerning consumer. The Right's case for the dominance of the market has always been based on the concept of 'consumer sovereignty' in which well informed and fully independent consumers operate as free agents exercising choice over the range of products on offer. Manufacturers then simply respond to these expressed desires through the mechanism of the market, adjusting their output according to independently determined changes in tastes and demands. It is freedom to spend which is the modern engine of growth from which everyone benefits.

The arrival of mass consumerism and the new individualism has presented much more of a challenge for the Left which has always felt uncomfortable with affluence. They clash with their traditional distrust of markets, of individualism and commercialisation. They have contributed to the decline of industrial society and the mass, male, manual working class which had been both the source of power and inspiration for the Left, leaving a gaping hole in their traditional base of support and philosophy. For the Left, the development of a diversified consumer culture offering identity other than through the solidarity of the workplace, the trade union, the football stadium or the working men's club has been a potent threat.

Yet these trends have been welcomed and exploited by much of the European Left. Many of the more modernised Left parties in Europe such as the Spanish and before their disgrace, the Italian Socialists, made virtues out of the consumer obsessions of the 1980s.

In Britain, the rise of a new consumer culture was seen as empowering by the former journal of the Communist Party, *Marxism Today*.

> Despite their profound contradictions, ideologies of affluence have had very real effects on large sections of the population. Some of these have been potentially liberating – consuming as a source of power and pleasure. They will need to find a place within our vision of the new times.[85]

The essential theme running through *Marxism Today*'s analysis was a view of consumer society as emancipatory. Many of the changes brought by consumerism, and the ending of the grey uniformity of the past, were viewed as progressive, bringing both greater individual freedom and new chances of self-expression. Rising living standards have brought more choice and new opportunities for most, enabling the majority to rise above the basic and limited lifestyle that had been the norm. Consumerism represents a rupture with the past, with tradition, with established and limited ways of living. It has brought a new sense of freedom, in which everyone's special, everyone's different. It has contributed to the breaking down of class barriers, of former hierarchies and systems of deference. What might be called a 'Fordist' technology of mass production is in theory giving way to a 'post-Fordist' one of greater individuality and differentiation, with more flexibility, shorter production runs and variation in products bringing increased diversity and choice.

The problem for the 'post-Fordist' theorists is that this revolution has been a partial one. The extra choice claimed for the consumer is easy to exaggerate. Items are more sophisticated and there is a much wider range of colours and styles. But claims of greater responsiveness and differentiation are overstated, except at the top end of the market. Clothing and furniture sales are dominated by a small number of multiple retailers that can be found in every high street. Outside the luxury and specialist market, the majority of cars sold fall into a handful of 'Euro-models', differentiated only by colour, power and the quality of inbuilt stereo.

An opposing trend has been towards global homogenisation. McDonald's is a near universal phenomenon as are C&A and

Benetton. The ubiquitous Coca-Cola has found its way to even the remotest and poorest parts of the world. Differences between nations are declining. Mass production and imitative consumption remain the dominant mode for the majority of consumers. One critic, for example, has argued that far from enabling manufacturing industry to become more responsive to individual tastes and preferences, 'the quest for new technologies, like that for differentiation in products, has connoted intensifying struggles for market share more than it has ushered in a new society of "empowered" consumers and designers.'[86]

The criticisms of consumerism have a long pedigree. The conventional Left critique of the consumer society has three basic strands – that individuals are manipulated by corporations, that consumerism is highly wasteful, and that it encourages alienation as individuals are increasingly forced to relate to each other through commodities. Central to this critique has been the question of the concept of the all powerful consumer. It is claimed that, far from being sovereign, modern consumers are manipulated by increasingly powerful corporations and their marketing teams. In search of expanded markets, they have created new and false or artificial desires.

This view was first expressed by a variety of North American 'liberal' and Left analysts writing in the 1950s and 1960s.[87] Although written from different political standpoints, the essence of these critiques was similar. They came from American authors first, because consumer capitalism arrived in the United States well before Europe. All attacked the alleged tendency of large corporations to adopt persuasive advertising to create increasingly superficial and artificial needs. For J.K. Galbraith, for example, the fundamental problem of modern capitalism has been how to maintain profitability with what he sees as essentially finite consumer *needs*, a dilemma resolved by the creation of false *wants*. A similar critique was mounted by the social theorist, Herbert Marcuse, who also drew a distinction between 'true' needs rooted in essential human and social interaction and artificially created 'false' needs.

The essence of these critiques is that capitalism's survival depends on the maintenance of rising consumer demand, secured through a twin marketing process of creating new wants and eliminating old ones. Without it, market-dominated societies would grind to a halt. Central to this idea is the concept of built-in obsolescence. There is in fact nothing new in the use of obsolescence by twentieth-century capitalism. As early as the 1930s big corporations in the United States began to adopt a business strategy that involved regular planned product and stylistic change as the route to expansion. As one of the early American architects of the strategy, the advertising supremo Ernest Elmo Calkins, bluntly put it as early as 1930:

> The purpose is to make the customer discontented with his old type of fountain pen, kitchen utensil, bathroom or motor car, because it is old fashioned, out-of-date. The technical term for this idea is obsoletism. We can no longer wait for things to wear out. We displace them with others that are not more effective but more attractive.[88]

After the war, obsolescence, and the dynamising of taste that went along with it, became an integral part of both business planning and consumer living. It helped to sustain the extraordinary stability and success of the long post-war boom. There was no obvious conflict. It helped generate the profits that underpinned the boom and it stimulated consumer satisfaction. The rapidity of social, cultural and stylistic change seemed in tune with wider social progress and consumer satisfaction. As affluence progressed the same processes became more imperative. Unable to survive by providing 'survival' needs alone, sustained profitability has depended on the development of new products and markets and more sophisticated marketing. With the needs and wants of today's affluent majority largely met, it is claimed, consumers have to be continually persuaded that their existing goods and lifestyles need updating.

This view has a persuasive ring. If today's consumers seem happy to indulge themselves in the increasing commercialisation of modern living, it can't be denied that they have been given more than a helping hand by the marketing professionals. In the last twenty years, manufacturing has given way to the image industry. This is increasingly the age of the market researcher, the advertising agent, the marketing manager, the producers, directors, designers, all engaged in packaging and selling.

In the process, marketing has become not only more sophisticated, but, some would argue, more intrusive as well. In the United States, commercialism's stamp is increasingly hard to escape. Ads are tucked in books, projected from subways and even bus stop monitors, pumped into doctors' reception rooms, inscribed on clothes, zapped through fax machines. Technology has added to the opportunities. Wall-sized video screens have been erected in shopping malls and at sports events. Even hot dogs carry edible slogans.

Another modern marketing device is *product placement*, a form of promotion in which manufacturers pay to have their products prominently displayed in influential films, soaps and dramas. This is huge business in the United States with the giant film companies earning large sums and the manufacturers gaining big audiences. When Tom Cruise wore Ray-Ban Aviators in Paramount's blockbuster *Top Gun* in 1989, sales more than doubled. Similar success was won by Tom Cruise wearing black Levi 501s throughout *Days of Thunder* made in 1990. Most big Hollywood films are crammed with such placements, from Domino Pizzas in *Teenage Mutant Turtles* to Subway Sandwiches, another young male dominated market, in *Terminator II*.

Sports sponsorship is also a booming business in the United States. Nike invested £7 million in 1990 on basketball-related promotions alone. The practice has extended to television series and has already crossed the Atlantic. It is rare to see a major sports event that isn't sponsored, with conspicuous site advertisements such as giant logos on test match pitches and participants displaying branded clothing and equipment. Several ITV series have been backed by lucrative commercial sponsorship. *Inspector Morse* came 'in association with Beamish Stout' and *Rumpole of the Bailey* with Croft Port. *Without Walls*, Channel 4's flagship arts programme, is sponsored by Financial Advisers Promotions. Aiming at the programme's upmarket viewers, they reportedly paid between £100,000 and £200,000 for ten-second logo and credit sequences at the beginning and end of each edition.

The ITV fast-moving drama series, *The Bill*, featured Holstein lager as a suitable drink for its principal characters who drive patrol cars supplied by Ford. In, reportedly, a five-figure financial deal, the BBC Anglo-American drama, *The Object of Beauty*, shown on television in February 1992, featured a scripted scene in which the leading actress, Andie MacDowell, orders a dozen bottles of Perrier from room service. The High Street in *Eldorado*, the BBC's now cancelled soap opera, included the shop fronts of Avis Car Hire, Thorn-EMI video rental and Texas Homecare. Specialist brokers supply free products for props departments which then appear prominently in television drama.

While the practice is not commonplace, the *New York Times* uncovered one instance of literary encroachment in a novel featuring a Maserati. It turned out that the author had cut a deal with Maserati that landed her $15,000 worth of book promotion in exchange for the mention. The risk is that the distinction between culture and commercialism is being increasingly blurred. The worlds of entertainment and business have been creeping together over the last decade for powerful commercial reasons, a trend which is probably unstoppable. Film and programme makers are gradually becoming more financially dependent on corporate support, with the real prospect that films could eventually become another form of advertising, in which form and content is compromised by the requirements of the promoters.

It is claimed that similar influence is at work in the sponsorship of the arts in the United States. American Corporations spent $22 million on the arts in 1967. Today the outlay is close to $1 billion. Few museums, exhibitions and shows are not underwritten by corporate money. This has had the effect of producing safe and unchallenging exhibitions which, according to one critic, are 'non-provocative and certainly unquestioning of corporate political economy'.[89] He quotes one curator as saying 'Most corporate sponsors finance exhibitions based on centrist ideals and uncontroversial subject matter.' Schiller goes on, 'Corporate sponsorship of museum exhibitions leads inevitably, as does advertising-supported television, to self-censorship, with the result that public awareness of social reality is continuously diminished.'

Another object of the promoter's gaze is children. Indeed children are one of the fastest growing target audiences in the United States. Companies spent about $500 million in 1990 to reach children aged two to twelve – five times what they spent in the early 1980s – according to James McNeal, professor of marketing at Texas A&M University. One specialist in marketing told the *Wall Street*

Journal, 'Even two-year-olds are concerned about their brand of clothes, and by the age of six, are full-out consumers.'[90] Advertisers are drawn to children because they have more buying power than ever before.

> Corporations long ago infiltrated the schools, emblazoning their logos on educational materials and offering rewards like free computers and pizza in exchange for brand-name recognition among the next generation of consumers. Whittle Communications, which is credited with some of the most innovative marketing practices of the 1980s, beams Channel One, a 12 minute TV news show that includes two minutes of ads, free to more than 8,900 schools. To sweeten the deal, Whittle gives the schools satellite dishes, VCRs, and TVs as well; all the teachers have to do is round up the kids to watch the spots for Burger King etc.[91]

In Britain, children have also become increasingly influential in bidding up household spending. Companies such as Tesco, W H Smith and Boots have introduced voucher schemes for school equipment in return for purchases. In supermarkets children behave as 'naggers' and 'trolley loaders' badgering parents and sneaking goods into the trolley. Saturday morning television is dominated by toy advertising, especially at Christmas. This raises expectations, a problem that is particularly acute for poor families whose children are equally vulnerable to the seductive power of possession advertising.

As John Pearce, Professor of Child Psychology at Nottingham University put it, 'Our children are becoming acquisitive and materialistic. Looking back, the toys you remember were not the ones that were very expensive but the ones you could do a lot with. Children often have too many toys now. They don't value them and they often get broken.' In Japan, average spending on children's toys is $450 and on clothes $770 a year, and some gem shops specialise in jewellery for children under twelve. Takayama Hideo, head of Tokyo's Children Research Institute, reports 'Today's mothers . . . want their children to match what they themselves wear. They buy fancy tableware and other goods for their children and . . . they're more fashion conscious.'[92]

Identity through consumerism

Another issue is the question of motivation. Modern consumerism is much less a narrow functional activity, about the meeting of material and bodily needs. It has become increasingly symbolic, about identity and the meeting of first social and more latterly psychological needs. This symbolic aspect of consumption has always existed, but until recently, only for a small minority. It first emerged in a 'mass' form with the development of youth culture in the 1960s, and the beginnings of the equation of 'identity with style'. The use of clothes and other products for the purpose of wider expression and symbolic communication was especially associated with the hippies and the mods and rockers in the 1960s and then with the punk movement a decade later, and has gradually spread to most levels of society.

One effect has been that satisfaction may be coming less from the act of consumption itself. Some spending still performs this role – the time saving and convenience from having a washing machine in the home, the pleasure of more adventurous holidays, the wider choice of viewing offered by the video recorder. But much of modern consumption is performing a very different role, providing symbols of how we want to appear. Image is more important than use. A four-wheel drive car in central London is not essential even to cope with the condition of modern roads. Expensive trainers and track suits are worn less for the purpose of sport than to carry a message about the type of personality we want to project. Parker pens, according to the advert, 'are guaranteed for a lifetime of self-expression'.

> How does the Saab owner see his car these days? Does he see it as a fast car? As a safe car? Not primarily. No. He sees the car in terms of its brand image. He sees the advertising. He understands how he, as a Saab owner, is supposed to think, to behave. He has bought an image of himself. And now he must try to live up to it.[93]

In modern societies products have become a means of communication. They are the modern means of expression, the new social props. Some products have value today less for what they do for us than for what they say about us. The French cultural theorist, Jean Baudrillard, has claimed, in criticism of Galbraith, that human needs are far from finite, that 'need is not a need for a particular object as much as it is a "need" for difference (the desire for social meaning)'. Today, he argues, consumption has become a form of 'language', with commodities and objects a 'system of signs . . . Marketing, purchasing, sales, the acquisition of differentiated commodities and object/signs – all of these constitute our language, a code with which our entire society *communicates* and speaks of and to itself.'[94] Objects still have functional attributes, but have also increasingly come to take on these more intangible, emotional and less predictable meanings.

These trends have been encouraged but not created by the marketing industry which has been quick to appropriate new meanings for once familiar products. Goods are promoted not for their functional qualities, but for what they do to our personalities. They are associated with desirable human traits, offering status, power, potency, dynamism, warmth. Products are the new lapel badges, our membership cards, our passports. They have taken on meaning in themselves. Meaning used to reflect use. A kettle was for boiling water. A track suit to go running in. No longer. Goods can make us more exciting, more amusing, more interesting, sexier. Gold Blend coffee provides new powers of seduction. The American Express Gold Card makes us exclusive.

In the past the selling industry was more closely linked to usage. Spending was dominated by the satisfaction of material and social needs and wants. But as those needs and wants have been met, consumerism has evolved, and marketing with it. Increasingly, everyday products are being repackaged to reflect core values. According to the design company used, the Maxwell House Coffee label has been redesigned 'to bring out the brand values associated with rich coffee: comforting, warm and approachable'. Diet food under the name of Limmits was relaunched with new packaging to appeal to the 'sophisticated, streamlined, sexy' taste. Persil now reflects the brand values of 'whiteness and caring'. Gini bitter lemon is 'modern and dynamic'.[95]

Advertising undoubtedly works. The Levi 501 ad launched in the 1980s was a model of how to reverse declining sales. Levi's put £10 million into promotion. The British agency, Bartle, Bogle and

Hegarty created two highly successful commercials: Nick Kamen undressing down to his boxer shorts and washing his jeans in a 1950s launderette, and James Mardle wearing his jeans in the bath. As one writer described the effect, 'This was enough to catapult the unknown model Kamen to high-profile superstardom as beautiful young man, actor, pop star or whatever. It was also enough to increase 501 sales from 80,000 in 1985 to 650,000 in 1986.'[96] It also had a dramatic impact on the sales of boxer shorts!

This is not to claim that modern consumers are gullible and defenceless victims of the marketing professionals or that the marketing process is all one way.

> A more serious look at advertising's dialogue with the market puts paid to the cliche that consumption is foisted on gullible populations by hype and the lust for profit. Advertisers and marketers are not simply the slaves of capital. They are the intermediaries who construct a dialogue between the market on the one hand and consumer culture on the other . . . To fail to recognise that marketing taps something of our pleasures and aspirations as consumers is to ignore the how and why of its success.[97]

It is arguable that consumerism is as much a product of the new, iconoclastic individualism as the other way about. Consumers are intoxicated with modern consumerism as much because they have been able to break out of the circumscribed roles of the past, as because they have been seduced by the professional salesmen. Modern consumerism has brought new forms of satisfaction, and led to more varied and interesting lives. In many ways, it has provided a convenient substitute for the lack of meaning provided through other routes. In this new climate, the marketing industry found it easy to repackage their messages to become more seductive. It was a process in which consumers and producers seemed only too happy to be part of a joint conspiracy.

A quick fix?

To some, the new meaning provided by consumerism is both desirable and inevitable.

... the fact is that greater and greater numbers of people –
with however little money – play the game of using things to
signify who they are. Everybody, including people in very
poor societies ... know that today's 'goods' double up as
social signs and produce meanings as well as energy. There is
no clear evidence that, in an alternative socialist economy,
our propensity to 'code' things according to systems of
meaning, which is an essential feature of our sociability,
would *necessarily* cease – or, indeed, should.[98]

There are several reasons for the growing attachment to
consumerism. We live in societies with fewer certainties, with a
waning emphasis on grand ideologies, on simple and meaningful
social orders. Values used to come from the family, the church, the
local trade union, from political movements. Each of these has
become a declining influence over time. Materialism was less
important in the past, not just because it was confined to a minority,
but because there were other aims and forms of authority to sustain
us. Gradually those alternative systems and aspirations have, one by
one, been eroded. The nuclear and extended family has lost much of
its former authority. So, too, has the state and its institutions.
Scientific developments have undermined the certainties once
provided by religion. Political systems that were born in hope and
idealism have proved false and ephemeral.

The rise of consumerist values can be viewed in two distinctive
ways. As the product of this process of splintering with materialism
stepping into the void created by the evaporation of old certainties.
Or, alternatively, as the cause of this very splintering. In reality, it is
not possible to separate the two. Affluence and social and
aspirational change are all part of an integrated process.

Not so long ago, the world had a much clearer social order,
hierarchical, elitist and authoritarian. The key social players and
power brokers in business, politics and the church had a strong
vested interest in maintaining it. People knew their place and were
either happy with their lot or could do little about it. Gradually this
old world has been overturned. We still want to 'keep up with the
Joneses' in the sense of aspiring to a higher living standard. The
difference between the 1960s and 1980s has been the nature of the
desire for imitation. Thirty years ago, 'keeping up' meant getting a

relatively narrow range of functional consumer goods – a portable radio, a colour TV, a washing machine. Today imitation is wholly different. The label is more important than the item. Designer clothes and gadgets are the new badges, bringing, at least in theory, a greatly extended range of choice.

It is also different in another way. A new motivation has been added, the need to 'keep away from the Joneses'. Consumer motivation has become a neat combination of emulation and imitation, on the one hand, and differentiation and distinction, on the other. Fashion is often a compromise between the two. While still conforming, people have been breaking ranks. Uniformity is mixed with diversity. There are fewer constraints to stick to the rules, and people have increasingly broken out of the social norms into which they had been placed.

Henley Centre research has shown that in 1992, a clear majority of Europeans expressed a desire to be distinctive, to wear different clothes and drink different beer, with few cross-country differences in the attitudes being expressed. The conflict between peer pressure to conform and to be individual and different was most marked amongst 16–24-year-olds. Roughly equal numbers (47 per cent of young people) wanted to 'keep up with the latest fashions' as 'wanted to buy things which other people don't have' (45 per cent). This duality is an added ingredient to the aspirant and leap-frogging culture that grew during the 1980s, and has had the effect of fuelling consumer demands.

The main source of this cultural upheaval has been the growing affluence that has gradually opened up new frontiers of opportunity to larger and larger numbers of people. Another has been the subversive effect of 'seeing backstage', the phrase coined by the eminent sociologist, Erving Goffman who, writing in the 1950s, used it to describe the importance to authority, social norms and social stability of keeping the 'audience' and 'actors' in social situations apart.

A classic example of this was when a photographer some years ago managed to take photos of the Pope about to dive into the swimming pool at his Papal residence in Rome, wearing, unsurprisingly, only swimming trunks. The release of the photo caused complete panic in the Vatican PR department. In a similar vein, the tabloids' unveiling of the British Royal Family in one scandal after another has steadily undermined Royalty's authority and mystique. Aided by the cinema, by TV and other media, seeing backstage is precisely what has been happening for the last 30 years. In the process, the role models, aspirations and activities that once seemed so inaccessible and intimidating have become much less so.

This process of escape from the limited roles of the past has not been taking place independently of the wider currents of change. Values have become increasingly relative. Nothing is better than anything else. Gradually, ethics has become more and more about vesting the ultimate value in individual action and choice. In the past, there was a greater emphasis on absolute values drawn from religious or other precepts that were above and beyond the individual. Today, the idea of such absolutes seems to belong to a past and authoritarian age, replaced by an era which sees little legitimate authority beyond the sovereign individual.

Contemporary philosophers have increasingly questioned the 'modernist' idea of universality in the sense of a final and eternal truth. The French theorist J F Lyotard has attacked what he called the modernist concept of the *meta-narrative*, the idea of some universal truth from science and humanism to religion and socialism, as fundamentally flawed, contradicted by the ephemeral nature of such ideas. Rather, he and other modern philosophers have posited the idea of diversity and the bounded, limited nature of knowledge.

The conflict between these two contrasting ethical systems is evident in the lingering tension that still exists between what people want and what they think they ought to do. Nevertheless, this change has been accompanied by a marked change in the respect we accord to traditional authorities, or what Samuel Beer, in criticism, has described as the 'collapse of deference'. So groups who have been the subject of declining respect and legitimacy as the mystique has gone include not merely politicians, Royalty and teachers, but church leaders, bank managers and newscasters too. The loss of these traditional sources of authority has led us to seek, or be seduced by, new ones. One of these is consumerism. In the past, who you were determined what you did or bought. Now its the goods you buy or the activities you undertake that denote who you are.

This analysis offers an explanation of the significance of modern consumerism, the grip that it has been able to establish because of the inexhaustible nature of the need for such meaning. But it also points to the central dilemma of the new dependency on consumerism, with its shallowness and unpredictability. The problem is that our links with others still depend upon shared understanding and experience as they always have done. But instead of being based upon stable social structures and objective physical criteria they now depend more and more on the subjective meaning that we assume the products we buy have.

This is a precarious world since such evaluation will always be vulnerable to misinterpretation and modification in a way that is less true of the functional purposes of things. Two people will agree about the mpg, acceleration, torque, colour and price of a BMW 7-series but may disagree violently about what it means to own one. This is a recipe for common misunderstanding and muddle. Past generations had a better understanding of whom they shared meaning with and what that meaning was. The most we can do today is assume that others with whom we wish to affiliate and make common cause through our actions and purchases understand the same as us by that action.

This is the irony of modern society. The success over the last thirty years in winning the freedom to be whom we choose and with whom we are affiliated may actually be destroying the basis for this shared social meaning; and in the process, contributing to a loss of social cohesion and mutual understanding. The essential problem is that we are increasingly unsure what, if anything, we mean to each other anymore. If we end up not meaning much to each other, we end up not mattering very much to each other either. Herein lie the seeds of social disintegration.

Since spending is less about meeting basic needs, style and fashion have become the arbiter of our purchasing patterns. In today's consumer society, much of the pleasure from consumption comes from the experience of seeking out and creating a new lifestyle. We no longer shop simply to replace worn items. Consumption is much more short lived, guided by changes in taste that are much more rapid than in the past. This is the disposable age. Items which in the past would have been considered 'durables' have very limited lives. Watches, electronic goods, computer games, even telephones and cameras are discarded way before their 'end-of-use date'. There is no standing still for long. Our homes look shabby and dated if they don't contain the latest designs in lighting, in furniture, in kitchen utensils. Fashion models are full-figured and assured one year, waif-like and vulnerable the next. The racing bike gets displaced by the mountain bike, Y-fronts by boxer shorts. It is difficult to resist the pressure.

The result is an ephemeral society, one guided by the need for instant gratification, of rapidly changing tastes and values, of detachment, impermanence and fads. As Christopher Lasch has argued, this carries the risk that '. . . the model of possession, in a society organized around mass consumption, is addiction. The need for novelty and fresh stimulation becomes more and more intense, intervening interludes of boredom increasingly intolerable.'[99]

There has been a compulsion about buying irrespective of quality. Take the unexpected warning from Gerald Ratner, the former Chief Executive of the retail jewellery chain. A huge commercial success during the 1980s, Ratners had expanded to over 1,000 stores in the UK, the product of high profile marketing. During a much quoted speech to the Institute of Directors in 1991, Ratner seemed to attribute this success to the marketing of cheap and shoddy goods, comparing the longevity of the company's earrings with that of a prawn sandwich and explaining that he could sell a decanter and sherry glasses for less than £5 because 'it was total crap'. Understandably, Ratner's own longevity as head of the company proved to be limited as well.

For a while, this world seemed to offer so much. In the colder climate of the 1990s, the meaning that products promised during the 1980s seems less certain. This has served to emphasise the problem of a consumer culture built on the quick fix. Now there is a new sense of concern about its impact on wider values. The more the excitement associated with the chase is dependent on something that is elusive and transient or superfluous, the more it is likely to become a source of uncertainty and doubt. The void that is emerging during the 1990s is at least in part the product of a gnawing unease with the consumerism that was on offer during the 1980s.

That is not all. In the 1990s, many nations have ended up paying the costs of the heightened consumerism of the 1980s. Societies came to expect an effortless and apparently never-ending upward cycle of material well-being. It could not last. The 1990s recession was, at least in part, the product of the unsustainable boom of the late 1980s, a consumer led burst, fed by the new values of the time and in several countries, an explosive increase in personal and corporate debt.

Herein lies the contradiction inherent in modern consumerism. It has led to more interesting and compelling lives for some. But it has simultaneously been a major source of growing instability. Expanded appetites are not easily consistent with the moderation required in running modern economies. The arrival of mass imitative consumerism has therefore contributed to the greater economic turbulence of the last two decades. Once, fashion was the preserve of the few, a dialect rather than a language. As it has spread beyond the reach of the minority, and to a wider range of goods, its appeal has become more widely available. But, in the process, it has produced strains on societies that are proving increasingly difficult to manage.

6. The Rise of 'Competitive Individualism'

That was somewhere near the middle of a modern gold rush. Never before have so many unskilled twenty-four-year olds made so much money in so little time as we did this decade in New York and London.

(Michael Lewis)[100]

Is this, then, where our vaunted individualism has brought us? To seek shelter in isolated lives, surrounded only by those who share our immediate persona, cultural and economic interests, while the larger society atrophies? What about our other ideals, such as concern for the community, religious and ethnic tolerance, equality before the law, thrift, and respect for hard work? Have they become irrelevant? Might we not strike a new balance for the Nineties, one that could redirect toward bettering our society more of the selfish energy that spurs people to work, entrepreneurs to create, yuppies to acquire, and corporations to streamline?

(*Fortune*)[101]

When the state is tired, the economy depressed, unemployment inexorable, the grand design undefinable and the construction of Europe a challenge which disturbs more than it mobilises, it's a time for each for himself.

(*Le Monde*)[102]

The 1980s was not merely a decade of triumphant consumerism and growing indebtedness. It was also the period when the long process of individualisation of societies and the steady erosion of welfare capitalism began to accelerate. Concern rose about welfare dependency, doubts grew about the efficacy of government, self-reliance emerged as the new creed.

The forward march of individualism

This is in sharp contrast to the prevailing mood of the post-war era when society was seen as more than a collection of individuals operating independently of each other. The character of society was seen as depending on the quality of the relationships between individuals and their interaction with the wider community at a local and national level. A new culture emerged which emphasised the importance of mutual obligation and interdependence, and in which individuals were seen as having rights as well as responsibilities.

Immediately after the war, the overriding public concern was with preventing a return of the insecurity, unemployment and extensive poverty of the 1930s. The political culture of the period accepted an enhanced role for government intervention to build a more secure and prosperous society. Most people saw their own interests as lying in a strong and intervening state committed to redistribution and reducing divisions.

It is these concerns and the former belief in the importance of the community and the power of the state that have been in long term decline. This does not necessarily mean that individuals have become more selfish over time; simply that their aspirations and perceptions of their own self-interest have evolved with changes in the social and cultural sphere in which they operate. As Donald Trump put it, 'People don't change; circumstances do.' Growing prosperity has made people more independent of their families, their local communities and the state, and more dependent on their own resources. We increasingly live and take decisions as individuals rather than as part of wider groupings or communities, whether at work or socially.

Issues that may have been on the public agenda after the war such as inequality, unemployment and welfare have gradually become peripheral to the wider majority. In the 1950s a much higher proportion of the population depended on the state for their social and economic needs such as housing, pensions and welfare. That is no longer the case. To some extent the successful welfare programmes of the post-war years have become a victim of their own success even in the most welfarist of societies. The growing affluence to which these programmes contributed has enabled a much higher proportion of the population to make their own provision. People have slowly become less dependent on public provision, less convinced of its effectiveness and more critical of big government.

Individualism is not necessarily in conflict with a commitment to community. Indeed, human nature has a natural affinity with the idea of society, often seeking and dependent on the approval and support of fellow citizens. How this interplay works is a vital element in the way communities function. Awareness of the inter-dependence can act as an important source of mutual co-operation and constraint. Individualism can be consistent with social responsibility as well as self-preoccupation. In itself individualism has in many ways been a desirable trend, encouraging and allowing greater individuality and self-expression, and reflecting a long term quest for more personal autonomy. The problem is that the individualism which has developed has become increasingly competitive, a person's position in society depending upon performance in relation to others, and vocational and community work being vested with lower status than entrepreneurial skills. It is this brand of individualism which clashes with citizenship. As *Fortune* put it,

> Individualism, an American ideal championed by Jefferson and Franklin, has evolved from the exuberant 'do your own thing' ethos of the Sixties, to the self-absorption of the 'Me Decade', to the all-consuming 'galloping greed' of the Eighties. Such glib monikers oversimplify, of course, but they do call to mind the French writer's [de Tocqueville] warning that unbridled individualism – perhaps the most hallowed of the American virtues – can foster not only personal opportunity and upward mobility but also civic complacency and collective decline.[103]

This process began in the 1960s when the children of the post-war generation showed the first signs of rebellion against conformity and political consensus. By the 1980s, that second post-war generation had quietly turned their backs on the protest movements of the 1960s and 1970s, and their own offspring began to embrace a very different set of political and social values.

The rise of 'competitive individualism' found its deepest expression in Britain and the United States where it was encouraged, though hardly created, by the New Right, anti-collectivist regimes of Margaret Thatcher and Ronald Reagan in the 1980s. But it was hardly unique to these nations. Similar, if less extreme, processes were also evident in most of continental Europe. They may have taken different forms, emerged from different starting blocks, and progressed more gradually but these nations were also succumbing to the same long term social and political trends unleashed by rising affluence.

For twenty or more years after the war, much of Europe had been governed by political parties that shared a common set of objectives and programmes. There were differences of emphasis but not of principle. This was an era of consensus across political parties and the public. There was a commitment to social protection through generous welfare benefits as well as wealth creation. There was a new emphasis on collectivism and on the active state, and an acceptance of the limitations of pure individualism and self-reliance. There was a lessened resistance to higher taxation to pay for improved social programmes. The immediate post-war era can therefore be seen as the birth of a new kind of 'ideological or ethically based politics', with new commitments to building fairer societies, the product of the debilitating impact of the pre-war recession and the effects of the war on the public mood.

The recession of the 1930s had shattered the political complacency of the time and its largely hands-off approach to government. In the United States in the 1930s, this rising concern found expression in Roosevelt's 'New Deal' liberalism. In Scandinavia, it contributed to sustained periods of social democratic rule. Indeed, the sense of consensus that emerged after the war has always been strongest in Scandinavia, built on the solidaristic political culture that brought Left parties to power during the interwar depression. The Danish Social Democrats went on to hold power for forty-two of the fifty-eight years from 1929 to 1987; the Swedish Social Democrats forty-nine out of fifty-five years since 1932 and the Norwegian Labour Party, thirty-six out of fifty-two years since 1935.

From the earliest days of power, these parties sought widespread support and consensus across the political spectrum for policies which concentrated on redistribution through public spending rather than socialisation. 'Here was the basis for the welfare state consensus which, along with economic growth, transformed the Scandinavian countries from poor, backward societies into rich and egalitarian societies.'[104]

A similar, if frailer, consensual social conscience emerged in much of the rest of Europe after the war, where similar, if weaker welfarism, was carried out even by Centre-Right governments with widespread public endorsement. During the 1950s and into the 1960s, the prevailing ideology of the German conservative coalitions led by Konrad Adenauer was that of the 'social market', a belief in redistributive welfarism alongside controlled, but not socialised, markets. In Britain, there was a similar era of political and public consensus with the welfare reforms carried out by the post-war Labour Government continued and expanded by the next three, essentially 'one-nation' Conservative governments.

None of this means that this consensus was deeply ingrained or never challenged. In France, the 1950s was a period of political instability. There were twenty-six separate cabinets and fifteen different prime ministers, largely centrist, between 1946 and the collapse of the Fourth Republic in 1958. In Germany, the 1960s was a period of political confrontation and public protest which led, according to one commentator, to the 'erosion of prosperity based consensus politics'.[105]

Nevertheless, the emergence of a new politics around the idea of an active state and a new commitment to social protection was pretty universal, as has been its steady erosion with long term social and economic trends. The sense of consensual politics around these commitments has started to crumble even in those nations with the longest and strongest sense of solidarity and commitment to welfarism.

The end of consensus?

The erosion of consensus is especially evident in Britain. Indeed, although a collectivist consensus undoubtedly existed in post-war Britain, it is arguable that it started to erode well before the 1970s, the decade with the clearest evidence of a turning of public opinion. While most people approved of the government's record in the

1950s and 1960s, disapproval became the majority opinion in the 1970s, while a belief in the responsiveness of local and national government also declined.[106]

Disenchantment with particular aspects of state intervention also grew. Some welfare policies began to be perceived as increasingly inefficient, bureaucratic and unresponsive, and there was a growing distrust of the power of trade unionism. Optimism about the future sunk to a post-war low, a reflection of a growing anxiety over the economic difficulties of the period which seemed to be increasingly blamed on excessive state intervention.[107]

Opinion also seemed to turn against the poor who became the convenient scapegoats for apparent economic decline which was all too easily blamed on an allegedly excessive generosity, in particular, to the unemployed and the 'workshy'. While a distinction between the 'deserving and undeserving poor' had prevailed throughout the post-war period, though with differing degrees of intensity, it became particularly widespread in the second half of the 1970s with the rise of a new mood of 'scroungerphobia' and 'a shrill and mounting antagonism to the welfare system and its clients'.[108]

While public opinion was clearly influenced by the voices and growing confidence of the new Right who at the time were espousing similar ideas, Mrs Thatcher was more the beneficiary than the architect of these changing views. Nevertheless it was on this disenchanted base that she tried to mould a more permanent set of public attitudes during the 1980s. Her undisguised goal was the promotion of the values of individual responsibility and the downgrading of those of collectivism. Her years in office added up to a crusade to break the post-war consensus and to change the heart and soul of Britain. 'I came to office with one deliberate intent. To change Britain from a dependent to a self-reliant society – from a give-it-to-me to a do-it-yourself nation; to a get-up-and-go instead of a sit-back-and-wait-for-it Britain.'[109]

She believed that what she viewed as Britain's post-war decline could be laid at the door of an overweening state, of an excessive concern with redistribution and too little concern with the creation of wealth. She launched attacks on the 'permissiveness' of the 1960s and the 'Nanny State' which were seen as destroying economic and personal initiative and encouraging over-taxation and under-achievement. The pursuit of self-interest was encouraged as more than OK – looking after one's own economic interest was the route to wider prosperity for all; private is good, public bad.

The 1980s was a decade geared to the achievement of a less governed and more self-orientated Britain. Nationalised industries were sold off, home ownership encouraged and the trade unions weakened. Between 1979 and 1989, the proportion of the public owning shares rose from 7 per cent to 20 per cent and the proportion owning homes rose from 55 per cent to 65 per cent. The number of trade union members fell from its peak of 13.3 million in 1979 to 7.7 million in 1992.

The 1980s were littered too with symbolic battles that all fitted this wider strategy. The Falklands war was, above all, an attempt to resurrect a flagging national pride ending with appeals for a wider application of the 'spirit of the south Atlantic'. The bitterly fought and protracted miners strike in 1984/5 was a set-piece battle over the future of collective struggle. The abolition of the Greater London Council and the Metropolitan County Councils, the steady reductions in the central funding of local government, the introduction of rate-capping and the 'poll tax' were all attempts to 'take out' other centres of 'collectivist' resistance to the vital task of rebuilding Britain.

Similar pressures towards greater individualisation have been at work on mainland Europe, though they have had to battle against different traditions and sometimes more developed welfare states, more successful corporate structures and, in many countries, a greater inherent sense of solidarity. Continental Europe has also lacked the equivalent of a Margaret Thatcher or a Ronald Reagan working to give these processes a more vigorous thrust. This has meant that the process of decoupling the state has been driven by less doctrinaire and more pragmatic ends. The Christian Democratic parties which have held power in Germany and the Netherlands since the early 1980s, for example, have a very different tradition of state paternalism with a strong element of catholicism and its Christian ethic of social solidarity. It would be difficult for Helmut Kohl or Ruud Lubbers, for example, to claim, along with Mrs Thatcher, that there is no such thing as society.

Despite this, the *direction of change* has been common. Over the 1980s, trade union membership fell by 9 per cent in Belgium, by 3 per cent in Germany, by 19 per cent in Italy, 12 per cent in the

Netherlands, 42 per cent in France and by 16 per cent in the United States. Most European nations have been slowly switching priority away from social to private housing programmes with new measures to encourage home ownership. By 1990, ownership averaged 58 per cent in the European Community, compared with 68 per cent in Britain.[110]

There have also been similar trends in underlying attitudes to the state and to welfare, even in the most staunchly social democratic countries with a stronger solidaristic tradition and more enduring sense of common responsibility. In 1973, the newly formed anti-tax and anti-state Danish Progress Party gained 16 per cent of the vote in the general election and became the second largest parliamentary party. The Progress party in Norway has also been successful in local elections, being in governing coalitions in Oslo and other major towns, and coming a close third in the elections of 1989.

In the Swedish general election in 1992, the newly formed Democratic Party, the country's first truly right-wing party committed to cuts in taxes and welfare and immigration curbs, obtained 6.7 per cent of the vote and enough seats to give it parliamentary influence. Although these anti-state parties have never achieved enduring success, and were slow to catch on in Sweden, they have helped to shape a new political agenda. One commentator has argued that in Scandinavian society, 'There is a great deal of evidence that the solidaristic values of reciprocal obligation and responsibility were generation specific' and that a 'growing egotism seems to be taking their place'.[111] As he went on

> For the older generation which had known poverty and periodic unemployment, the benefits of the welfare state were worth almost any cost in bureaucratisation. But for the younger generation which had grown up with full employment and relative affluence, the mechanisms that made the welfare state work became the target for protest.[112]

One effect of this changing mood has been a steady chipping away of the generosity of welfare systems in most countries. As table 6.1 shows, the rapid growth of public spending in the 1970s was largely halted during the 1980s. The dominant trend in both government and welfare spending over the last twenty years has been expansion

Table 6.1: Government spending as percentage of GDP

	changes	
	1970-79	**1979-89**
OECD	8.5	1.2
Europe core	7.9	−0.1
Corporatist	10.5	1.3
USA	2.4	2.1
Japan	10.2	0.6

Source: Glyn, 1992, p 80; The European core includes Belgium, France, Germany, Italy, Netherlands, Switzerland and the UK; the corporatist group includes Sweden, Norway, Finland, Denmark and Austria.

followed by containment, even in the 'corporatist' countries like Sweden, Norway and Denmark with their tradition of higher taxes and more generous welfare systems. Moreover, increases in spending on welfare have typically reflected the growing numbers dependent on benefits, rather than greater generosity. Despite these changes, most welfare systems had been capped but not rolled back by the end of the 1980s. The 1990s, on the other hand, has been marked by a new phase of retrenchment, the product of both global economic crisis and growing public unwillingness to finance generous welfare benefits.

The rise of the 'me generation'

The growth of 'egotism' as a new creed proved a greater force in some countries than others. In Britain and the United States, the pursuit of materialism and the virtues of competitiveness were backed by governmental authority. Making money was not just acceptable but desirable. In the United States, the revival of conservatism and the new sense of indulgence was described by one commentator as 'the passage from the "yippie" to the "yuppie", from the "we generation" to the "me generation"'.[113] The 1980s seemed a decade of corruption and financial scandal. Tax fiddling became widespread and acceptable. In the United States, Government surveys in the mid-1980s showed that 30 per cent of taxpayers had deliberately under-reported their incomes, particularly among the rich, compared with only two per cent in the 1940s.

As Anthony Sampson put it, 'Moral attitudes to money-making

were now going through a major turn, as the new prophets of capitalism insisted that people had no reason to be ashamed of pursuing personal gain.'[114] In the five years from 1982, stock markets rose right across the west as never before. In America, the Dow-Jones index went up by 230 per cent, while the FTSE index rose fivefold. Huge salaries were being earned through the financial boom. Indeed, the biggest gainers were those involved in finance rather than manufacturing – in Britain, the City dealers, the property developers, the investment fund managers, the financial lawyers and bankers; in the United States, the Wall Street lawyers and investment bankers.

> The British now found fewer arguments against money-values ... The signs of money-worship multiplied. Newspapers fattened with business supplements. TV channels competed with money programmes. Banks and credit card companies pressed customers yet more stridently to borrow more money. Tycoons, after years of discretion, became the subject of bestselling memoirs or biographies.[115]

The new spirit of the times was captured in Caryl Churchill's play *Serious Money*, in Tom Wolfe's novel *The Bonfire of the Vanities*, in Oliver Stone's film, *Wall Street*. The endorsement of greed was echoed by Gekko, the central character of the film, 'Greed is good. Greed is right.' The new obsession with money and possessions was caricatured on both sides of the Atlantic by the 'Yuppies' – the affluent young on the make and out for pleasure. They were fashionable, spendthrift, culturally barren, stereotypes with their filofaxes, Golf GTIs and car phones, but all too real as well.

While only a minority of the population of the United States and Britain were participating in the get-rich-quick ethos of the time, it set the standard and the goal for society as a whole. It encouraged borrowing and consumerism and made getting into debt acceptable. It gave authority to the pursuit of private advantage rather than public accomplishment, and encouraged the turning away from the concept of the 'public realm'. As Paul Goldberger, architectural critic for the *New York Times* described the process,

> Today in Los Angeles and Miami, in Boston and Chicago, as

well as New York, we build great, shiny skyscrapers, but they are private not public. We build enclosed arcades and shopping malls, but they, too, are private. Corporate office towers but not housing, private arcades but not parks: these choices stand as the symbols of our age . . . If there is any legacy of the Reagan years, it is to have devalued completely the importance of the public realm and to have raised dramatically the value we place on the private realm . . .[116]

The new market reverence was also reflected in an apparent erosion of the limits that had governed acceptable business and political behaviour. The period brought a wave of scandals which suggested a declining integrity and growing corruption. In Britain, city scandals hit the headlines with monotonous regularity – Guinness, Blue Arrow, Maxwell, British Airways. Insider dealing seemed the norm rather than the exception. Executive salaries and perks continued to soar during the recession, often in reverse relation to performance, while business leaders continued to preach moderation to their employees and the nation as a whole. New schemes such as executive share options and huge pay increases in the year before retirement were devised by City experts to enable directors to divert profits from shareholders and employees.

There were similar trends on the continent. 'Yuppies' became a global description of a group of younger professionals in advertising, the media and financial services with large incomes and spendthrift lifestyles. In France they were known as the 'young wolves', in Sweden the 'financial pups'. The generational shift was common. In Italy and France, the yuppie generation in their thirties succeeded to influential positions, displacing in part the older groups who had dominated commerce, industry and business, and in the process bringing a different set of values. There were business and political scandals in Italy, France and Germany.

There were similar changes in aspirations. In Italy in the 1970s, as elsewhere, it was fashionable for the young to espouse leftist values, a product of the impact of the upheavals of 1968. By the 1980s, this influence had largely dissipated, a change reflected in a switch from Left to Right, or 'Red' to 'Black'. During the 1980s, the Italian Socialist Party under Bettino Craxi, determined to break the political stranglehold of the Christian Democrats, deliberately set out to become the champions of the new consumerism espoused by the yuppie generation. Craxi's success in becoming Prime Minister for much of the 1980s was more of a triumph of style than of socialism.

In France, similar processes were reflected in the development of the politics of the 'interest group' in which powerful lobby groups – students, lorry drivers, farmers – were able to manipulate decision-making in their own interest. The contrast between the student riots in the lycees in 1990 and those in 1968 is striking, the former motivated by a self-centred preoccupation with the quality and quantity of teaching, and the latter with external ideology. In a survey of 16–22-year-olds carried out in October 1990, the person thought to best represent their outlook on protest was Colouche, the comedian who sought to stand in the 1980 Presidential election as 'Le Candidat Nul'.

These aspirational changes were reflected in consumer booms throughout most of the west. In the Anglo-Saxon nations, these booms were financed by a huge increase in private borrowing, a trend encouraged by financial deregulation and easier credit. There were large increases in household debts which rose in most leading nations during the 1980s from the range 60–80 per cent of income to 80–115 per cent. The rise was sharpest in the UK and Japan, and only Germany and Italy maintained debts of less than 20 per cent of income in 1990. Consumerism in the 1980s was also fuelled by the raiding of savings. Between 1979/80 and the late 1980s, the household savings ratio fell by 7 percentage points or more in the UK, France, Norway, Italy, Sweden and Finland.[117]

From collectivism to individualism

How far the wider trend towards greater individuality can be viewed as a deep-seated cultural shift has been a matter of controversy. Whatever Mrs Thatcher's intentions, for example, how far have attitudes and aspirations been transformed as she sought; and if they have, how far are they the product of her tenure? The 1980s was widely viewed at the time as a period of substantive change, with the 1987 election result seen as the final triumph of the 'Thatcher Revolution'.

In Britain, however, some opinion surveys appear to show a contrasting trend – a swing back from the apparently growing anti-collectivism of the 1970s. The annual British Social Attitude Surveys (BSAS), for example, found a steady increase in the level of public support for increases in state welfare and an apparent readiness to pay increased taxes to finance them. In 1990, well over a half opted for extra social spending compared with around a third of respondents in 1983.[118]

They have also found strong support for the principle that the state should be the dominant supplier of medical care and a shift towards a collectivist or welfarist position on a series of other questions. Thus in 1989, 39 per cent agreed that 'the welfare state makes people nowadays less willing to look after themselves' compared with 52 per cent in 1983. The same report concluded that there is 'a growing consensus among supporters of all parties for a switch to welfarist, rather than individualist, taxation and social spending policies'.[119]

An alternative set of five surveys carried out between 1963 and 1987 by the right-of-centre Institute for Economic Affairs purported to show the opposite finding.[120] The Institute claimed that over the last twenty-five years there has been consistent support for alternative, private arrangements for publicly provided services such as health and education.

Neither approach provides a reliable way of measuring real attitudes. The BSAS approach is likely to elicit excessively generous responses by failing to make the costs of backing higher spending clear. Indeed, other questions by the BSAS show less generous attitudes when the price tag is made clearer. Thus, while 46 per cent supported higher taxes for higher social spending, more than two-thirds thought their own tax rate was too high and less than one per cent too low – people support more state spending if someone else is footing the bill. As the BSAS concluded, 'Whatever you think about tax rates and income inequalities, redistribution has more charm when it enables you to put your hand in someone else's pocket.'[121]

Another problem with these approaches is that people are assumed to fall neatly into the 'individualist' or the 'collectivist' camp. The reality is much more complex. People are a mixture of both. They also change with circumstances. Collectivism is not the same thing as altruism, and individualism is not the same as self-interest, though surveys sometimes tend to treat them as if they were equivalent. A vote for collectivism (such as higher spending

Figure 6.1: A typology of values

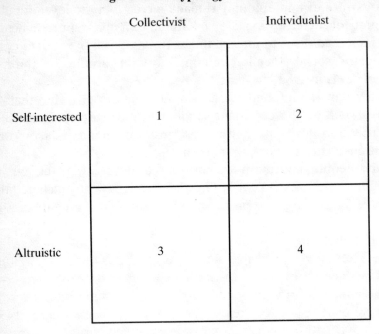

and taxes) is often interpreted as reflecting a spirit of altruism, and a vote for individualism (lower spending and taxes) as support for self-interest. Values are more likely to correspond to the four-way breakdown shown in figure 6.1 than the usual two-way breakdown assumed in surveys.

People who are predominantly motivated by self-interest can be either collectivists or individualists depending on their job, their class, their income, their aspirations. 'Self-interested collectivists' (cell 1) supporting higher taxation might include the better off whose income depends on work in the public sector such as doctors and teachers and the better off high welfare users as well as the poor whose income depends heavily on the state. It would also include those with a strong sense of 'enlightened self-interest' who, while having a short term interest in an individualist position, believe that their longer term interest lies in a more cohesive society created by greater collectivism.

The 'self-interested individualists' in cell 2 would include those who work in the private sector who have a weak dependency on the state or who aspire to be able to afford private health care or education, and who are not worried personally by the effects of declining social cohesion. 'Altruistic collectivists' in cell 3 would include the wealthy who could afford private services but are happy to back higher taxes for higher public spending because they favour a more egalitarian society even if it is against what they perceive as their own vested interest. Cell 4 would include those whose vested interest lies in collectivism but, for whatever reason, vote for individualism – maybe because they are persuaded that society would be a better place as a result.

How the population divides between these groups is difficult to know because most surveys pool the collectivist and individualist camps. The effect of this simplification is an implicit assumption that cells 1 and 4 do not really exist. This may be a reasonable assumption in the case of cell 4, but it is not in the case of cell 1. If anything, the opposite is likely to be true, that is that most collectivists are so because of self-interest not altruism.

Surveys by the Henley Centre can be used to make an attempt to allocate people between these cells. Figure 6.2 combines the results of two survey questions: 'Does the responsibility for solving the social and economic problems lie with the Government [assumed to be a collectivist response] or ordinary people [individualistic]?' and 'Is the quality of life best improved by looking after the community's interests [assumed an altruistic position] or by individuals looking after themselves [self-interested]?'

The results confirm the domination of 'self-interest' (60 per cent support) over 'altruism' (40 per cent), and if anything are likely to understate its importance for the reasons given above. The largest group (41 per cent) falls in the 'self-interested collectivist' camp – those supporting both individuals looking after themselves *and* government action. This confirms the dominance of what might be called 'pragmatic self-interest' in determining behaviour.

Even this dichotomy is an over-simplification. Most people are a complex mix of different values, both altruistic and self-motivated, with the balance varying with different issues and changing circumstances. They mostly take a pragmatic rather than ideological attitude on issues such as private versus public provision. Most people do not adopt straight 'pro-state' or 'pro-market' positions on core services like health and education.[122]

**Figure 6.2: The dominance of 'pragmatic self-interest',
Great Britain, 1992**

| Quality of life is best improved by . . . | Responsibility for solving social/economic problems lies with . . . | |
	Government (collectivist) %	Ordinary people (individualist) %
individuals looking after themselves (self-interested)	41	19
looking after community's interest (altruistic)	25	15

Source: The Henley Centre, Planning For Social Change Survey, 1992

Attitudes then become a question of availability and performance. Most people back universal education and health services because they can't afford private provision. But this does not mean that they are opposed to the principle of private availability. The BSAS shows that 49 per cent agreed that 'those who can afford it should be able to pay for better health care' and 46 per cent for better education.[123] People might well prefer private education or health care if they could afford it, but because it is out of reach, back more taxation for the service which is accessible to them.

Surveys have shown, for example, that close to a half of parents aspire to private education if they could afford it. This probably reflects a perception of performance, rather than of ideological superiority. If state schools were viewed as being more successful, the 'preference' for private education would falter. Those who can afford the private service might still opt for public provision if it is deemed as good or superior.

Pragmatism also helps to explain why people appear to want to have things both ways. They would like better funded and more generous public services but not if it affects their own pockets too heavily. This characteristic of 'social schizophrenia' is common to most western societies as they have become more affluent. Even in the United States, there was a big consensus during the 1980s in favour of increased government spending on education, crime prevention, health care and environmental protection combined with big opposition to higher taxes.[124] People will, on the whole, back higher taxation up to the point at which they feel they will benefit personally from the payment. 'Whether on taxes or services, people tend to ... "think of others" only when the cost to themselves is minimal.'[125]

This explanation is underpinned by evidence on the highly selective nature of opinion on welfare spending. Surveys have revealed a highly stratified view on particular services with much stronger support for 'universal' areas like health, pensions and education and a much weaker commitment to 'minority' areas such as housing, unemployment and single parent benefits. Far from revealing a strong sense of altruism, this suggests a sophisticated understanding of self-interest.

People are only too well aware of how their personal interest is injured by poor health care and education. Inter-class comparisons of views on the tax/spending trade-off confirm this awareness. The BSAS show that the middle class is more willing than the working class to pay increased taxes to finance an expansion of government spending on both health and education from which it benefits. It is, in contrast, much less willing to finance spending on non-universal benefits such as unemployment benefit and housing.

Support for the welfare state remains partial and conditional. There is a strong consensus on only two issues – state responsibility for the sick and for the elderly. On other areas of welfare policy – the government's responsibility to provide a job for everyone who wants one, to reduce income differences and to provide a decent living standard for the unemployed – there is a strong division. There are also good reasons for believing that support will continue to decline, and that this disagreement will extend to other areas.

Take expectations, which are, arguably, a better guide to the way society is heading, and certainly a powerful determinant of actual behaviour. Henley Centre 'Measures of Health' in 1990, for example, found that nearly 50 per cent of respondents expected hospital treatment to become a private good requiring payment within the next ten years. The expectation was higher among younger respondents. Nearly 35 per cent thought that visiting the GP and nearly a third that care of the elderly would be paid for privately after ten years. The corresponding figure for education was 25 per cent.

The tax revolt

This interpretation is also reinforced by the apparent contradiction between the generosity shown in surveys and the more 'selfish' values revealed in voting behaviour. Both the 1987 and 1992 British general elections, for example, were won by the Conservatives despite the electorate's apparently greater espousal of the welfarist and redistributive values of the Labour party. This contradiction is usually explained away by the electorate's opposition to Labour on other grounds – its internal divisions or its ability to manage the economy.

These results suggest that the electorate's commitment to welfarism is at best weakly held. The 1992 general election campaign in Britain was dominated by Labour attempts to reassure the electorate that they were no longer the party of high taxation or of growing public spending. They knew that society would not tolerate significantly higher taxes. Labour's commitment to increased taxes and national insurance on the top fifth of income earners (those over £22,000) was seen throughout the campaign as Labour's Achilles' heel by the Conservative party managers and was hounded day in day out. Although Labour was at pains to reassure voters that eight out of ten would be better off, Labour's tax proposals were an important factor in their unexpectedly heavy defeat. The third of the electorate belonging to the skilled working class were especially hostile to higher levels of taxation which were at odds with their aspirations to move to a higher income bracket and which were widely perceived as a cap on upward mobility.

One of the reasons for Bill Clinton's victory over George Bush in the 1992 US Presidential election was his realisation of the electoral unpopularity of taxation, a lesson that he took to heart from Labour's defeat. One of Bush's most potent weapons against Clinton was the latter's allegedly high tax and spending policies. This failed to stick because Clinton managed to persuade the electorate that only a very narrow group of the very rich would pay more, while wooing the dominant middle classes with promises of small tax concessions.

For twenty years, people throughout the affluent west have been flexing their muscles against high taxation. In the United States in the 1950s, less than half the public felt they were paying an unfair amount of tax, a figure that had risen to three-quarters by the late 1970s. The proportion believing that government 'wastes a lot' rose from 47 per cent in 1964 to 64 per cent in 1984.[126] This growing disquiet encouraged the tax revolt that began with Proposition 13 in California in the 1970s when voters rebelled against high property taxes. That rebellion was repeated in many other states and has continued ever since. President Carter talked passionately about bringing the federal government under control, about improving efficiency and cutting waste. In 1981, Ronald Reagan's tax cuts on the rich aimed at increasing incentives triggered a worldwide shift towards lower rates of direct taxation on the better off.

Along with the rise of anti-tax parties in some European countries, other evidence of growing hostility to high personal taxation includes a growth of moonlighting, social security fraud and a steady growth in levels of tax evasion. In Italy, tax evasion is commonplace. An estimated one-third of the Swedish population regularly evades taxes, while there has also been a steady decline in public opposition to such evasion, with 51 per cent of the Swedish population strongly opposed to tax evasion in 1981 compared with 63 per cent in 1968, and a fall in the proportion agreeing that penalties for evasion are not severe enough from 24.5 to 10 per cent over the same period.[127]

This is confirmed by attitudes to tax *levels*. Table 6.2 shows some evidence of resistance to high levels of taxation particularly on middle and lower income groups. Only small minorities in all seven countries, with some variations, believe that taxes on the rich are too high. On the other hand, much larger proportions believe that people on middle and low incomes face excessive taxation.

The response to this growing public hostility has been a general trend away from progressive taxation (table 3.2). Few countries have been able to reduce the overall burden of taxation, but most have switched from politically sensitive and visible direct taxes to what are seen as less conspicuous indirect taxes. Even Centre-Left parties have become increasingly aware of the limits to taxation. The British Labour Party has abandoned its commitment during the 1970s to heavy taxation on the rich. The American Democrats have done the same, though from a lower base of commitment, while other Left parties in Europe have been reviewing their traditional stance.

Table 6.2: Attitudes to taxation, 1987

Taxation is much too high for those . . .

	. . . with high incomes	with middle incomes	with low incomes
West Germany	12%	49%	80%
USA	17%	68%	67%
Italy	18%	61%	84%
Britain	24%	40%	85%
Netherlands	25%	57%	76%
Australia	34%	59%	69%

Source: Smith, 1989, p 64

In Germany, the limits to taxation are illustrated by the difficulties Chancellor Kohl had in raising taxation in the West to pay for the costs of reunification. Kohl had originally sold unification with a promise of no extra taxation, yet badly underestimated the costs of modernisation, and was forced to impose an initial 'solidarity surcharge' on tax bills of 7.5 per cent for one year from July 1991 to July 1992. This decision contributed to the wave of strikes over wages that began in April 1992, led to a much more generous settlement than the Chancellor wanted and came close to causing the downfall of the Government.

This dislocation reflected the unwillingness of the workforce in the former Federal Republic to share the burden of improving the living standards of their poorer neighbours in the East by foregoing some increases in their own living standards for a period. Kohl had similar difficulties in trying to sell what he referred to as a 'solidarity pact' in the winter of 1992/93, in effect, a further attempt to persuade the West to make sacrifices on behalf of the East.

Once electorates get used to lower rates of taxation, and steady increases in living standards, reversing them becomes increasingly difficult. Indeed the pressure lies in the other direction. The same applies globally. The more open and interdependent economies become, the greater the pressure to adapt to the position of the country with the lowest rates. The United States started the trend towards lower personal taxes, was then followed by Britain, so setting a new pattern that is being widely followed.

The individualisation of society

These changes in social attitudes have their roots in growing individualism which has contributed to a very different agenda. In the post-war years unemployment, inequality and welfare provision were high priorities. Today they are more marginal to the wider majority. The key issues that concern modern electorates are taxes, health, education, interest rates and economic well-being. The effect of these changes has been an increasing self-dependency.

Increasingly, people are faced with finding private solutions to the ordinary problems of their lives. It is not that people have become more selfish; apparently selfish behaviour has become more necessary. 'Private hopes and aspirations of a particularly narrow, materialistic kind have come to have precedence in how people arrange their lives, construe the future and allocate their political support.'[128]

This shift in climate has been fuelled by other social changes. Gradually, individuals have become more independent not merely of the public sphere but of other individuals. Europe, and especially northern Europe, has seen a steady trend towards smaller households and more single person households. There has also been a decline in the importance of the extended family. In Britain between 1961 and 1991, the proportion of households consisting of adult individuals living alone rose from 11 per cent to 26 per cent – the elderly, the unmarried, the divorced, single parents. Within households decisions are increasingly taken on an individualised basis. We are less involved in other traditional collective forms of activity and democratic forms of decision making including political parties, trade unions, tenants' and community associations.

Established sources of authority from the family and the church to politics and schools have also been weakening, contributing to a decline in the importance of former social networks, and making us more self-reliant and independent. Between 1953 and 1983 the proportion of the West German population attending church dropped from nearly 40 per cent to less than 20 per cent. There were similar falls in the United States and Britain, and a steeper drop in France.[129]

These changes have also been reflected in a growing hostility to the social and economic institutions that govern modern societies.

Figure 6.3(a): Lack of confidence in institutions, 1981–1990

(Europe as a whole)

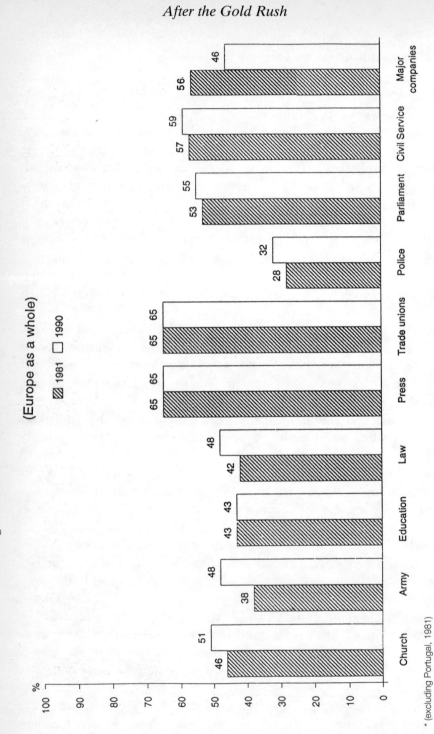

▨ 1981   ▢ 1990

	Church	Army	Education	Law	Press	Trade unions	Police	Parliament	Civil Service	Major companies
1981	46	38	43	42	65	65	28	53	57	56
1990	51	48	43	48	65	65	32	55	59	46

* (excluding Portugal, 1981)

Figure 6.3(b): Lack of confidence in institutions, 1981–1990

(Britain)

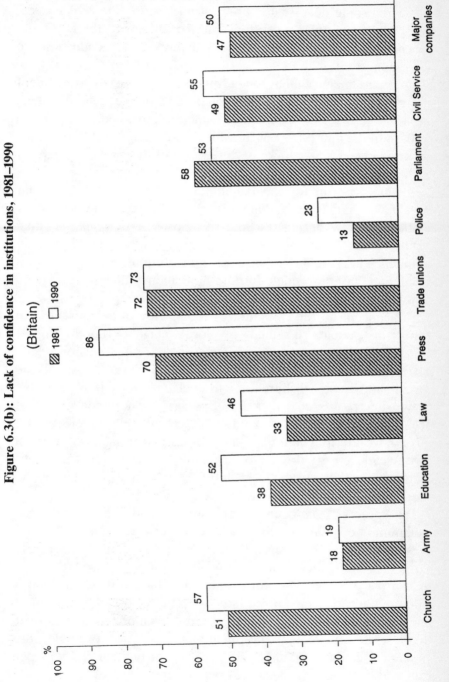

Source: The European Social Value Surveys, 1981 and 1990; Timms and Ashford, 1992

In Britain, there is barely a national or local institution that is not facing some deep-seated crisis of authority – the civil service, the school and university system, the Royal Family, the BBC, the judiciary, the police, the large company. Other countries are beginning to follow.

There has been a similar long term decline in trust in government and political parties in and out of power. In the United States, public support for government remained relatively high during the 1950s until the mid-1960s but then 'declined precipitously' to reach a post-war low in 1980 with only 25 per cent of the public saying they could trust the government, and only 21 per cent believing that government is run for the benefit of all.[130] There was a similar erosion of public confidence in Britain, while in Germany confidence grew during the first two post-war decades and then began to fall from the 1970s. Figure 6.3 shows the decline in confidence in a number of traditional institutions over the 1980s, a trend that has proceeded further in Britain than on average in Europe.

The concept of 'the community' in the sense of a coherent local entity of people sustained by local neighbourhood support structures and networks seems increasingly a phenomenon of the past. Local institutions such as the workplace, library, hospital, the corner shop, the local church, the football club, local transport have been slowly eroded, first by the large-scale redevelopment programmes of the 1960s, and more recently by wider cultural forces. We are moving out of local buses and trains into our own private cars. We are driving to the all purpose leisure centres rather than popping down to the local club. The hypermarket is hitting the shops of the local high street.

This process has been accompanied by the decline of the 'community economy' in line with the increased commercialisation of society. In some areas, the traditional community is nearly extinct. In the United States, many neighbourhoods are little more than a place to sleep, where neighbours share little more than a video rental and a convenience store. Figure 6.4 shows the extent of the decline in traditional community organisations in Britain over the last twenty years, with membership of, for example, the Women's Institute, falling by 25 per cent, of the church by 24 per cent and of the girl guides by 24 per cent.

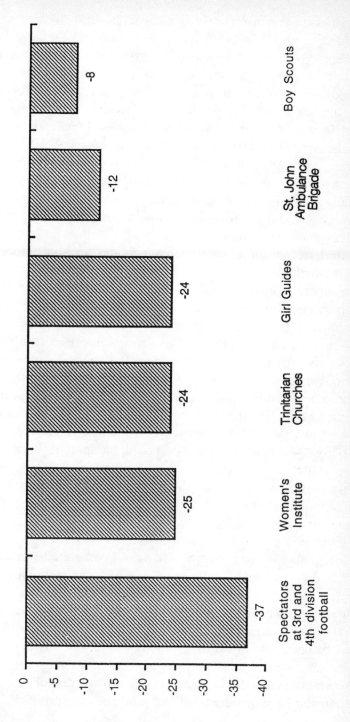

Figure 6.4: Decline in involvement in traditional community organisations, Britain

(% change in members 1971–1990)

Source: organisations involved

Affluence has brought rising material living standards but it is also bringing more self-sufficient, isolated and segregated lives. Technology and modern media mean that it is not even necessary to leave the home for entertainment or sometimes even work, a withdrawal into comfortable private worlds known as 'cocooning' in the United States. The VCR, the video shop and Sky movies have transformed the home into an individualised entertainment centre. This has contributed to less communal, less neighbourly and less gregarious lives and less aware communities. The wider support mechanisms that were provided through social networks have been eroding, making us more insular, weakening social cohesion and awareness, and contributing to a slow erosion of communitarian values and commitments.

Modern consumerism has contributed to the same process. Increasingly, ordinary people are being forced to behave as consumers, as the atomised individuals of economic textbooks, rather than as social beings as part of a community. The processes of living that used to be social and communal have become more commercial and functional. This process has been compounded by the arrival of the hypermarket and the shopping mall. Malls are most common in the United States, but have also been sprouting in Europe. At the beginning of the 1980s, superstores away from town centres accounted for less than 9 per cent of total food sales through supermarkets and local shops. In 1993, the superstores' share is expected to top 50 per cent. Spain is planning to triple its ninety-odd centres. Italy has relaxed its controls on mall development. Even in France, the microwave and the mall are edging out the once popular local bakeries, dairies and farmers' markets. As one writer has described the process:

> The mall is not a community. It is a commercial enterprise, designed in minute detail to prompt impulse buying . . . It excludes those who cannot afford to spend on a par with the rest of the consuming class. And rather than grounding people in attachments to their neighbors and their place, it fosters a sort of care-free anonymity.[131]

In Britain, all the big grocery chains are planning a continued expansion in large stores. Tesco and Sainsbury both have bigger

132

capital spending programmes than British Rail. As one senior supermarket executive described the forces in operation, 'Factories are closing, timber yards are closing, hospitals are closing, schools are closing. There has never been a better flow of potential new sites.'[132] The superstore has transformed our lives, in one sense for the better. It has brought wider choice, more interesting food and savings in time. Few people would want to put the clock back. But there is also a big downside. It has contributed to the decline of the community. As *The Independent* of 27 February 1992 described the process,

> . . . each time a superstore replaces a local shop, there is a tiny increase in alienation, depression, stress, vandalism, anti-social behaviour and crime; that what the punter saves as a consumer he may be forced to spend as a taxpayer or ratepayer, and it will almost certainly cost him dearly as a citizen.

The trip to the supermarket is the exemplar of the domination of the consumer role. Shopping used to be more of a social and human experience. Today, human interaction is minimal. We enter a turnstile and pick up a mass produced basket or trolley. We select from a vast array of goods catering for a variety of tastes and lifestyles and we do it at speed. We do not speak to the mass of other people who are doing the same. We check out through an electronic recorder which will soon be fully automatic, and probably pay on credit.

We have fulfilled our material needs but in a machine-like way, almost devoid of human contact and social interaction with others. When Margaret Thatcher told the readers of *Woman's Own* that 'There is no such thing as society, only individual men and women, and their families', she was not just expressing her own philosophy, she was also, perhaps inadvertently, describing modern living. In major elements of our lives, 'society' has been or is being effectively dismantled. We are consumers first and social beings second.

The rise of 'competitive individualism'

It is not so much individualism but 'competitive individualism' that is the hub of modern consumer societies. Competitiveness and

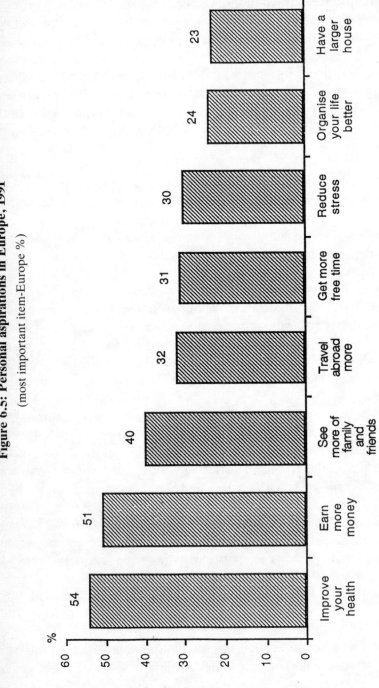

Figure 6.5: Personal aspirations in Europe, 1991
(most important item-Europe %)

Source: The Henley Centre, Frontiers Survey, 1991

prosperity have marched hand in hand. The increasing competitiveness of modern societies stems from a number of sources. Internationally from the increasing globalisation of the world economy, the growth of world trade and the increasingly competitive environment of the multinational corporation. Nationally, from the increasingly competitive nature of labour markets, and the growing dependence on personal skills, qualifications and entrepreneurialism for work. Politically, from the nature of party competition. Individually from the growing importance of consumerism in determining status.

Surveys may show that people would prefer to live in a caring, more co-operatively organised environment, but that sort of society seems increasingly elusive. The trends of consumerism, of greater self-reliance, of corporate culture, of an increasingly privatised system of welfare are all pulling in the same direction – towards more competitive and divided ways of operating and living.

The process has been at work in all affluent societies, though with greater impact in some than others. In Japan, one survey has shown that when asked to select the philosophy that most closely approximates their own, the proportion selecting 'live a pure and just life' fell from 29 per cent in the mid-1950s to 9 per cent in the mid-1980s, while the share opting to 'live a life that suits your own taste' rose from 21 to 38 per cent.

In the United States between 1967 and 1990, the share of students entering college who believed it essential to be 'very well off financially' rose from 44 to 74 per cent, while the share who thought it essential to develop a meaningful philosophy of life dropped from 83 to 43 per cent. High school seniors display similar aspirations with the proportion ranking 'having lots of money' as extremely important rising from less than a half in 1977 to almost two-thirds in 1986, making it first on a list of life goals well above 'finding purpose and meaning in life'. The same survey showed a big jump in the desire for second cars, vacation homes, appliances and other consumer items.[133]

Figures 6.5 and 6.6 show just how dominant material self-interest seems to have become in European attitudes and behaviour. While 'improving your health' came top with 54 per cent, 'earning more money' was the second highest motivation across Europe with support from 51 per cent. Other aims came much lower – 'seeing

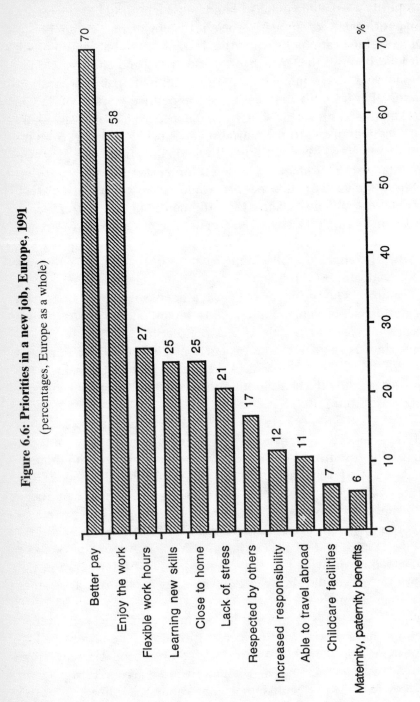

Figure 6.6: Priorities in a new job, Europe, 1991
(percentages, Europe as a whole)

Source: The Henley Centre, Frontiers Survey, 1991

more of family and friends' (40 per cent), 'getting more free time' (31 per cent). There was not a single European country where these priorities did not broadly hold. Earning more money was relatively more important than improving one's health in France and Italy.

The priorities in figure 6.6 do not vary much across nations either. 'Better pay' was the most important consideration in a new job for 70 per cent of Europeans. Others, like flexible work hours (27 per cent) and increased responsibility (12 per cent), were a much lower priority. Moreover the desire to earn more was much stronger among younger workers. There were no clear differences even in those countries with a deeper tradition of co-operation and 'solidarity' such as Sweden and West Germany.

In Britain, competitive individualism has been encouraged but not caused by the Thatcherite politics of the eighties. Competitiveness is the watchword not merely of the individual and the modern corporation but the public service too. Schools have to compete for pupils, universities for students, hospitals for patients. These groups have become 'customers' to be competed for in the market place. The introduction of market forces into public services, a move that is being followed elsewhere, is designed to encourage efficiency and accountability, but has also had the impact of intensifying the nature of social competition. John Major's Citizens' Charter is not about the restoration of citizenship. It is a charter for customers, and hence another element in the commercialisation of relationships.

Rising prosperity has brought many gains – greater independence, new opportunities, more choice, for most, an escape from the authoritarianism and scarcity of the past. But the same processes that have brought new freedoms have also contributed to a decline in social cohesion and an erosion of a sense of community. The idea of the close-knit community seems increasingly at odds with wider social trends – the weakening of networks, the decline of the local association. Former vigilance has been replaced by the security camera, former child autonomy by a growing fear of leaving children unattended.

Growing affluence has brought an end to scarcity for the majority but not all. Previously the key problem facing society was how to tackle widespread poverty. Modern societies face a new dilemma – reconciling the apparently contradictory interests of a newly

Figure 6.7: Attitudes to private health care, 1992

"The government should be encouraging people to take out private health care"

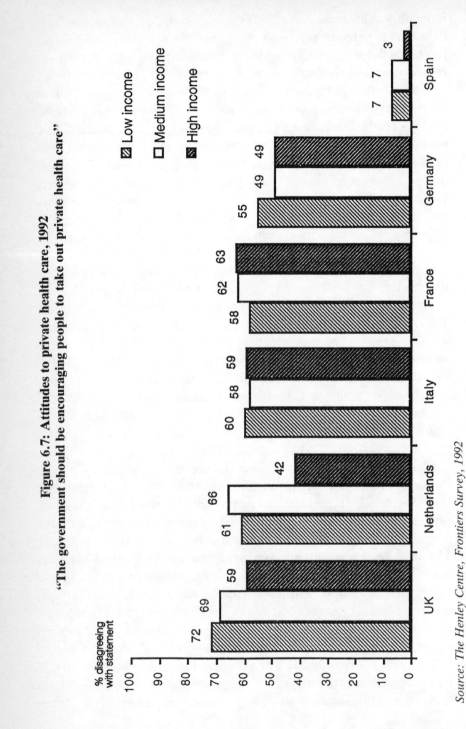

Source: The Henley Centre, Frontiers Survey, 1992

independent and aspirant majority, and of the insecure and still dependent minority who have been left behind by economic and social change. There has been a declining population with a strong vested interest in the kind of redistributive strategies of the past.

All governments are having to contend with a new set of essentially individualised value systems and it is this which has contributed to the difficulties of countering growing inequality with traditional policies of redistribution. The danger is that the interests of the housed and the homeless, the employed and the unemployed, the rich and the poor are becoming increasingly at odds; that the greater communal values that provided the motivation for the earlier commitment to social cohesion, and in the process, contributed to the rise of mass affluence, have been steadily eroded.

Reconciling these conflicting interests depends, in essence, on an appeal to altruism, to fear or to enlightened self-interest. This chapter has argued that people are and have been primarily motivated by their perception of their own self-interest and are only weakly motivated by altruism. In the early years after the war, most people went along with the co-operative spirit of the time because it was perceived as fitting their longer term interests. It is the shift in this perception to one of greater individualism which has contributed to the subsequent political and social trends. How these perceptions evolve will be a key determinant of the course of trends over the 1990s and beyond.

The more dependent people become on their own resources the less willing and able they will be to support collective forms of help, or the more strained their commitment will become. The more they are forced to buy into private health care, private education and private pensions because of the perceived inadequacies of public provision, the less willing they will be to fund high state pensions and state schools and the more inevitable a two-tier provision will become. Figure 6.7 shows the greater preference of higher than lower income groups for private health care across Europe, but especially in the Netherlands and the UK. Similar pressures apply in the case of pensions where there is also likely to be an increasing switch from public to private provision.

This may seem an unlikely scenario. The great majority of the European population depend on state schools and public health care, and satisfaction with both is relatively high. In the past,

139

dissatisfaction with other public services such as housing and public transport led to increasing resort to the private option. The same could gradually happen to health and education. If private provision starts to be used by larger numbers of people, the more attractive it becomes to those who are left. As more people leave the public sector, those left behind will increasingly compare what they are getting with what is on offer elsewhere.

Modern societies have been facing a powerful current of change that has contributed to growing social fragmentation. Whether this trend can be halted and reversed will be one of the major issues of the 1990s. The signs are mixed. The public generally take a sceptical view. In a poll in 1989, reviewing changes over the decade, 58 per cent of Britons believed that the country had become more prosperous over the period, but 84 per cent said that the country had become more arrogant, 78 per cent more selfish, 70 per cent less honest, 69 per cent less tolerant and 57 per cent less happy. A majority, 55 per cent, agreed that Britain was heading in the wrong direction and that major changes were needed while only 35 per cent agreed that the country was heading in the right direction with no major changes needed.[134]

Attitudes in Europe are also pessimistic. In 1990, the proportion agreeing or strongly agreeing that 'social behaviour will continue to get worse' stood at 63 per cent in Britain, 60 per cent in the Netherlands, 58 per cent in France, 57 per cent in Belgium, 53 per cent in Italy, 50 per cent in Sweden, 42 per cent in Germany and 51 per cent across Europe as a whole.[135]

7. From 'Ethical' to 'Managerial' Politics

We used to think that you could spend your way out of recession, and increase employment by cutting taxes and boosting government expenditure. I tell you now in all candour that the option no longer exists.

(James Callaghan)[136]

I believe that we have started government on a different course, different than anything we've done in the last half century since Roosevelt began with the New Deal.

(Ronald Reagan)[137]

This election is not about ideology, it's about competence.

(Michael Dukakis)[138]

James Callaghan's speech to a shocked Labour Party Conference during the 1976 economic crisis marked a turning point in post-war history. It was to prove a signal of the end of the era of optimism about the role of the state, and of the dominating ethos of post-war politics.

The rise of the interventionist state

The central feature of the new post-war politics was that citizens were viewed as having clear rights, and society and governments clear obligations. There was an acceptance that the market alone could not deliver these rights, and a new commitment to ensuring that all citizens should share in economic and social progress. This commitment was embraced in varying degrees by all west European democracies in the post-war period even those with Right-of-Centre governments.

This new era of strengthened and welfarist government was inspired by the social ethics of Christian Democrats and Liberals and the socialism of Social Democratic and Labour parties. If there was a single theme running through the social legislation passed in Britain in the post-war years, for example, it was an attempt to provide the 'essential means for achieving the goals of social solidarity'.[139] In Germany's post-war Christian Democratic Government, the Finance Minister, Ludwig Erhard, asserted that 'the state will never again be pushed back into the role of nightwatchman'. Even though the commitment to public welfare in the United States was always weaker, there was still an acceptance of a new responsibility which was crystallised in the 1940s in Roosevelt's call for the famous 'four freedoms' – of speech, of worship, from want, from fear.

This is not to exaggerate the speed of change, or the degree of consensus of the time. Nevertheless, the catalytic environment created by the depression and the Second World War helped to usher in a new era of active states with new commitments – to full employment, welfare for all and a mixed economy. Over this period, the state grew more and more influential and public spending grew. Of course, there were differences of detail and emphasis between Left and Right over issues such as the boundaries of public ownership and the role of welfare, and countries proceeded at different rates.

Nevertheless, the pre-eminent ideology was one of social democracy or the social market, an acceptance of a joint role for governments and markets in meeting economic and social goals. Thus even France under de Gaulle, Germany under first Konrad Adenauer and then Ludwig Erhard, and Britain under Harold Macmillan presided over active states.

In Europe, the 1950s and 1960s can be seen as a period of broad political consensus around a Centre-Left axis. While political differences persisted, this was a period of broad convergence. This shift was partly a matter of electoral need, with socialist parties seeking the votes of the middle class and conservative ones those of the working class. But it also reflected ideological change.

On the Left, the Scandinavian Social Democratic parties had

accepted the importance of mixed economies in the 1930s. In 1956, Anthony Crosland's influential book, *The Future of Socialism*, had laid out what he saw as the core values of social democracy – political liberalism, a mixed economy, the welfare state, Keynesian economics and a belief in equality. Similar views were also embraced by the German SPD in its historic conference at Bad Godesberg in 1959, a meeting which both threw off its Marxist heritage and laid out a new vision of socialism. For the Left, this revisionist formula offered a solution to the problem of how to reconcile socialism and the market, opening up the possibility of a third way between communism and capitalism. The managed or welfare capitalism of the 1950s and 1960s was the outcome of this 'historic compromise'.

The Right, too, were engaging in revisionist politics, turning their backs on the pre-war preoccupation with free markets. For them, the new intervention meant a means to electoral success and the economic growth which underpinned liberal capitalism. So complete was this process of political realignment across western democracies that the American political scientist, Daniel Bell, as early as 1960, was able to herald 'the end of ideology'.[140] A new way of running societies had apparently been discovered yielding high and stable growth through co-operation between once antagonistic groups, and free of extreme ideologies. Life no longer followed a zero-sum game in which winners would be balanced by losers. Now everybody could be a winner as long as they played by the rules.

The decline of consensus

This optimism was premature. The seeds of the collapse of consensus first became visible with the rise of the student protest movement that swept North America and much of Europe from the mid-1960s. The revolt by essentially young, middle class and well-educated students was a protest against what was seen as political complacency, excessive materialism and growing bureaucracy. These movements against the impersonalisation of society spawned the new ideological and fringe political campaigns of the 1970s – the women's movement, the anti-nuclear protests and peace campaigns, and the stirrings of the environmental movement. They contributed, too, to the slow process of political de-alignment that affected the popularity of the mainstream political parties from the mid-1970s.

A decade after Bell's pronouncement brought a serious international recession and a new era of stagnation and economic upheaval. From that point on, the political and intellectual domination of the social democrats began to fade. There was less talk of the end of ideology, and such consensus that had existed began to break down. Steady and stable growth and full employment were replaced by economic instability, rising unemployment and one economic crisis after another. The post-war era of managed growth and social reformism that, from the perspective of hindsight, seemed so successful had run its course.

The demise of social democracy was to be slow and drawn out. During the 1970s, it was governments of the broad Left – Labour in Britain, the Democrats in the US, the SPD in Germany – that were most deeply affected by the growing crisis. Indeed, it was Left-of-Centre governments that first began to implement the reversals in policy that marked the end of the era.

In Britain the Labour Government of 1976 found itself bowing to the austerity measures dictated by the International Monetary Fund (IMF) in order to gain access to external financial aid. In the United States, the Democratic President, Jimmy Carter, found himself facing similar economic and social problems of rising inflation and unemployment, growing public disenchantment and an increasingly unresponsive political system. In 1974, the reformist SPD Chancellor of Germany, Willy Brandt, was replaced by the pragmatist, Helmut Schmidt, bringing a new era of economic stringency, the subordination of social reforms and a retreat from long standing party commitments.

The end of social reformism was seen in France. In 1981, the election of the first Socialist President, Francois Mitterand, brought a full blooded and 'go-it-alone' programme of reflation through increased public spending, extended public ownership and a substantial increase in the minimum wage. One of the boldest socialist experiments of the post-war era, it had to be brought to an abrupt halt after barely a year. The French experiment coincided with another world recession. The effect was an increase in inflation, a worsening of the balance of payments and a fall in the value of the franc. Mitterand's Government was forced into a series of spectacular U-turns including devaluation, big cuts in public spending and the introduction of wage controls. It was being forced into the same policies of retrenchment and economic liberalisation that had been initiated by other Left governments in the 1970s and accelerated by Right governments in the 1980s.

It took some while for the economic and social problems of the 1970s to translate themselves into electoral and ideological change. In the 1970s, the Left clung on to power in many countries including Britain, the United States and Germany. But, simultaneously, the parties of the Centre-Right were beginning to distance themselves from the old consensus, preparing themselves for a quite different approach to economic and social management. In 1979, the Conservative Party in Britain began a period of uninterrupted power committed to a new policy of market liberalism, while in the United States, the Republican Party won the 1980 and the next two Presidential elections with a similar agenda.

In the Netherlands the Centre-Left coalition lost power in 1982 to a Centre-Right one led by Ruud Lubbers who stayed in power throughout the 1980s. In Germany, the SPD-led coalition collapsed in 1982, and the SPD fared badly in the 1983 federal elections seeing its vote decline from an average 43.3 per cent in the 1970s to 38.2 per cent. Its vote fell further in both the 1987 and 1990 elections leaving the Christian Democrats under Helmut Kohl in power for more than a decade. In Denmark, the ruling Social Democrats were forced to hand over power to a Right-of-Centre coalition in 1982, a coalition which held until 1993. If the dominating ethos of the 1950s and 1960s had belonged to the revisionist Left, the 1980s belonged to the new Right.

In Britain, the three governments of Margaret Thatcher set about reversing the political tide of the post-war era with a new ethos of minimal government. Monetarism replaced Keynesian demand management. State subsidies to industry were reduced, there were new attempts to slow down the growth of public spending, state industries were privatised, and financial markets deregulated. Trade union power was weakened and the institutions of corporatism largely dismantled. The post-war aim of reducing inequality was downgraded and a new emphasis given to self-reliance in welfare policy. Social benefits were made less generous and some welfare programmes were cut sharply, notably in public housing.

In the United States, Reaganism brought a similar mix of monetarist economics and anti-welfare ideology. Of course, the

United States had always stopped far short of the European social democratic model, with both a less generous and less comprehensive system of welfare. Nevertheless, Roosevelt's 'New Deal' programmes of federal help for the poor begun in the 1930s, became the dominating political ideology for almost a generation. Reaganism was an attempt to reverse even these modest programmes of state redistribution, and signalled the end of forty years of New Deal liberalism, the weaker equivalent of European social democracy. Reagan came to power committed to cutting taxes, reducing government spending at home, balancing the budget. Reaganomics held that reducing taxes would stimulate effort and the economy, bring higher prosperity, and so, higher tax revenue. In the summer of 1981, Congress passed two historic pieces of legislation, one cutting taxes on the better off, the other, cutting federal spending especially on programmes for the poor.

The Reaganite and Thatcherite agenda was less powerful, but still influential, on the continent. Monetarism and the new emphasis on fiscal rectitude became as universal a creed in the 1980s as Keynesianism had before it. Similar approaches to economic management and welfare were followed in countries with socialist governments including Spain and France. Anti-inflation displaced full employment as the new driving force behind economic policy. The austerity programmes of the Mitterand regime together with the commitment to a strong currency inevitably led to sharp rises in unemployment. Many countries also followed Britain's lead in privatisation including France and Italy and the Labour governments of Australia and New Zealand.

In the developing world, state intervention was also being replaced by free markets, a process encouraged by the practice of making aid dependent on deregulation. The economies of Latin America and most of Asia have become more and more capitalist, while even China's communist mandarins are embracing free markets. The end of the 1980s brought a further boost to neo-conservatism with the final collapse of communism in Eastern Europe. One by one the command economies and one-party states fell to the pressure of both internal political demands for democratisation and the international requirements of competition. This collapse gave a new impetus to neo-liberalism as both the scale of the economic, environmental and social problems were unveiled and solutions were sought in highly competitive market economies.

The political history of the post-war era of the west can therefore be divided roughly into decades. The 1940s and 1950s saw the birth and expansion of managed growth and social and economic reformism. The 1960s brought first consolidation and then the early signs of decay. The 1970s brought failure, disillusion and retreat. The 1980s saw the final curtain fall on the social democratic experiment and its replacement by market liberalism. The 1950s and 1960s were decades of broad political consensus, where parties of both the Right and Left were committed to the idea of an active state. These gave way to a new period of division with the Right moving away from interventionism and the Left slowly having to adapt to the new agenda after early resistance. The 1990s are likely to prove another decade of transition. Transition to what is a subject examined in chapter 10.

The decline of social democracy

The central explanation for this political evolution from social democracy to market liberalism was the growth and spread of prosperity. The consensual politics of the period became the victim of its own success. The gains of the post-war era could not be sustained. Indeed, they contributed to their own undoing.

By bringing different aspirations and concerns, rising affluence changed the conditions that had created rising prosperity. After the war the principal concern was with preventing a return to the insecurity and instability of the past. The post-war consensus suited the circumstances of the time which were characterised by a convergence of interest that straddled most of the political spectrum, that embraced both sides of industry and the mass of public opinion. The paternalistic model of government also suited the needs of reconstruction. The public were happy to accept a transfer of social responsibility because, as individuals, they neither had the means nor the power to provide work or better housing or improved social protection. The breakdown of social reformism that began in the 1970s has its roots in the transformed and ultimately unsustainable social and economic conditions that gave rise to the initial post-war boom.

One reason for this was that the consensus was partly a matter of political expediency. Parties of both Left and Right depended for electoral success on the votes of the mass working class whose support depended above all on economic and social prosperity and security. Delivering this depended critically on building a base of mass consumption on which industry could thrive. Hence, a commitment to growth, to full employment and to welfare expansion. The fusing of markets and welfarism was always a marriage of convenience. When it no longer served the electoral interests of the Right, it could be quietly abandoned.

The same expediency applies to individuals. By breeding a new generation that would no longer share the same symbiotic relationship with the state, growing prosperity was bound to undermine the very political base on which it had been created. Here was another element to the paradox of wealth. Prosperity brought with it a challenge to the collectivism that had helped to create it. Periods of hardship can promote collectivist values but give way to greater individualism as those hardships are overcome for the bulk of the population.

In the conditions of scarcity that existed after the war, most people had reason to look to the state for help. That is no longer the case, and a rising proportion of the population of the west now seeks to make its own provision in housing, pensions, health and to a lesser extent, education. Nevertheless, while increasing numbers have been enjoying growing independence from government, economic retrenchment and rising inequality have simultaneously increased the dependency of a substantial minority. The effect has been to compound the ambiguities underlying government interventionism. As Daniel Bell has put it, the dilemmas

confronting Western societies derive from the fact that we have sought to combine bourgeois appetites which resist curbs on acquisitiveness, either morally or by taxation; a democratic polity which, increasingly and understandably, demands more and more social services as entitlements; and, an individualistic ethos which at best defends the idea of personal liberty, and at worst evades the necessary social responsibilities and social sacrifices which a communal society demands.[141]

While the politics of social democracy worked well in periods of scarcity, its ideological base was always relatively shallow. The post-war consensus on social reformism was never rooted in a fundamental and underpinning philosophy. A piecemeal and pragmatic approach to social reform through little more than an appeal to social conscience was never sustainable. A successful welfare state depends upon what William Robson has described as a 'welfare society', a strong sense of national consensus or unity, a commitment to wider community values including redistribution, if it is to survive.[142] This may have existed in some parts of post-war Europe, especially in Scandinavia, but it never represented a deep-seated and permanent cultural shift elsewhere and was, therefore, always going to be a temporary phenomenon. Its gradual replacement with a much more individualistic ethos, in which behaviour is governed by maximising self-interest, is the antithesis of Robson's 'welfare society'.

This lack of a deep-seated social philosophy put additional strains on the inevitable tensions at the heart of the social democratic agenda and its twin objectives of managed growth and redistribution. The history of post-war intervention has been a compromise between collectivist welfare and economic regulation on the one hand, and individualism and free enterprise on the other. This compromise contained inevitable ambiguities and contradictions. Success depended on a degree of co-operation and compromise between the competing players. Profits competed with wages, taxes with income, investment with consumption.

A central source of tension was that between redistribution and growth. The higher taxes needed to pay for redistribution were bound to influence the business and individual incentives on which economic performance depended. The requirement of a strong economy placed a limit on the redistributive objective. As intervention grew, tax rates increased and spread to more and more of the population. This growing tax burden imposed a further limit on the speed with which governments could deliver their claims of improved services and benefits while provoking growing antagonism towards public institutions.

Over time these inherent conflicts became increasingly difficult to resolve. The moderate Left assumed that they could be resolved with growing prosperity through a 'growth dividend', that higher levels of wealth would enable the redistribution that would bring social justice alongside improved economic performance. This formula worked more or less successfully in the relatively high growth and consensual climate of the 1950s and 1960s, but has proved more difficult in the more turbulent economic environment since then. Here was another ambiguity inherent in the rise of prosperity. Prosperity was a necessary condition of more generous welfare provision, but it also placed a growing strain on its survival.

Sustained growth also brought expectations that were rising faster than they could be met. Society expected more of government and welfare, individuals wanted better living standards and business wanted higher profits. Politicians happily participated in this process, promising more than they could deliver because of the requirements of political competition. Such expectations would have been difficult to meet even in favourable economic circumstances. But faltering economic performance created even greater strains, rising public disillusion and the growth of inflation. Demands on the welfare state grew at a faster rate than willingness to pay, creating what some Left-wing critics have coined 'the fiscal crisis of the state', and some on the Right, the problem of 'overload'.

The onset of stagnation revealed the vulnerability of Keynesian interventionism, and hit at the very heart of the post-war project which depended on increasing affluence providing the means to redistribution without social hostility. Here was the essential problem for the moderate Left. The first element of their package – social reformism, depended on the success of the second – the managed economy. The failures of the second because of the weakening power of Keynesianism meant that the first was no longer achievable. In the 1970s, successive governments attempted to respond to this growing crisis with new and extended forms of intervention but these failed to deliver an improved economic performance and simply hastened the growing disenchantment with the formulas of the past.

For the new Right critics, the compromise was equally unsustainable but for different reasons. To them, growing instability was the product of excessive government intervention. There were several elements to the Right's critique. First, it was claimed that high and growing state spending was simply 'crowding out' private activity and was therefore self-defeating. Second, that high taxes for the rich discouraged effort and motivation, and that generous benefits for the poor acted as a disincentive to work. Third, that the high fiscal deficits caused by soaring government spending and increasingly financed by monetary growth were stoking inflation. For the new Right, the onset of economic stagnation could therefore be laid at the door of excessive state interference in the mechanisms of the market, encouraging inflation, and discouraging the wealth creation that comes from private initiative. The solution was simple – less government.

The main counter argument to the Right's thesis was that high government spending was the consequence, not the cause, of the economic crises of the 1970s. Deficits and tax rates were rising mainly because of increasing unemployment and falling revenue. Nevertheless, the Right's critique was gaining added resonance from another source, a growing public disquiet with some aspects of government intervention. Societies experiencing growing consumerism and taxation were bound to apply more stringent tests to government programmes. The competence of the state to run not merely the economy but universal welfare programmes and public services became an increasingly vital issue of politics. There was a growing concern with the efficiency of public programmes and with the vested interests and terms and conditions of public sector staff. By the middle of the 1970s, the love affair with the state had noticeably cooled, and along with it, support for high public spending and taxation.

Globalisation and the declining power of the nation state

The success of the post-war era also contributed to the waning of the social democratic domination in another way. Its achievements changed the rules of economics in a way that undermined its powers. Economic progress led to a steady expansion in world trade and in the influence of multinational companies. As a result, economic regulation at the national level became progressively more difficult. Keynesianism depended on the ability of national governments to adjust the level of demand. The growing openness of national economies resulting from the relaxation of trade restrictions, combined with the globalisation of trade and capital markets and intensified international competition have undermined the economic autonomy of national governments. This has made it more difficult to reduce unemployment by stimulating demand without creating acute balance of payments and currency problems.

As first the Wilson/Callaghan Governments in Britain and then the Mitterand Government in France found to their cost, it became progressively more difficult for countries to reflate their way out of recession unilaterally. This undermined the advocates of 'socialism-in-one-country'. The solution advanced by some groups on the British Left in the late 1970s and early 1980s of 'an alternative economic strategy' based on reflation behind a protective wall of import controls, extended public ownership and withdrawal from the European Community, was never a realistic option in an increasingly open world.

It also failed to allow for the implications of the arrival of the big transnational company which weakened another instrument of economic planning in the Left's armoury, that of nationalisation, now giving power over what economist Robin Murray has described as a 'lowland plain rather than the commanding heights'. When threatened by nationalisation, international companies are easily able to switch the heart of their production to other countries, leaving socialist governments in charge of 'empty buildings'.

Faced by global recession in the early 1980s, a group on the European Left turned to another approach, an attempt at co-ordinated international reflation, in recognition of the problems associated with running economies at out-of-synch levels of demand, and with the disruption caused by 'beggar-my-neighbour' deflation.[143] Such a co-ordinated strategy was never a realistic option given the different political persuasions and situations of the leading powers, and most major nations continued to operate on an individualistic basis.

Since then, economic interdependence between nations has accelerated. Economic decline in major trading nations rebounds on the global economy. Decisions in Frankfurt, New York, London and Tokyo can affect financial markets around the globe. This interdependence has grown too with the development of the European Community. Membership of the European Exchange Rate Mechanism (ERM) imposed severe limits on domestic macroeconomic policies by depriving countries of the option of exchange rate flexibility. During 1992 and 1993, high German

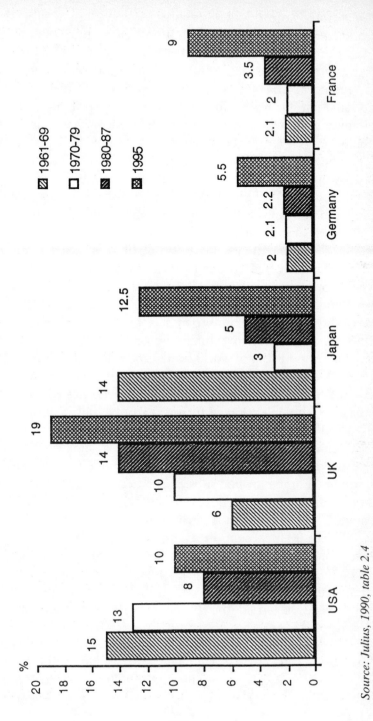

Figure 7.1: Outward foreign investment as a proportion of exports

Source: Julius, 1990, table 2.4

interest rates forced other countries to operate with high real interest rates. This had the effect of prolonging the global recession of the time. With the end of the traditional reflationary option, interest rates became the central instrument for controlling demand. Yet unilateral changes in interest rates were ruled out unless individual nations were willing to accept the possibility of currency realignment. It was this that ultimately encouraged the currency speculation that led to the eventual collapse of the ERM in 1993.

The undermining of the sovereign state has also been fostered by the growing significance of the multinational corporation, a shift encouraged by the internationalisation of technology and the removal of controls on the flow of capital. In the continuing search for cheaper sources of production, capital is moving freely across borders. The components and assembly of a car or a computer may include materials and labour from many countries. Transnational corporations use global strategies to secure their markets and often form joint ventures in a variety of countries in the process. As a result, direct investment abroad has been growing in all major countries, and direct investment flow in advanced countries has been outstripping that of world trade especially since 1985. As figure 7.1 shows, this has been especially important in the UK and is predicted to continue to grow. The same process has also led to a big increase in foreign exchange turnover from a daily average of $300 billion in 1986 to nearly $900 billion by 1992.

Foreign-owned firms now account for a significant share of domestic output, employment and investment in most advanced economies. Foreign owned subsidiaries account for well over 30 per cent of manufacturing turnover in Australia, Belgium, Canada and Ireland, 20–30 per cent in Austria, France, Germany, Portugal and the UK, 10–20 per cent in Denmark, Italy, Norway, Sweden, Turkey and the United States, but less than 10 per cent in Finland and Japan.[144] The main industries involved have been chemicals, pharmaceuticals, automobiles, electronics and computers.

This trend began in the 1960s with the rapid growth of US investment in Europe but has gradually extended to other countries, especially Japan and Britain, and to a lesser extent, Germany and France during the 1980s. This new transnational capitalism is now dominated by Japanese companies, though their influence has been declining since 1991/92 with the fall in the size of Japan's trade surplus. Take Japanese cars in the United States. Compared with 1979, the car market has not grown from its 9 million units, but Japanese cars now account for 2.6 million of them – 1 million being produced in the US, directly or under a joint venture arrangement.

It is a trend that has been stimulated by the strategy of transnational companies to centralise office and other functions in a single cheap and efficient country, often one of the newly successful developing nations. Swissair, for example, handles all its revenue accounting in Bombay. Asian countries are being increasingly used by European multinationals, while US companies were developing links with Mexico even before the negotiations over the North America Free Trade Agreement.

This trend is likely to continue. According to the United Nations, 'International production has become a central structural characteristic of the world economy.'[145] It is being encouraged by the communications revolution which has allowed companies to integrate more fully with their overseas subsidiaries. Further trade liberalisation would also increase the incentives for firms to locate production in low cost countries from which they can export. On the other hand, the process could slow or even go into reverse if growth remains slow, if technology transfer proves disappointing or if world markets get closed through protectionism.

The significance of such inward investment for individual economies has been the subject of a good deal of heated debate, especially in the US over the question of the role of Japanese companies. It has been argued that by encouraging competition, such increased economic integration has contributed to improved productivity and growth. It is arguable, for example, that in the US, Japanese inward investment during the 1980s helped the US economy, contributed to its rising productivity and its new trade surplus with Japan.

On the other hand, it has also created a new layer of volatility and uncertainty, opening up the possibility of huge and unpredictable transfers of industrial power, creating in the words of the British Labour MP, George Robertson, 'a bonfire of the certainties'. The potential for such transfers was well illustrated at the beginning of 1993, by the decision of the US owned Hoover Company to move its European production base from Dijon to Glasgow, and the decision of the French firm, Nestle, which had taken over Rowntrees a few years earlier, to move its plant in the opposite direction from Glasgow to Dijon. As the Royal Institute of International Affairs has put it,

> This rosy picture of direct investment-led integration and growth is what the ivory-towered economist sees. From corporate headquarters, or in Whitehall or Washington, things look very different. Exchange rates lurch, as one news item overtakes another, and sometimes ride off in the 'wrong' direction for weeks on end before jolting back to reality. Familiar indicators like trade balances and monetary aggregates misbehave capriciously, confusing the corporate planner and provoking the government spokesman into more and more convoluted justifications of current policy.[146]

A new consensus?

These long term changes set in train by rising affluence have had a profound impact on the political and electoral climate. First has been the declining popularity of the mainstream parties reflected in their declining vote, the greater volatility in voting patterns, and the steady rise of fringe parties. The last twenty years has seen the rising popularity of regional and ethnic parties in Belgium, Finland, Italy, Spain and the United Kingdom; the rise of anti-state parties in Norway, Denmark and, more recently, Sweden; the rise of Green, Ecology and fringe Left parties such as the Socialist People's Party in Denmark; and the rise of hard Right and racist parties in France, Germany, Italy, Belgium and Spain.

These newer parties have made elections less predictable and coalition government more unstable. Their rise reflects, in part, a growing disillusion by electorates with mainstream parties and politics, a problem accentuated by rising national economic impotence. It also reflects the growing complexity of modern electorates. In the past voters could be seen as more homogeneous in their outlook and their voting patterns. Individualisation has led to what political scientists have called 'partisan dealignment' with voters showing less commitment than in the past to a single party.[147] This has led to a more 'pick and mix' voting pattern, with electors less willing to endorse complete programmes of particular parties.

Affluence has had the greatest impact on parties of the Left, reducing their traditional electoral base. The decline of the working class might have mattered less if political loyalties had changed but in Europe 'class dealignment' has been minimal. This has meant that the Left can only win elections by wooing a higher proportion of the votes of the expanding middle ground as well as attempting to maintain support among its traditional but shrinking base. The electoral and ideological dilemma for the Left has been that the interests of these two groups have often been at odds.

The same dilemma applies in the United States. Between 1950 and 1990, the proportion of the population living in suburbs rose from a quarter to a half. Although inner city dwellers are still staunchly Democratic, those who have moved to the suburbs are more inclined to vote Republican. As in Britain, the suburban view of government is very different from the urban. When people move to the suburbs, they do so in search of privacy, security and lower taxes. 'Suburbanization means the privatization of American life and culture. To move to the suburbs is to express a preference for the private over the public.'[148] There is an even stronger anti-government, anti-tax coalition in the United States than in Europe, one fed by a resistance to taxes among the suburban middle class and a cynicism about government which is especially strong among the urban poor.

This process of political dealignment has, in turn, contributed to the blurring of the boundaries between Left and Right and to a new process of convergence between the main parties, as, first, they have to compete for a declining share of the total vote, and second, external forces make the idealistic models of the Right, and especially the Left, less appropriate.

The initial impact of the critique of active government was the collapse of the cross-party consensus on the role of intervention. In most countries, this led to a new period of political discord, with Conservative and Christian Democratic parties moving to the Right and the Social Democratic and Socialist parties maintaining, at least initially, their former commitments. Gradually, however, that divergence has narrowed as first, Left parties accommodated themselves to the newly emerging economic and welfarist orthodoxies, and then, Right parties began to moderate their own position in response to the perceived failures of market liberalism.

Approaching the mid-1990s, it is arguable, a new and less ideological consensus has begun to emerge.

The initial beneficiaries of this changing climate were the neo-liberal thinkers and their political allies. During the 1980s, the Thatcher/Reagan strategy of reduced government had been widely admired, and extensively, if not universally copied. By the beginning of the 1990s, Keynesianism was widely discredited, as were the tools of nationalisation and state planning. All governments were having to grapple with attempts to reduce the burden of public spending and taxation. Welfare programmes were being rethought. Market processes were being encouraged.

Despite this, the new deregulated capitalism has been far from successful, even in its own terms. Its advocates would claim major changes for the better – the breaking up of self-serving corporatism, the busting of inefficient monopolies, more meritocratic and opportunistic societies, a more individualistic culture. Perhaps the most profound impact of the rise of neo-liberalism has been on political culture, shattering the relative complacency and sterility of the politics of the 1970s. The lasting legacy of Thatcherism and Reaganism has been a shift in political mood, a change in the terms of debate and a seachange in the character of the opposition parties of the Left.

Few of the neo-conservative's specific goals were realised, however. It is unproven whether the reforms of the 1980s have created the revolution in enterprise and values sought. Changes there have been in aspirations and motivation, but these have been more the product of wider structural than of political shifts. Success on the economic front has also been mixed.

In the United States, the recession of the early 1980s combined with rising military spending meant that tax levels and the budget deficit were higher when Reagan left office than when he entered. Mrs Thatcher also had only limited success in controlling the overall level of taxes and public spending and in creating a more competitive Britain. The new economics was relatively successful at reducing inflation but at the price of growing economic instability and inequality and rising unemployment. Economic progress is now more uneven and uncertain than in the past. Deregulation has delivered poor growth rates and higher unemployment by post-war standards. The conquest of inflation has not, to date, proved to be the route to future economic success.

The much heralded British economic miracle of the second half of the 1980s brought renewed growth and rising productivity, the product it was claimed of deregulation and liberalisation, but it was short lived. The beginning of the nineties brought a new world recession that the new economics seemed singularly ill-placed to tackle. The former, but discredited, solution of Keynesian reflation was no longer viable in the new world of free capital markets and interlocking economies. The new economics had contributed to the making of the recession. After a decade in the ascendancy, the ideology of the new Right seemed a lot less confident.

Even if the neo-conservative alternative seemed less relevant to the problems of the 1990s than it was to those of the 1980s, its brief dominance had a dramatic impact on the political landscape, and especially on the position of the opposition parties. Under the collapse of social democracy and the growing influence of neo-liberalism, Left parties across the western world suffered growing identity crises, culminating in the watering down of doctrinal socialism.

In Britain, the Labour Party's immediate reaction to the problems of the 1970s and the rise of Thatcherism was a swing to the Left, as political and economic failure was blamed on revisionism. Just at the point when the French Socialists were shedding some of their more dogmatic policies, the Labour Party fought and lost the 1983 general election on a more Left-wing platform, including withdrawal from the European Community, unilateral disarmament, extended public ownership and expanded public services.

After a third successive election defeat in 1987, Labour was forced to take its declining support more seriously and began a prolonged period of self analysis that ended with an attempt to move to the centre ground of politics. Previously cherished beliefs on Europe, on unilateralism and on public ownership were ditched. Commitments to reverse the process of privatisation and trade union reform were abandoned. This move to the centre was to prove no more successful. Labour lost its fourth election in a row in 1992.

In the United States, the Democratic Party followed a similar pattern of electoral failure, losing three Presidential elections in a row, and forcing a similar period of internal reflection. The

Republicans were the party in tune with the 1980s and its new creed of self-reliance and less government. By 1992, the Democratic Presidential candidate, Bill Clinton, was offering a package that seemed more in tune with the times. Gone was the former commitment to big government, replaced with a revived interest in private enterprise, 'responsibility' and 'opportunity'. It was to prove a successful formula. Aided by the recession, an unpopular Bush and a discontented electorate, Clinton became the first Democratic president for twelve years, albeit on a minority vote.

The Left in mainland Europe was also having to come to terms with the new world, the new individualism and the growing doubts about the benefits of state intervention. During its political exile from 1983, the German SPD was also forced into political rethink. Because of its earlier accommodations, this process was less radical and less convulsive than the one in Britain. The twin catalysts to change were the long run change in social composition, and the rising electoral success of the Green Party formed in 1980.

By 1988, the party had adopted a good deal of the environmental agenda, committing itself to the phasing out of nuclear energy within ten years, 'the ecological modernisation of the economy' and the introduction of quotas for women's representation. The party's new programmes accepted some of the arguments about the limits to growth with proposals for 'qualitative growth' that allowed for the social and environmental costs of rising material living standards. This ideological shift did little to improve the party's electoral performance which continued to worsen in the federal elections of 1987 and 1990, with its vote declining further to 37 per cent and 33 per cent respectively.

While other Left parties were suffering electoral decline, the Swedish Social Democratic Party (SAP) more or less held its vote throughout the 1980s, but then suffered its most serious result since the 1920s in the general election of 1991. The election campaign was dominated by debates about reform of the public sector, the future of the welfare state and tax rates as well as the deteriorating economic situation. The election brought a new government under Karl Bildt committed to privatisation, deregulation, cutbacks in welfare spending and taxation and the encouragement of individual initiative. It has given Sweden à dose of 'moderate Thatcherism' ten years after Britain, and called into question the future of the most successful socialist experiment in Europe.

Even before the election, cracks were beginning to appear in the Swedish success story. Its economy was becoming increasingly uncompetitive, unemployment had started to rise, and its high public spending programmes seemed increasingly unsustainable. Sweden's problems are similar to those facing other countries – growing unemployment and the soaring of welfare spending beyond the capacity and willingness of the country to finance it. It is a crisis that has simply come later than elsewhere. The SAP backed some of the policies of retrenchment introduced by the new government, confirming the political convergence that emerged in the early 1990s.

Before they lost office, the SAP had recognised that they had reached the limit of personal taxation, with the younger generation less tolerant than their more solidaristic parents. They reduced marginal tax rates and raised VAT and capital taxes. Although it did not reduce the overall level of taxation, it was seen as a recognition of the Right's argument that high taxes harm the economy.

Although the French Socialists held power for most of the period from 1981 to 1993, their economic policies epitomised the problem for contemporary Left politics. Following the reflationary debacle of the early 1980s, the Socialists essentially emulated German economic policy with the aim of reducing inflation and maintaining a strong currency. After the devaluations of the early 1980s, the franc held its value against the mark for a decade. Successful economic management, however, meant abandoning some cherished socialist beliefs. The policy led to some impressive economic gains – low inflation, new overseas markets and a greatly improved trade balance. But these gains exacted a high price, soaring unemployment, the highest youth unemployment in Europe and growing urban instability. This was despite increasing spending on training and other initiatives which trebled as a proportion of GDP.

The economic strategy also failed to win public approval. France under ten years of Socialist rule seemed increasingly a country adrift, losing the political inspiration of earlier periods. The disillusion in the country was shown in the big No vote in the 1992 referendum on Maastricht, the growing unpopularity of Mitterand and the devastating defeat of the Socialists in the 1993 general election. The Party had seemed to stand for little more than effective day-to-day management of the economy and this was not enough to hold on to power. The defeat left the Socialists in disarray and locked in bitter internal feuding, reminiscent of the British Labour Party in the aftermath of the 1979 defeat. In the arguments that followed, the outgoing Prime Minister, Pierre Beregovoy, committed suicide amidst rumours of scandal. The Socialists' defeat ushered in a new government of the Right under the Gaullist Edouard Balladur, committed to more privatisation, tax and spending cuts and tighter immigration controls.

Over the last fifteen years, parties of the Left have been in gradual electoral decline. Most Euro-socialist and social democratic parties are experiencing some combination of ideological doubt and electoral unpopularity, as they are grappling to accommodate themselves to the structural changes taking place, and facing up to the dilemmas of how to run affluent modern societies. Socialism as a body of ideas and a recipe for radical change is undergoing fundamental reappraisal everywhere. As yet this soul-searching has delivered no ready answers. Is it possible to continue to back high taxes and generous welfare benefits? Is universal welfare sustainable? Is a return to anything like full employment possible? Are redistribution and electoral success compatible? Though these questions would have been unthinkable even a few years ago, they are now at the centre of the policy debates within European parties of the Left.

In Spain, the Socialist Government has been reducing its commitment to generous health provision and imposing cuts in unemployment benefit. 'It's not healthy to have a society in which people of working age live off subsidies,' according to the Spanish Finance Minister. At the German SPD's Congress in 1992, the Party's then leader, Bjorn Engholm, told delegates that the 'era of the redistribution of growth is over'. In Britain, several influential voices in the Labour Party have begun openly to question the merits of universalism.

The effect has been a steady abandonment of traditional policies and solutions, and a downgrading of the commitment to the state and to collectivism, but with little of substance replacing these former beliefs. At the same time, the emerging weaknesses of the neo-liberal approach have led to some reappraisal on the Right. With the Left shifting to the Centre, and the Right backtracking on some of its more extreme postures of the 1980s, there are signs of the emergence of a new common ground on both economic and welfare policy. This may not yet add up to a new political consensus, but it does represent a narrower range of views around a new Centre-Right axis. The problem is that this new convergence seems to offer little prospect of tackling the deep-seated problems besetting modern societies.

The new conventional wisdom is less comprehensive than the one that it replaced. It is also likely to prove less robust, representing a convergence on what we're against as much as what we're for. So, central planning, state ownership, large fiscal deficits, excessive state regulation, inflation and high personal taxes are all out, on the Left as well as on the Right. There is also some agreement on a more minimal role for government and a greater reliance on markets in both economic and social activities. There has also been a similar straddling of the political divide on some aspects of social policy, including a growing acceptance of the state as an enabler rather than a provider, of a greater role for competition and markets in welfare provision, and a need for greater responsibility on behalf of the welfare recipient. These changes add up to the downgrading of state collectivism in favour of individualism and a new emphasis on opportunity and responsibility rather than dependency.

The key issue of difference is that of equality and redistribution. The European Left remains committed, in principle, to a more equal society to be achieved, at least in part, by state policies of income redistribution and generous welfare provision. The Left's problem has become how to achieve it. The Right, on the other hand, has abandoned any former attachment to greater equality that it may have held in the early post-war era, and now believes that greater equality is neither desirable nor achievable. Ronald Reagan and Margaret Thatcher's policies were strongly anti-egalitarian, specifically designed to reward the successful and penalise the unsuccessful. The theoreticians of the Right from Von Hayek to Keith Joseph argued that equality of outcome was inconsistent with economic efficiency, and that the poor could better be helped by economic success than by expensive social policies, a view that has not been moderated.

Political parties across the western world are increasingly distinguished less by ideology and moral certainties than, as Michael Dukakis put it in the 1988 American Presidential election campaign, by 'competence'. Gone is the former distinction between the fundamentalists and the revisionists of the Right and the Left, between the puritans and the pragmatists. Politicians are increasingly functionaries rather than ideologues, and it is hardly surprising that it is the parties of the Right that have accommodated most successfully to this new world. The political winners today are those who offer the most effective management of a market dominated economy in an interdependent world, not its replacement or reconstruction. Capitalist mixed economies now have no rivals. The only question left in politics is how best to manage them.

This new managerialism is also reflected in a subtle and tentative erosion of the humanism that all 'respectable' ideologies and political parties felt that they needed to adopt in the post-war period. The principles that underpinned the 'ethical politics' of the era were drawn from a set of convictions drawn from Christianity or socialism, a belief in the essential goodness of humanity, and the ability to be able to harness that in creating better societies. The slow erosion of this optimism ushered in a much more cynical mood. Faced with horrific crimes, such as the murder of three-year-old James Bulger in Bootle in 1993, and seemingly intractable social problems, the big political idea of 1993 then became the rediscovery of evil and the need for much more draconian policies on 'law and order' and against minorities.

Such an idea finds it easier to take hold in a society devoid of an ethical base and lacking alternative ideologies. The danger is that persistent social instability will lock societies even more into a downward cycle, making it easier to blame the problem on a rotten, irredeemable core. Once this becomes part of the vocabulary and the conventional wisdom, it opens the door to a more authoritarian culture and the creation of easy scapegoats for a malaise stemming from other quarters. People and communities can then easily be written off. Responsibility lies with the individual and the individual alone.

Contemporary politics has become less ideological and more pragmatic. Modern government has increasingly looked to shifting responsibility elsewhere, to companies, individuals and quangos. The latest fashion is for the creation of independent central banks on the model of the German Bundesbank, with responsibility for monetary policy and interest rates, thereby taking at least part of economic management out of the political arena. In Britain, the organisation of traditional public services such as health and education are being viewed as entirely a matter of management. The underlying presumption is that many issues of contemporary management such as the level of interest rates, the control of the money supply and the provision of local services are essentially apolitical. Being purely technical matters they can then be taken out of the hands of government and the political process.

The Left's shift has been largely negative, the product of a reluctant, but inevitable, rejection of the old solutions rather than the discovery of a new road. The Right's conversion was borne out of a belief in the individual and a new emphasis on self-reliance, but has ended up around a more pragmatic agenda. The result of these fading ideologies has been the birth of a more apolitical era, a time when politics is driven by economic and social technicalities, and by political and party self-interest.

With the possible exception of the United States, the general elections of 1992 and 1993 – in Britain, France and Spain – were in essence about the ability to govern, rather than about different social visions. The result has been the shedding of ethically based politics and a new concern with processes, with management, with the art of the possible. Election campaigns are a triumph of style over substance. This would be all right if societies had been able to solve social and economic problems, but this is far from being the case.

An essential argument of this book is that successful economic and political management is not simply a matter of efficient technical control and adjustment. Since the Second World War, countries carrying out broadly similar maco-economic policies and with similar growth patterns have, for example, experienced very different levels of unemployment. Employment opportunities and economic stability are as much if not more a matter of social culture and values as of economic competence.

The relatively short-lived nature of the neo-liberal economic experiment has left modern societies in a political vacuum, and with a new crisis of government. Social democracy has effectively departed. Neo-liberalism is in retreat. Pragmatism reigns. Yet this has little to offer in the management of contemporary economies.

Part Two:
Out of Malaise?

Part one has presented a largely pessimistic account of the state of the economically developed world as it approaches the end of the century. The shift from scarcity to affluence and from welfarism to consumerism since the war has had a mixed impact. It has brought rising living standards for a majority but also changing values and aspirations which have simultaneously put increasing strains on the way societies function. Today's consumerist and individualistic societies are less sympathetic to co-operative action which a majority feels no longer serves its immediate interests. They have also become less willing to meet the costs of rapid social change. These internal forces have reacted with wider external trends to create more unstable and unequal societies.

Part two examines the prospects for the future. Can modern societies find new ways to tackle these emergent problems of the management of affluence? Or have they lost the power to prevent a more troubled and uncertain future?

This depends ultimately on the interaction between external events, public opinion and political ideology. Indeed, post-war history can be seen as the product of the interaction of these three forces. The immediate post-war era was characterised by a combination of favourable external events and a new political philosophy which captured a public mood hungry for change.

In the 1970s, a more hostile economic backdrop meshed with changing public attitudes to sow the seeds of the political changes that were to follow. It was the sliding of public sympathy for the high tax, welfare and interventionist ethos of social democracy which led ultimately to its electoral and ideological decline and the emergence of the market experiments of the next decade.

During the 1980s, political ideology and public opinion were marching hand in hand. Both Margaret Thatcher and Ronald Reagan gave authority to the competitive individualism that was being encouraged by wider social changes. The individualism that found expression in mass, imitative consumption and in the pursuit of a less restrained self-interest was encouraged and proclaimed from the political pulpits of those in power on both sides of the Atlantic. By the depths of the 1990s recession, they were marching to different tunes. Moulded by the impact of rising unemployment and falling living standards, public confidence began to slide. Unbridled individualism seemed a less persuasive creed, consumer capitalism a less successful model for organising affluent societies.

As they approach the end of the century, most affluent societies face a situation of uncertainty and instability. There is a good deal of unease about the future, about the prospect for work, about living standards and about social stability. There is a whiff of drift and decay and, in some nations, of spreading corruption. It is doubtful that societies will get by simply by sitting tight. If so, most societies are poised for a further period of change. The question is in which direction?

External forces are likely to remain a source of uncertainty and pressure, but also carry the potential for much improved opportunities. Technological improvement which increases economic efficiency and productivity offers the prospect of more choice, more leisure and improved working conditions if it is managed properly. If it is exploited for the benefit of the few, it will mean more uncertainty and insecurity and further upheaval in the pattern and distribution of employment. The problem of meeting the costs of welfare will be aggravated by demographic shift which is bringing ageing populations. Continued population growth and rising consumer demand will put more pressure on the world's resources.

Growing political and economic interdependence and intensified competition will affect the global pattern of winners and losers. Traditionally successful regions and nations face the prospect of relative decline while some poorer areas could take their place. The risk is that the effect of this continuing upheaval is likely to be a further widening of the gaps between the rich and the poor, both between and within nations, as jobs get restructured and redistributed and systems of social protection prove increasingly difficult to maintain.

The real danger facing modern society is that unfocused technical change and jobless growth together with the market requirements of intensified international competition will create workless and desolated communities. The political task is to minimise the malign effects of these forces without inhibiting economic performance, to marry the needs of the market and social cohesion.

Whether it proves possible to grasp the opportunities and minimise the disruption depends on the political and public mood. The recession brought a much more nervous outlook and more moderate consumerist aspirations. This mood is unlikely to remain static. Persistent economic problems could bring deep-seated insecurity and growing public discontent. Sustained economic recovery could bring a return to the explosive and unsustainable appetites of the 1980s, to a contented but largely politically apathetic and indifferent majority. Alternatively, that era may prove the aberration, giving way to a new maturity, a more generous culture and a greater sense of social responsibility. A greater awareness of the limitations of a competitive, leap-frogging culture could permit an alternative, and more co-operative, approach to the management of affluence.

Politics is also uneasily poised. Despite the claims of Francis Fukuyama of the 'end of history', of the final triumph of the free-market, democratic state,[149] the current and convergent approach to social and economic management is unlikely to hold for long. Despite the inevitability of the mixed economy and of the domination of private production and the market-led economy, it is doubtful if societies have achieved the final resolution of the great questions of governance. The fact is that the present managerial orthodoxy is not up to the difficult tasks facing modern societies. As yet, an alternative model is not in sight. Finding a more successful approach capable of lifting the malaise and creating more harmonious societies will depend, above all, on a combination of a sustained change in social behaviour and new political leadership.

8. Consumerism:
Is There a Limit?

. . . our civilization is holding ever more tightly to its habit of consuming larger and larger quantities every year of coal, oil, fresh air and water, trees, topsoil, and the thousand other substances we rip from the crust of the earth, transforming them into not just the sustenance and shelter we need but much more that we don't need: huge quantities of pollution, products for which we spend billions on advertising to convince ourselves we want, massive surpluses of products that depress prices while the products themselves go to waste, and diversions and distractions of every kind. We seem increasingly eager to lose ourselves in the forms of culture, society, technology, the media, and the rituals of production and consumption, but the price we pay is the loss of our spiritual lives.

(Al Gore)[150]

The regular budget of the UN, excluding emergency costs is some $8 billion a year. It is about what Western children spent last Christmas, or what US citizens spend a year on cut flowers and potted plants.

(Erskine Childers)[151]

Sharing plenty has proved a much harder task than sharing shortages. Part of the explanation is the pull of modern consumerism. The world's ability to manage its future wealth in a way which creates a better balance will depend heavily on the course of consumer aspirations.

173

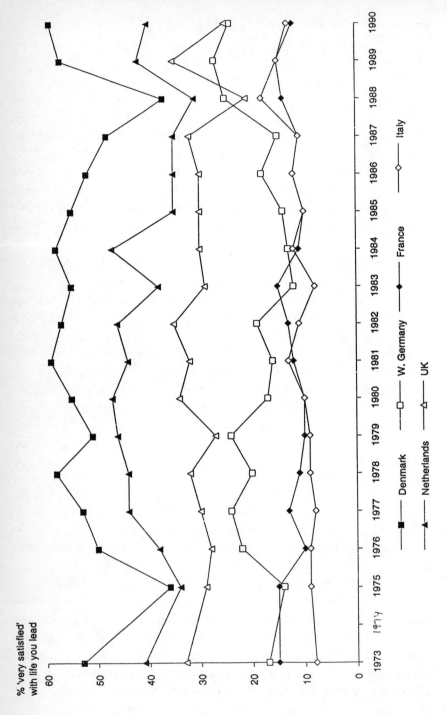

Figure 8.1: Satisfaction with the life you lead 1973–90

% 'very satisfied'
with life you lead

Denmark ■ W. Germany □ France ♦ Italy ◇
Netherlands ▲ UK ◁

Source: Commission of the European Community, 1991 (b)

Consumer satisfaction

Figure 8.1 shows the proportion of the population of six European countries who were 'very satisfied with the life you lead' based on surveys of all EC countries carried out by the European Commission since 1973. The most striking characteristic of the results is the remarkable stability over the period despite the rise in per capita incomes over the seventeen years. A similar pattern of long run stability is found when respondents were asked about their level of happiness, and in the other countries sampled. The pattern suggests that individual satisfaction is relatively stable over the long run, independent of rises in living standards within the country, but subject to short-run fluctuations related to expectations which rise and fall in relation to economic activity. In general, longer run improvements in material living standards within nations are not associated with improvements in happiness.

There are two main explanations for this trend. First, a person's or nation's material living standard is not the sole determinant of welfare. Non-material factors such as family life, work satisfaction, leisure and friendship are as important, if not more so, than the quantity of consumer goods in determining the quality of life. A survey by the Henley Centre in 1987 showed that of a list of seventy-nine items, those like 'honesty', 'fulfilled by family life', 'have people who care about you', and 'fit and healthy' came much higher up the scale of importance than 'to buy expensive things' which took 66th place in the list.

The second reason lies in the distinction between absolute and relative levels of consumption, and in the rise in the importance attached to relativities in affluent societies discussed in chapter 2. The more satisfaction depends on relative living standards, the less satisfaction will rise with material improvements, and the more expectations will remain unmet.

The other key feature of figure 8.1 is the wide variation in satisfaction between countries, with, for example, Denmark and the Netherlands well ahead of the average and France and Italy well below. The differences are, at least in part, the product of cultural and social factors: some countries with similar levels of economic well-being have happier populations than others for other reasons – they may be less preoccupied by materialism and relativities, they may have more manageable expectations, they may be at different stages of political development.

The rising costs of affluence

Given the apparently weak relationship between satisfaction and material well-being, the question arises as to whether there is an eventual limit to the desire for ever increasing levels of consumption. One factor that could contribute to such a limit is the growing costs associated with affluent lifestyles. These costs are both personal and external and have the effect of offsetting the gains from higher consumption. Eventually they will exceed the benefits. The problem is that these costs are often largely ignored in either individual or collective decision making. If they were taken account of more explicitly, they would lead to a very different set of material priorities.

These costs include, first, the private costs incurred solely by individuals. For example, it is widely argued that affluence has had the effect of creating more overloaded, harried and unmanageable lives, of putting increased pressure on time. There are really two elements to what has become known as 'the problem of running out of time'. First is the question of working hours, and the extent to which richer societies choose to take the gains in productivity from economic advance in the form of more consumption rather than more leisure. Second, there is the question of how far leisure itself becomes increasingly congested and therefore less pleasurable in affluent societies. That is, how far are the higher material living standards resulting from growth bought at the cost of a much more demanding worklife and of losing the essential characteristic of leisure – relaxation?

The evidence on hours worked over time is mixed. Over the very long run, hours worked have risen sharply. Most of us work much longer hours than before the industrial revolution. But compared with the nineteenth and first half of the twentieth century, hours of work have fallen. In Britain, the average worked by full time male manual workers fell by around three hours a week between the mid-1930s and 1990.[152] The pattern is similar in other developed countries – there is a clear negative relationship between hours worked and economic development. The only exceptions to this general rule are Britain and the USA during the 1980s which both showed increases in hours worked against the long run trend.

In the United States one study found an average increase in working hours over the last twenty years of around 8 per cent – the equivalent of an extra month a year.[153] This dramatic rise is common across industries and occupations affecting men and women and professionals and low-paid service workers alike. Commuting time is also up – by an average of twenty-three hours a year – and paid vacation time is down by 3.5 days a year.

This trend, according to Juliet Schor, has contributed to rising stress and less time spent on sleeping and eating, and less parental devotion to children. She reports 30 per cent of adults complaining of high stress nearly every day and 59 per cent reporting high stress once or twice a week; a third of the population say they are rushed to do the things they have to do, up from a quarter in 1965; up to 7 million children were left caring for themselves while their parents were at work; one reported study found that between 1960 and 1986, the time per week parents had available to be with children fell between ten and twelve hours; another linked this 'parenting deficit' to poor school performance, mental problems and drug and alcohol abuse.[154]

In Japan working hours are even longer – 400 hours a year more than in Europe – though they have been coming down. According to a survey by Recruit Research in 1991, Japanese employees take an average of 7.9 days paid leave a year and put in an average of 62.5 hours of overtime a month during the busiest seasons. This is the product of intense competition, loyalty to the company and a strong work ethic. The Japanese pay a high price for this commitment. The country has a special word for death from overwork – 'karoshi' - and there are ten thousand victims a year. Bus drivers, nurses and teachers as well as corporate executives have fallen victim. Burnout is commonplace. When a leading Japanese newspaper conducted a nationwide poll in January 1991, half the respondents admitted to fears of becoming a 'karoshi' victim. This may help to explain the low levels of satisfaction in relation to income found in Japan.

In Britain hours worked are less than in Japan and the United States, but an average four and a half hours longer per week than on the continent. The stress levels associated with long hours have more than doubled in the past seven years, according to Professor

Figure 8.2: Stress in Europe, 1992
(Proportion saying stress is a major concern)

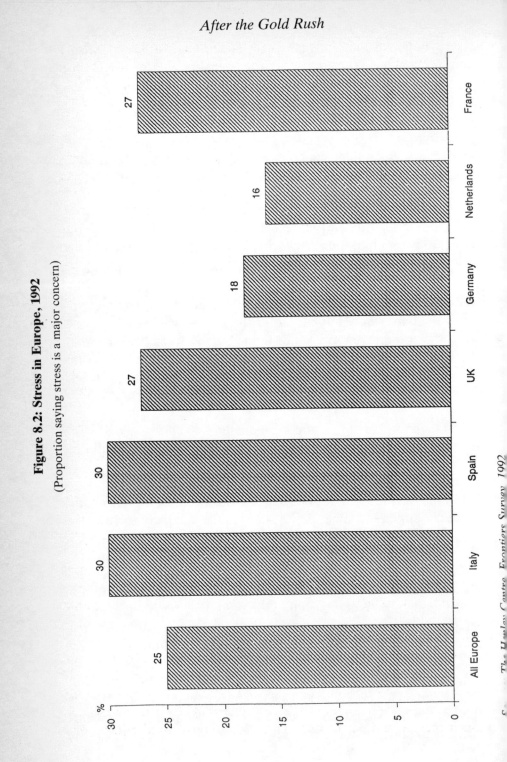

Source: The Henley Centre, Frontiers Survey, 1992

Cary Cooper of the University of Manchester Institute of Science and Technology. The proportion of company chairmen and chief executives who mentioned hours-related stress rose from a fifth in 1985 to a half in 1990. Another survey by Professor Cooper of 200 executives found that half were at their desks by 8am and a quarter were still there at 6.30pm. Fewer than half took their full holiday entitlement and a quarter worked every weekend. Fear of the sack and of denting career prospects in an increasingly competitive environment has fuelled the pressure to work long hours. A study by the mental health charity MIND, published in March 1992, showed that the office was now the biggest cause of stress, afflicting groups such as librarians, bank managers, quantity surveyors and insurance clerks as well as executives. Figure 8.2 shows that stress is a problem for a quarter of Europeans.

The problem of stress is closely related to the growth of competitive individualism and a dominating consumer culture. The increasing importance attached to relative performance in work, in leisure, and in personal attainment brings tension and the risk of failure. Increasing workloads, personal debt and pressures to succeed can be attributed to the rising aspirations of modern living. We need more money to meet the rising obligations, demands and goals of today's lifestyles. Stress is thus closely related to the growth of a 'leap-frogging' culture, and to pressure outstripping the capacity to cope.

A similar influence is at work in the way we use our leisure time. Arguably, this is becoming more and more congested. Commentators have long been warning that consuming takes time, that growing affluence would lead to more and more consumer goods and opportunities but less and less time to enjoy them.[155] Staffan Linder argued that time has become more and more squeezed with economic development, with traditional societies enjoying a surplus of free time, intermediate societies having what he termed 'time affluence' and advanced societies like the USA suffering from 'time famine'.

He foresaw societies becoming increasingly crowded and frustrated, with leisure becoming less and less 'leisurely' and people switching away from activities that take time like long and leisurely walks and relaxed dinner parties to things that can be done quickly. Such increased time pressure has, according to Fred Hirsch, also

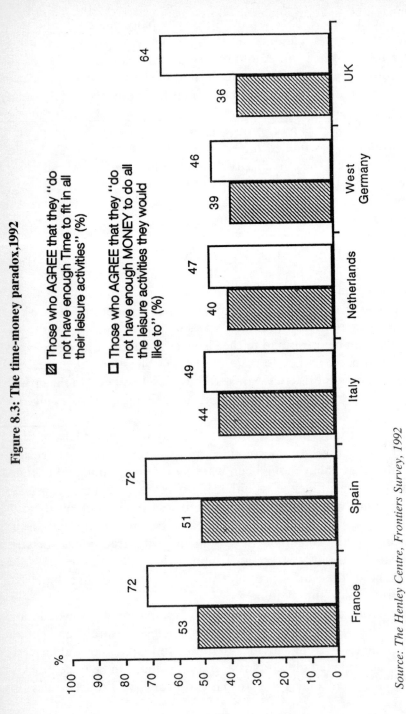

Figure 8.3: The time-money paradox,1992

☒ Those who AGREE that they "do not have enough Time to fit in all their leisure activities" (%)

☐ Those who AGREE that they "do not have enough MONEY to do all the leisure activities they would like to" (%)

Source: The Henley Centre, Frontiers Survey, 1992

contributed to a 'decline in sociability and, specifically, friendliness. Friendliness is time consuming and thereby liable to be economised because of its extravagant absorption of this increasingly scarce input'.[156]

This provides another explanation for the growing contradictions of affluent consumer societies. People need more money to fulfil rising expectations and aspirations *but* are denied the time to enjoy the consumer and leisure pursuits being sought. 'Time is money' is a phrase that has less resonance in poorer societies. Psychologists have shown how, from walking, talking and shopping speeds, the pace of life accelerates with affluence and commercialisation. A study of six nations showed that Japanese urban dwellers move fastest followed by Americans, English, Taiwanese and Italians. Indonesians moved most slowly of all.[157] This has encouraged the commercialisation of leisure and hence the need for even higher incomes. This paradox is shown in figure 8.3 which indicates the constraints of time and money shortages across Europe in pursuing the growing pressure for more leisure. The data, from our own survey, also showed that this conflict is more severe among the better off who are more likely to complain of lack of time.

One impact of this has been to increase the demand for time saving services such as taxis and take-away food which can be viewed as an additional cost rather than a benefit of modern living. It has in turn led to the commercialisation of a number of formerly non-market activities. These include care of the elderly and of children which were once the responsibility of families and communities. As one study in the United States has put it,

> As social bonds turned into commodities, families and communities began contracting out their functions to the market economy. Let Kindercare watch the toddlers. Let preschool open their eyes to life. Hire counselors for neglected, latchkey kids. Buy entertainment from Nintendo and the video store. For adults, turn time away from work into a 'leisure industry', which sells camcorders and motorized treadmills in place of visits to the side porch and walks through the neighborhood. In virtually every corner of family and community life, the things people used to *do* have been turned into things they have to *buy*.[158]

It is this tendency which has fuelled the increasing commercialisation of leisure. We are happy to be organised if it buys us time. We gain on time and convenience by using readily supplied fun – the theme parks and leisure centres. But there is also a downside. Leisure seems too often to have become less an escape from the pressures and stresses of work than another part of the competitive society. The commercialisation of leisure means that we need more money to relax. But equally, we are encouraged to use our spare time, not as simple pleasure or relaxation in itself, but as a means of self-improvement. Leisure is increasingly about striving, about self-image. And it is big business.

For most people, this analysis rings true. Lives seem more harried and less relaxed. But this is also not the whole story. In total, leisure has risen in most western societies because people retire earlier and live longer, though arguably it comes when it is least needed and can be least enjoyed. If time congestion is an inevitable part of modern living, whether this is desirable or undesirable is a matter of judgment. Many people thrive on fast working and living. Some cultures, including North America, live off ambition, achievement and self-fulfilment. Exhausting and frustrating it may be, but it is not wholly negative. Nevertheless, whatever the gains, the costs cannot be ignored and may eventually lead to re-evaluation of social behaviour.

The rising social costs

To these personal costs should be added the growing social costs which are borne by others as well as ourselves. One example is the more congested cities associated with burgeoning car ownership and the process of urbanisation. Initially the advent of the car brought considerable gains to the few able to afford them. As car ownership has spread, the benefit for the minority of initial owners has fallen, partly because of the loss of the satisfaction from exclusivity, and partly because of growing congestion. The congestion caused by escalating car use imposes high and mounting costs on other car users and the whole community.

Tourism illustrates the same problem, that increased participation changes the nature of the experience. Tourists, in their search for something special, undermine that difference by their very enjoyment of it. Travel has brought undoubted benefits of pleasure, fulfilment and discovery to millions. But it has also brought environmental and cultural damage. The Mediterranean now has the most urbanised coastline and the dirtiest water in the world. In Spain, France, Italy and parts of Greece, there are few undeveloped coastlines left. Spain is now engaged in a mass programme of environmental improvement – cleaning beaches, greening resorts, banning cheap hotels – yet much of the damage is irreversible. What has happened to Spain and Greece is now shifting elsewhere. Previously remote and unexplored areas of the world are being turned into building sites for the next wave of tourists.

Mass tourism has endangered two of the world's most fragile ecosystems – the Alps and the Mediterranean. It has threatened habitats and endangered species from the monk seal to the loggerhead turtle. Forests have been cleared for trekkers, golf courses and ski runs. By overloading waste disposal and sewage systems, tourism has become a principal source of pollution. Pollution in the Caribbean is destroying mangrove forests, seagrass beds and coral reefs. It is this spoiling that makes the process unsustainable. Sooner or later, the search for more secluded holidays will run out of opportunities.

The costs of modern consumerism include not merely the problems of congested lives, cities and holiday resorts, but more seriously the growing problem of pollution. Rising car ownership is not merely bringing extra congestion, it is a principal source of pollution. Across Europe, more than a fifth of households have two or more cars (table 2.1). In the United States, the average number of cars per household is two. In the past twenty years, the number of cars worldwide has more than doubled from 200 million to 480 million. Cars are the fastest growing source of carbon dioxide, the gas mainly responsible for the greenhouse effect and thus for the climate changes, flooding and hunger forecast for the next century. Cars account for 74 per cent of EC carbon monoxide emissions and a fifth of carbon dioxide. Yet the European Commission also expects total car mileage to increase by 25 per cent between 1990 and 2010 and the stock of cars to rise by 45 per cent.

Global warming is one of the alleged consequences of rising consumption. The depletion of the ozone layer is another, the result primarily of the growing use of CFCs and other man-made and, especially, industrial chemicals. Half of the original tropical forest has already gone, and at the present rate of deforestation another third will be gone by 2030. Europe has no old-growth forests left, and only a few remain in North America. An area about the size of China and India combined has suffered moderate to extreme soil degradation in the last twenty years, the result of agricultural activities, deforestation and over-grazing.

Over the last twenty years, the loss of fish from the world's oceans has nearly doubled from 56 million to 90 million tonnes a year. The Food and Agricultural Organisation reported in 1990 that most traditional marine fish stocks have reached full exploitation. We are also slowly poisoning the globe with mercury, cadmium, heavy metals, chlorine and a variety of other substances leading to an accumulation of oils and plastics in the ocean. The US Congress's Office of Technology Assessment estimates that 179 million tons of toxic chemicals are discharged annually leading to an estimated 20,000 extra cases of pesticide-linked cancers in the US alone.

How serious these problems are and how far we should go to tackle them is a matter of intense controversy. Scientists still disagree about the significance of global warming and it may be another decade before we know for certain. Partly in consequence, the policy responses needed have been a matter of dispute. The strongest action to date has come in relation to the problem of the depletion of the ozone layer. In 1987, the Montreal Protocol signed by the world's leaders proposed a 50 per cent cut in CFC emissions in industrial countries by 1998. In 1990, after new evidence showed an acceleration of ozone loss, a new deal was signed to phase out CFCs completely by the year 2000. It took the world twenty years before it acted on CFCs which were first warned of in the early 1970s. It may take a similar time before equally tough measures are taken on global warming, despite its potentially more serious consequences.

How sustainable current rises in consumption are also remains a matter of disagreement. The world's richest nations consume approximately five-sixths of the world's resources among a population of around one billion. The poorest nations consume one-sixth to be shared among a population of over 4 billion. On average, a person living in the north therefore consumes around twenty times that of a poor person in the south (though different methods of calculation give slightly different ratios). Simply to bring today's 4 billion poorest up to the present lifestyles of the one billion richest would require a twentyfold increase in world consumption.

If nations continue to expect an increase of consumption of say 2 per cent a year, consumption in these countries would increase fourfold after sixty years. Over this period, it has also been predicted that the world population will double. To bring the whole world up to the average standards of the richer nations over a 60 year period while allowing for modest increases in consumption and continuing population growth would require a one-hundred-and-sixtyfold increase in consumption per head. If this is considered unsustainable or undesirable on other grounds, the alternatives are to reduce population growth, restrict consumption growth in the north or maintain or increase the current divide between north and south.

Experts are divided as to the maximum sustainable consumption that the earth can accommodate. The Brundtland Report envisaged an increase of between five and tenfold in economic activity over the next fifty years without serious alarm. Green campaigners have been more pessimistic about the physical limit to the level of consumption imposed by finite resources. The most apocalyptic forecast has come from the *Limits to Growth* Report published by the Club of Rome in 1972 and updated in 1992.[159] The first Report forecast that infinite needs would rapidly come up against the problem of finite natural resources leading to global catastrophe and called for a halt to growth altogether.

This dire warning has proved to be greatly exaggerated as the world has found other sources of energy such as North Sea oil and new reserves of natural gas. Indeed, the standard economic argument against such doomsday scenarios has been the possibility of substitution through technical progress and use of alternative sources. Nevertheless, it is doubtful if the world can grow at the rates identified above without intolerable consequences. If so, something will have to give. The world is left with a clear choice between lower relative, and maybe absolute, living standards in the north, *or* creating irreparable ecological damage, *or* permitting gross inequalities between north and south to persist or widen.

While the more extreme forecasts by some environmentalists have proved highly inaccurate, the growing problems of pollution and resource constraints are being taken seriously. The United

Nations Earth Summit held in Rio de Janeiro in June 1992 brought together the heads of state of 130 countries along with 15,000 negotiators, lobbyists and activists to discuss the fate of the earth. Three years in the planning, it dwarfed in scale its 'predecessor', the Stockholm environment conference of 1972, yet with largely inconclusive results. There were lofty speeches from world leaders and signed, but vague and non-binding, agreements on promoting sustainable development and protecting the global environment.

In the year after the conference, most of the trends that inspired the conference had worsened, while many wealthy countries had cut their aid budgets. World leaders signed two treaties at the Summit on conserving bio-diversity – the planet's wealth of animal and plant species – and on atmospheric pollution. One year on, less than half the nations needing to ratify the Treaties before they can come into force had done so.

Left behind

The impact of rising inequality throughout much of the west over the last twenty years can also be added to the tally of growing and offsetting social costs. The principle of relativity in satisfaction applies as much to the poor as to the better off. The more that satisfaction depends upon one's relative and not absolute position, and that discontent is a function of 'relative deprivation', then the more rising inequality will have the effect of increasing consumer dissatisfaction. The consumer boom of the 1980s was certainly a restricted party, from which the bottom third were largely excluded.

Some of the better off may not have improved their satisfaction much despite their relative advance against the poor because they compare themselves with others who have also been pulling away. The poor who have fallen further behind will experience a loss of welfare because their reference groups have become middle income groups rather than other groups of the poor as in the past.

Growing division has certainly been accompanied by a new sense of resentment felt by the bottom third of society. The poor as well as the better off are bombarded by the seductive images of modern consumer culture, and are subject to the same acquisitive instincts. This has inevitably affected social behaviour. It has distorted individual priorities as traditional wants have been reordered. The shell suit, the Reebok trainers and the Nintendo game are as much the uniform of the poor as the newly affluent working class. Single parents and unemployed families struggling on social security are hardly immune from the pressures of the 'loadsamoney' culture and the 'pester power' of their children. The child whose parents have not bought the latest video game feels ashamed to invite their friends home. But meeting these addictions has all too often proved a costly business, driving more of the poor into debt, and sometimes into petty theft.

It is hardly surprising that consumerism has enhanced the feelings of rejection and boredom felt by many of the young unemployed, and that this has contributed to an upward spiral of vandalism, drug addiction and petty and more serious crime that has added to rising social instability. During the riots that shook Brixton, Liverpool and Bristol during the 1980s, one of the lasting images will be of the looters who calmly helped themselves in front of the television cameras to the trappings of consumerism on offer in the high street stores of those areas. In the aftermath of the Meadow Well riots on Tyneside in 1991, many of the young unemployed teenagers who inhabited the estate made it only too clear that they refused to be denied the trainers, track suits and mountain bikes that had become the new badges of affluence for their employed peers.

The personal and social cost of rising crime is another item to be added to the bill for modern consumerism. Higher levels of crime have had to be paid for not just by the victims, but also by society at large. Increasing numbers of the elderly have become trapped in their homes because of fear. The same applies to children who are missing out on the greater freedom and opportunities enjoyed by their parents. In 1971, 80 per cent of 7–8-year-olds walked to school. Now it is 9 per cent.[160] Today, parents' deepest fear for their children is of abduction or assault.

We have all had to foot the bills of higher crime prevention, greater home and shop security and swelling insurance premiums. In the United States, it is now commonplace for suburban houses in major cities to carry iron grilles and even warning signs of 'armed responses 24 hours a day'. North Americans now spend more on private security guards and burglar alarms than they pay through taxes for public police forces.[161] Urban schools have had to invest heavily in security screening systems because of widespread carrying of guns by schoolchildren. New York city's school security force employs 2,600 people. In Parkland, a middle class suburb of Tacoma, Washington, the vice-principal has been issued with a bullet-proof waistcoat, and in Rochester, New York, teachers can get a discount on a $16 desk alarm, courtesy of the local teachers' union. Security systems are expensive. Walk-through metal detectors cost $10,000, while X-ray varieties cost $17,000. They make schools look like prisons and playgrounds like compounds.

The future of growth?

There are therefore several reasons to question the unqualified benefits of a persistent growth in material living standards. To the extent that satisfaction depends on relative rather than absolute consumption, rises in consumption may simply fuel inflationary pressure rather than raise welfare. There are also substantial costs associated with rising consumption that can be viewed as a negative by-product of growth.

The evidence is that these problems have become more acute with rising material prosperity. Some critics have gone on to argue that the damage caused by ever rising consumption is now sufficiently severe that the cherished growth objective should be abandoned. Others have argued that growth remains the only means of tackling some of the deepening problems of contemporary societies, and that what is needed is not an end to growth, but a change in its composition.

Two conditions would be needed to justify the 'no-growth' stance. First, it would need to be shown that societies have now reached the point where the extra costs of growth outweigh the benefits. Second, it would need to be demonstrated that the composition of growth could not be altered to make the balance sheet more favourable. Neither criterion is easy to assess. There are significant measurement problems and value judgments involved. Nevertheless, several attempts at evaluation of the first condition have been made.

Changes in GNP per capita over time are accepted to be an imperfect guide to changes in general welfare. They inevitably ignore many factors that contribute to welfare but that cannot be measured in pure economic terms such as the quality of the environment, the availability of leisure, security, the strength of family and community ties and the quality of and access to work. As a result, changes in GNP and other aggregate measures of output and consumption remain the only single available indicator. Yet such measures remain a poor guide even to economic progress. Increases in consumption per head may be a poor guide to welfare, especially if there has been a simultaneous shift in its distribution. Nor do they make allowance for the costs associated with rising consumption, even though these can be significant.

Some items of expenditure can be viewed as forms of intermediate spending, purchased not for their own sake but in order to permit other forms of consumption. The inclusion of such 'defensive' items (sometimes termed 'regrettable necessities') in the national accounts then constitutes a form of double counting. The concept of defensive goods was first applied to certain items of public spending such as defence, police, and fire protection. The concept also applies to a variety of private expenditures which can be viewed as the hidden costs of industrial growth by individuals. These would include spending on time-saving goods and services, and on items bought to offset some deterioration in the individual's position such as the double glazing bought to reduce the noise from a new motorway or new runway.

These costs rise with growth. A study in Germany has concluded that such defensive expenditures grew nearly four times faster than GNP between 1970 and 1985, rising from 5.6 per cent to 10 per cent of GNP. The growing need for such defensive or involuntary spending as material living standards rise has also contributed to the preoccupation with ever higher incomes and the apparent paradox that higher 'real' incomes appear to bring only limited increases in well being.

Another factor excluded from GNP calculations is the depreciation associated with the loss of natural resources in production including minerals, forests, soils and fossil fuels. The idea of putting a cash value on such resources has always been a controversial one, but was given more credibility with a report commissioned by the Department of the Environment which proposed that the national accounts should attempt to allow for changes in the stock of environmental resources and the costs of pollution.[162]

There have been several attempts to produce a more accurate measure of welfare than that provided by the standard GNP

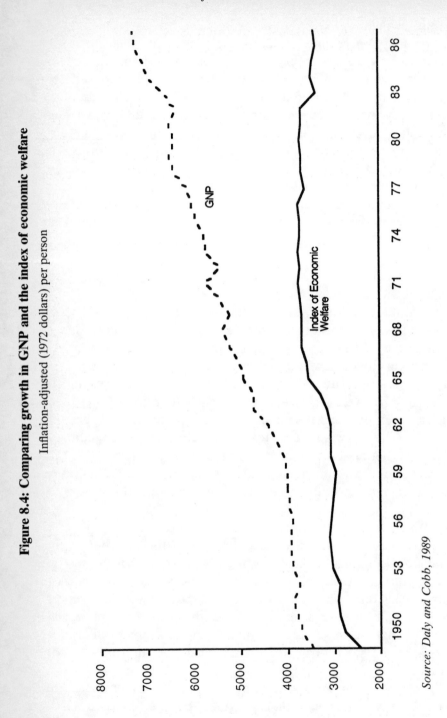

Figure 8.4: Comparing growth in GNP and the index of economic welfare

Inflation-adjusted (1972 dollars) per person

GNP

Index of Economic Welfare

Source: Daly and Cobb, 1989

measure. One of the most comprehensive is the Index of Sustainable Economic Welfare shown in figure 8.4. This index is subject to a number of qualifications noted by the authors and is derived, broadly, by subtracting the costs of items such as road accidents, commuting and pollution from consumption. It also makes an allowance for the destruction of natural resources. In the US, the index rose slowly between 1950 and 1970, though more slowly than per capita GNP, remained roughly static during the 1970s and declined during the 1980s. In contrast, GNP per capita continued to rise.

On the first criterion, the benefits of growth are therefore being at least partially offset by rising costs. Nevertheless, this conclusion is the subject of several qualifications, and until better tools have been developed for measuring these changes, it is necessary to remain sceptical of the superiority of a policy of slower or zero growth. Moreover, there is no guarantee that such a policy, even it were politically feasible, would reverse these relationships and produce higher welfare.

Advocates of continued growth argue that achieving higher wealth remains essential to tackling the problems of affluence. Improving the relative living standards of the poor in both the developed and third world will depend on growth. It was the 'growth dividend' that paid for the welfare and redistributive policies of the post-war era, without cutting the absolute living standards of the affluent. Some of the arguments of the anti-growth school seem to border on the extreme, such as one proposal for exclusively horse and horse-drawn vehicle towns and a ban on all international air travel.[163] As critics of the pure anti-growth school have argued, the arguments against growth are often highly elitist, made by the better off who, as Anthony Crosland put it, 'want to kick the ladder down behind them'. As Crosland went on,

Affluence is obviously more agreeable when it is a minority condition. Driving around the country was much pleasanter when the roads were nearly empty. Venice and Majorca have been ruined for the minority since the *hoi polloi* invaded in their charter flights and the local peasantry bought noisy Vespas. And a rural retreat was safer and more serene, before demands for lower housing densities began to decant the urban masses into the countryside.[164]

Crosland's dream that most of his constituents would eventually be able to enjoy the pastimes of the rich has become at least partially true over the twenty years since he wrote this polemic. Many of the activities which he wanted ordinary people to enjoy have moved from being minority to majority activities. The problem is that just as those on average incomes have started to catch up, the rich have found it necessary to want to pull away, leaving a significant minority further behind while giving another upward twist to the apparently never ending spiral of consumerism. It is this upward and at least partially self-defeating cycle of consumption which is distorting priorities and which may ultimately prove unsustainable.

Advocates of growth concentrate their arguments on the question of its composition, on qualitative as opposed to quantitative growth. Societies face three sets of choices about the proceeds of rising wealth: between consumption and investment, between public and private spending, between rich and poor. How these choices are resolved will have a critical effect on the character of future societies.

The second half of the post-war era has seen a very different division than in the first half, with a growth in inequality and with private consumption taking precedence over both investment and public spending in many countries. Increasingly, there is a new presumption in many consumer societies – that private consumption, of whatever form, is superior to other forms of spending, adding more at the margin to the quality of life than, for example, improving the frequency and comfort of public transport, reducing the impact of pollution or tackling the problem of street homelessness.

This is a matter of social and political priorities rather than economic judgment. The intensification of competitive individualism has meant that we need more money to stay on the escalator, with the side-effect that we have become less willing to pay the costs of social consumption. Growth has always been seen as the route to better societies enabling both higher personal well-being and the resources to tackle the problems of scarcity. Yet, despite growing material wealth, governments of all richer nations are finding it increasingly difficult to finance programmes of redistribution and public investment, including those necessary to counter the external costs of affluence. Hence the growing contradiction at the heart of modern abundance. Rising prosperity has brought increases in discretionary spending for the better off along with deepening inequality, rising absolute poverty and deteriorating public services – poorer and more expensive transport, more meagre social benefits, dirtier and less well serviced cities.

The weaknesses of the arguments of the anti-growth school have led others concerned to minimise the costs of growth to advocate a kind of 'green' or 'qualitative' growth, sometimes described as sustainable development. This approach takes issue with the implicit assumption of the anti-growth advocates that there is a fixed relationship between economic output and the physical resources needed to produce that output, and accepts a degree of flexibility in this relationship. The more this is true, the less serious is the trade-off noted above between rising living standards in the north, ecological damage and persistent inequality.

Nevertheless, even the advocates of 'green growth' accept its limitations. 'I am not saying that green growth can be never-ending; nor that it will be easy to achieve, for it will probably require ever more demanding environmental policies; nor that there is no place for any moral restraint on the demands we place on the planet.'[165] Green growth would mean being prepared to pay more to provide cleaner rivers, pollution free cars and safer pesticides. It would mean more effective urban and rural planning, and higher prices as consumers and industry are forced to pay the full costs of the pollution they create. It would mean trading some current consumption for an improved environment, taking greater account of social priorities and giving less rein to free market forces.

It is now increasingly accepted, for example, that western nations cannot carry on increasing car usage indefinitely. There must be both a limit to the level of congestion that is acceptable, and to the level of associated pollution. To halt global warming would require much tougher cuts in carbon dioxide emissions from exhausts than are currently being achieved, and car ownership is predicted to continue rising sharply. Cars can be made cleaner and more fuel efficient and electric cars can be encouraged. Physical curbs such as the banning of cars from city centres could be introduced. People could be encouraged to use other forms of energy efficient transport.

To be effective, all these measures would be costly. A carbon tax on fossil fuels such as petrol designed to cut car usage and encourage demand for more fuel efficient cars would have to be levied at a high rate to bite. A study by the Green Party concluded that even a petrol price rise of 170 per cent would only cut carbon dioxide emissions by 42 per cent, only a half that needed to halt global warming. Expanding and improving public transport sufficiently to persuade owners to leave their cars at home would also be expensive.

Ultimately, the success of such measures would depend on public willingness to accept them. The signs are mixed. Opinion polls seem to suggest some support for tougher measures such as higher car taxes and city centre bans. In practice, tough measures usually meet with strong resistance. Attempts in some European capitals to introduce urban road pricing have been deeply unpopular. In the United States, there has been strong opposition to increases in petrol taxation from its currently low levels. President Clinton's attempt to introduce an energy tax on all forms of energy consumption to help reduce the spiralling budget deficit met with such opposition that he had to make widespread exemptions to get it passed. Henley Centre research indicates that support for 'radical action to cut down on car use' is not widely matched by an equivalent willingness to use public transport.

It is economically and technically possible to reconcile economic growth and planetary protection, to increase living standards without destroying the quality of life and the environment. But it will require effective international action and some curbs on both personal freedom and the operation of free markets. Whether this proves politically feasible is the critical issue. Whether it proves possible to alter our priorities to tackle these wider issues depends partly on the question of the continuing power of the 'relativity' thesis. Persistent growth has always opened up the possibility of a slowing consumer addiction and even eventual saturation. That at a certain height, the rich would be happy to slow down or step off the escalator of rising demands. They would eventually settle for what they had already achieved, opting for more leisure, becoming more altruistic and creating new scope for a more rational use of our economic potential.

9. The Abstinent Consumer?

The novel swings of fashion which enlivened the self-indulgent Eighties have lost some of their charm in this leaner, meaner decade.

(Lands' End)[166]

. . . equality now implies a more modest standard of living for all, not an extension of the lavish standards enjoyed by the favoured classes in the industrial nations to the rest of the world. In the twenty-first century, equality implies a recognition of limits, both moral and material.

(Christopher Lasch)[167]

Nonetheless, the unqualified pursuit of expansionism harbours much potential danger. This may be the time to realize that the world cannot grow its way out of every problem under the sun.

(Noriko Hama)[168]

In the age of scarcity, the central measure of progress was one of economic advance. In today's more affluent age, the merits of ever-increasing material well-being have come to be more widely questioned. During the global recession of the opening half of the nineties, the question of the benefits of consumerism took a back seat. The central concern was with the unwillingness of consumers to spend. The recession had a sobering effect on consumer confidence, ushering in greater caution and discretion in spending patterns throughout the west, and to a greater extent than had occurred in earlier recessions. This has raised the issue of whether affluent societies are undergoing a simple *cyclical change* or whether they are experiencing the first signs of a *cultural shift* reflecting a more permanent switch in attitudes towards material consumption.

Attempts to find solutions to the growing problems of economic and social instability will depend critically on the development of more moderate material aspirations by the affluent majorities of the west. So what is the likely course of consumerism and expectations in the nineties and beyond? Will societies be back on the escalator of ever-rising materialism with the lifting of the recession, or are they in the process of a steady shift towards a more 'cautious and caring' era? If so, what are the implications for the management of affluence?

Consumer confidence

The second half of the 1980s was a period of high consumer confidence in the world's most mature economies. Personal spending outgrew incomes in several countries, financed by cuts in savings and rising personal indebtedness. This pattern was especially strong in Britain, the United States, Australia, Canada and Japan. In Britain, the saving rate halved from 10p to 5p in the pound between 1984 and 1988, while borrowing rose by a third. In 1984, individuals owed an average £66 for every £100 of income. By 1988 that borrowing had increased to £94. The rise in confidence was also fed by growing personal wealth, the product of booms in house prices and other assets.

Similar, if weaker and less volatile forces were at work elsewhere. Most of the leading economic nations experienced some mix of falling saving, rising asset prices and increased borrowing in the late 1980s. Italy financed its consumer boom through a cut in saving rather than a rise in borrowing. Between 1980 and 1989, the ratio of financial assets to disposable income increased by 76 per cent in the UK, by 58 per cent in Italy and France and by 31 per cent in Germany.

From then on, this trend went into reverse, with spending growth falling behind incomes. Borrowing was cut back and the saving ratio began to rise, albeit slowly. Consumer behaviour changed, affecting both the *level* and *pattern* of spending. In general, consumers coped with cutbacks, not by buying cheaper goods, but by buying fewer goods of equivalent quality. In markets such as holidays and cars,

British consumers tended to postpone purchases or reduce purchasing frequency rather than compromise on quality and go downmarket. The experience of affluence has been a rise in quality expectations and a reluctance to abandon them. The effect on the high street was dramatic. In the early 1990s consumers became less preoccupied with frivolity and superfluous gadgets, with flashy clothes and cosmetics, with upmarket and designer labels, and more with value-for-money. As a result, shops went back to basics, with a lesser emphasis on high fashion, and advertisements began to give different messages. The retail design industry suffered a catastrophic recession.

A similar trend occurred in the United States where the recession had its biggest impact on the luxury market from BMWs to premium chocolates. According to Peter Kim, chief of strategic planning at the advertising agency, J Walter Thompson, 'People are looking for greater value in what they buy, whether it's a $30,000 car or at the supermarket.'[169] The new concern with value led the high priced European car manufacturers – Mercedes, BMW and Audi – to alter their marketing campaigns with a new focus on engineering excellence and safety rather than status.

Rolex pointed to a shift in sales away from fancier, diamond studded watches to more practical, and cheaper, stainless steel models. Even exotic travel was being repackaged with fewer frills. Peter Stisser of Yankelovich Clancy Shulman, the leading American market research firm, said that consumers no longer hanker after the social badge that luxury confers, 'They are not depriving themselves. They just don't want it.' As the *Financial Times* put it, 'Welcome to America in the 1990s, where cheap is chic. Recipes for meatloaf are in vogue. Keeping the old car is in. Flaunting it, even if you still have it, is out.'[170]

What is unclear is whether this reversal represents a temporary or more permanent shift in consumer behaviour and attitudes. Will recovery be associated with a return to the high expectations, grasping self-interest and extravagant spending of the past, with a continuation of the new concern with quality and value, or a permanently more moderate approach to consumerism? There are two broad sets of factors which could lead to a structural shift in consumer behaviour in the nineties or beyond.

The first would be associated with a more permanent denting of consumer confidence, arising not from a shift in cultural or moral attitudes towards materialism, but from anxiety about work and/or welfare provision. The recession of the early 1990s certainly brought a new sense of introspection and a decline in the fascination with the conspicuous and often frivolous consumption that arose during the 1980s. The main reason for this was a rise in economic uncertainty, with increasing numbers worried about work and their economic future.

The nineties is likely to prove a decade of persistently high unemployment, with both limited job opportunities and greater insecurity in work. If so, the insecurity of the early 1990s which led to lower spending and attempts to reduce high levels of personal indebtedness may persist, especially if job uncertainty continues to affect the higher consuming classes – professional, white collar and skilled manual workers.

Other, essentially economic and external factors might also contribute to a more cautious nineties. A more stable economic environment which avoids the huge upheavals of the 1980s would encourage greater stability in consumer behaviour. It is unlikely that there will be a repeat of the unprecedented and credit-financed consumer boom of the 1980s, for example, if only because lessons have been learnt about deregulation and the control of credit. Intensifying international competition and progress towards European Monetary Union, if it proceeds, might also put a brake on credit-financed booms, and also contribute to less erratic growth rates. For similar reasons, the hike in asset values which fuelled the consumer confidence of the late 1980s might be less likely to recur.

Government policy towards welfare provision is another factor. Economic pressures, shifting public preferences and a move to the Right have led most affluent nations to review their welfare programmes. The more this trend towards the greater individualisation and privatisation of welfare continues during the nineties, the more consumers will have to rethink their spending priorities to consider making more private provision for areas like health, pensions and unemployment which were previously largely provided for by the state. This would bring another shift in the pattern of spending.

Cultural shift?

The second set of factors are associated with cultural shift. Irrespective of the course of consumer confidence, are societies likely to become the subject of a more deep-seated change in consumer behaviour? Were the consumer obsessions of the 1980s a temporary phenomenon, a phase that affluent societies have to go through, but one which they eventually grow out of, now or at some stage of higher consumption? Put another way, do societies go through different phases as they progress from minority to majority affluence and beyond?

In chapter 2 it was argued that as societies get richer, many of the social processes at work become subject to an affluence effect – individuals become more materialistic in their values and

Figure 9.1: Competitive individualism and affluence

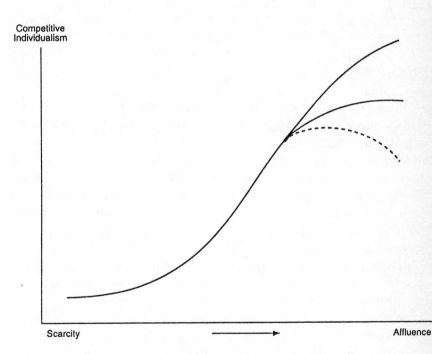

aspirations, more rather than less acquisitive, and more competitive in their behaviour. As societies move closer to the point of the affluent majority, aspirations change, the desire for upward mobility spreads and a higher proportion of consumer demand becomes subject to 'the relativity effect'. The result, shown in figure 9.1, is that the extent of 'competitive individualism' is minimal in poor societies, but begins to accelerate with rising affluence.

The future path that modern societies take is heavily dependent on whether this process has an eventual limit. There are three possible scenarios outlined in figure 9.1. First, the rise of competitiveness continues apace. Second, the level of competition eventually slows down and levels off. Third, it first levels off and then begins to diminish. Each of these scenarios has very different implications for the future functioning of societies. The first carries the seeds of an increasingly explosive and self-destructive cycle. It implies an unlimited demand for material possessions and services, that needs and wants continue to expand more rapidly than society's capacity to meet them. This would encourage inflationary pressure and make it more difficult to introduce the policy measures necessary to tackle unemployment. Inequality would persist and even intensify, and social conflict along with it. It would carry growing social and environmental costs and is ultimately unsustainable.

The second and third scenarios carry very different, and more benign, implications. They suggest a quite different pattern in the process of evolution through affluence in which the process of rising materialism that fuels competitive individualism first accelerates and then either levels off or wanes, implying a slowing down and a possible eventual limit to consumer appetites. This pattern would allow a different approach to the use of resources and carries different implications for the future of inequality and social instability.

So which of these paths are today's societies likely to take? There are certainly some pointers to a more fundamental shift in behaviour, in which the recession can be seen as a catalyst to a more profound re-evaluation of consumption in our lives. In France, there was much media talk of *deconsommation* – literally, deconsumption. Henry Racamier, the ex-chief executive of Louis Vuitton, the international upmarket luggage and leather-ware manufacturer, has argued that there is now 'less flaunting of one's money and . . . the end of an era in which the-more-expensive-it-is-the-more-it-is-admired'.

A similar view was aired in the United States. According to Kenneth Hey, the president of the consultant advisers, Inferential Focus, 'In the 1980s, Americans associated spending and acquisitiveness with happiness. More recently, happiness for many Americans has involved security, simplicity and modesty, values that favour less flamboyant purchases and more basic expenditures.' In Britain and elsewhere in Europe, it was being widely claimed that the nineties would see the end of the greedy and acquisitive values of the eighties and bring a new decade of 'caring and sharing'. In Japan, Koji Nakano's book on the virtues of frugality, *The Concept of Honest Poverty*, became an immediate bestseller.

Whether a more permanent reduction in competitive individualism will occur depends on a number of factors. The first is reaction to the stress associated with high living standards and 'volume consumption'. Chapter 8 showed how rising prosperity has been associated with more harried and congested lives and a rise in work and 'leisure'-related stress. There is some evidence of rebellion against the stress associated with modern living. Small but growing numbers have been opting for less pressurised jobs and lifestyles throughout western societies. There is a rising preoccupation with health, relaxation, and 'new age' activities.

Henley Centre research shows that changing diets, drinking less and even conventional medical treatment of ailments now come a long way behind 'reducing stress', 'getting more sleep' and 'taking more holidays' as a 'means of improving one's health'. There is also considerable support across Europe for working fewer hours.

A second factor involves the attitude towards the consumer and material values of the 1980s. There is some evidence, again, of quasi-moral antagonism towards excessive consumerism. This is partly associated with a sense that the recession was a consequence of the unsustainable, debt-induced boom of the 1980s and a kind of penance for its excesses. We had our fun and then had to pick up the bill. Environmental fears may also affect consumption patterns. But there is also a sense that there are other more important and sustainable routes to welfare and happiness than material wealth. As Kenneth Hey has put it,

North Americans have gone sour on supporting their wants

and have started to focus on their needs. To more and more people, happiness no longer depends upon material wealth and conspicuous consumption has become a sign, not of success, but of a spiritual vacuum – and of greed, immorality, arrogance and antisocial behaviour. Learning has started to supplant buying as a hallmark of a life well-lived.

The rise of 'post-material values'

Which path is followed depends on whether values evolve as societies become more prosperous. During the 1980s, an improvement in material living standards became an increasingly dominant preoccupation in most western societies. Will this continue to be the central goal as living standards continue to rise? Or will the upward spiral of affluence bring a change in values? It has been argued that rising prosperity eventually brings the development of what have been called 'post-material' values. As people satisfy their material needs, their interests turn elsewhere to a concern with the wider quality of life. They become more concerned with leisure and the environment, less self-centred and more altruistic.

The main advocate of this view is the American political scientist Ronald Inglehart. He argues that as societies develop and become better off, what people want out of life begins to change. They become less concerned with satisfying immediate material needs, with economic and physical security, and become more interested in outward-looking concerns emphasising the quality of life and self-expression. He also believes that economic development out of scarcity has led to a 'gradual shift in which needs for belonging, esteem, and intellectual and aesthetic satisfaction become more prominent'.[171] Inglehart's explanation of this 'cultural shift' comes from two premises. First, that what people value most stems from scarcity. Second, that value priorities are related to socialisation, to both one's family situation and to wider economic and political conditions. The effect of the rise of affluence will then, eventually, be the erosion of material priorities.

Inglehart has attempted to measure such differences in 'material' and 'post-material' values by using a four-point scale, based on a number of cross-national surveys carried out during the 1970s and 1980s. In the surveys, respondents were asked their first and second preferences out of four policy aims. The order of choice in 1981 was as follows:

1. Maintaining order in the nation (62 per cent made this their first or second choice)
2. Fighting rising prices (54 per cent)
3. Giving the people more say in important government decisions (38 per cent)
4. Protecting freedom of speech (38 per cent).[172]

Inglehart identified those preferring 'maintaining order' and 'fighting inflation' as holding 'materialist' political values, and those backing 'more say in government decisions' and 'freedom of speech' as holding 'post-material' values. Those choosing a combination hold mixed values lying between the two 'pure' value types. Table 9.1 shows that the dominant group are those with mixed values, and that over the last decade Europe has seen a modest shift towards post-material priorities. Southern Europe experienced the largest change, and Scandinavia was the only exception. The results for individual countries also show a slow movement away from materialism for most countries over a longer time period beginning in 1970.[173]

Table 9.1: Materialists and post-materialists

	Europe %		N. America %	
	1981	1990	1981*	1990
Materialists	33	21	22	14
Mixed	53	58	62	62
Post-materialist	14	21	16	24

* Canada only

Source: Barker, 1991

Inglehart believes that these results provide support for his basic thesis. His argument is that younger, better educated people, growing up in the post-war environment of greater affluence and security, have gradually shifted away from materialistic to more humanistic goals. There are, however, two problems with

Inglehart's interpretation. First, the reliance on a very small number of indicators. Second, the conclusion that the shifts noted are a product of growing affluence. The results certainly show a strong age trend with younger people more likely to display post-material views. They are also correlated with religious beliefs and moral attitudes.

Materialists are more likely to adhere to traditional Judaeo-Christian norms and traditional authority – that is, to attend church, to attribute greater importance to God in their lives, and to take a less liberal view on abortion and homosexuality. This means that the move in values may reflect as much a growing secularisation among the young and a more permissive morality as economic development. What these findings show is, according to one analysis, 'not so much a rejection of materialist, economic concerns, but rather a move away from the acceptance of authority and the maintenance of order at the cost of change and reform'.[174]

The evidence also suggests that, whatever the causes, there are limits to the trend. In Denmark, where the proportion of post-materialists was highest in 1981, the proportion fell over the decade. 'Secular, egalitarian and enjoying high levels of subjective satisfaction with life, there are indications of a reaction in the Nordic countries against the prevailing social democratic hegemony.'[175]

In chapter 2, it was argued that the history of consumer behaviour suggests a natural hierarchy in human wants. In poorer societies, there is little room for a concern with other than the basic needs of food, clothing and shelter. Richer societies, on the other hand, have seen a rising concern with material wants and desires (figure 2.1). The question of the future course of affluent societies will depend heavily on the existence of a higher level of 'non-material concerns', with a higher priority given to the wider quality of life, to ideas and a better environment.

Inglehart's studies provide some evidence – if inconclusive – of the existence of post-materialism. Others have pointed to the rise of the youth protest movements of the 1960s and the subsequent peace, green and feminist movements as supporting evidence. In 1968, the brewing student rebellion finally boiled over in sit-ins in the US and Europe, in violent confrontations between police and the protestors in the streets of most major capitals and in near-insurrection in France. The events of 1968 which shook much of the industrialised world could be seen as a sign of 'post-materialism on the march', the first stirrings of the demand for greater individuality, participation and freedom. The rise of social and political ferment, the anti-war demonstrations and the student movements of the 1960s were, of course, made possible by the onset of affluence, and the forward 'march' has subsequently slowed as economic crises have brought a return to more traditional concerns. Nevertheless, these movements did contribute to the wider concerns with peace, feminism, equality and the environment that emerged in the 1970s and 1980s.

Affluence seems to have brought contradictory influences. People have become swept up by consumerism while also displaying a concern with a number of wider issues, another example of social schizophrenia. Large numbers in the 1970s and 1980s got involved in protest movements, in the anti-racist rallies, animal rights campaigns, anti-nuclear protests and events such as Live-Aid, Farm-Aid and Hands Across America. The 1980s brought a rise of green consumerism. By and large, however, these expressions of public concern remain essentially weak, and often minority, activities. It is material aspirations that remain dominant. The argument of the post-materialists is that these interests will become stronger with prosperity; that protest is a luxury good.

There is some evidence in support of this. People generally seem less concerned with essentially external political issues during periods of economic hardship. Their discontent then becomes more personal – jobs, mortgages, paying the bills. Periods of economic success, such as the second half of the 1980s, have been associated with some, though a relatively muted, rise in generosity, though this is probably associated more with 'conscience appeasement' than altruism. Moreover, the problems of affluence suddenly seem less acute, or become more hidden, during economic booms. This is reflected in people's volatile attitudes towards the state, supportive of intervention when times are hard, but often indifferent and even hostile when things are going well.

The rise of environmentalism and social concern
Public behaviour throughout most affluent nations reflects a new diversity of values. Materialism may remain the dominant

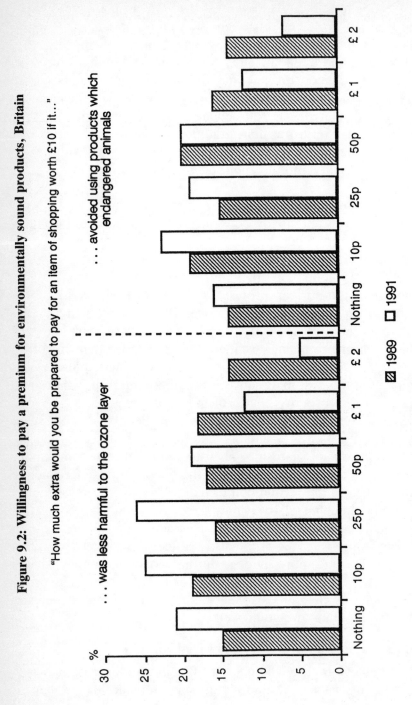

Figure 9.2: Willingness to pay a premium for environmentally sound products, Britain

"How much extra would you be prepared to pay for an item of shopping worth £10 if it..."

. . . avoided using products which endangered animals

. . . was less harmful to the ozone layer

▨ 1989   ☐ 1991

Source: The Henley Centre: Planning for Social Change Surveys motivation, but post-material values have had their influence. The most potent example has been the rise of environmentalism. Public concern with the quality of the physical environment began to take root in western societies from the 1970s and has been rising ever since. Despite this, the impact of such concern has varied considerably both within and between nations with the environmental lobby having its greatest success in Germany and the Netherlands.

More important than attitudes, however, is behaviour. People overstate their generosity in surveys where no clear price tag is attached. In the case of the environment, action is weaker than declared concern, though environmental considerations have influenced consumption habits. Growing numbers have participated in a variety of green practices – recycling glass and paper, buying low energy light bulbs and organic products. Henley Centre research shows that in Britain in 1991, one in ten consumers claimed that concern *always* influences the products they buy, three out of ten that it does *most of the time*, and nearly half that it does *some of the time*. Nevertheless, this change in behaviour is limited largely to areas which require least sacrifice. This is reflected in the success of 'green' products. Fifteen per cent of the toilet paper market and 21 per cent of the kitchen towels market is now accounted for by recycled paper. The phosphate-free share of the world detergent market rose from 6 per cent in the early 1970s to 60 per cent in 1988. Consumers also expect businesses to develop environmentally-friendly alternative products.

Concern has its limits, however. Figure 9.2 shows the proportion willing to pay a premium for two kinds of products in Britain. In 1991, 30 per cent claimed to be willing to pay at least 5 per cent extra for products which did not harm the ozone layer, while 35 per cent would pay the same for products which were not harmful to animals. In total, 11 per cent of the sample endeavoured to ensure that everything they buy was environmentally sound.

Another indication of greater social awareness and concern has been the emergence of 'affinity cards' – charitable credit cards issued by banks where a small percentage of the transaction goes to a charity – and the rise of ethical investments. Ethical investment trusts were first introduced in 1984 in Britain, and by 1992 had reached a total value of £400 million. Several major companies have introduced ethical pension schemes, and a number of local authorities and trade unions have attempted to restrict the outlets of their pension fund portfolios. There have been comparable developments elsewhere.

These trends probably reflect a rise in awareness of the social costs of modern consumption or a growth of 'conscience appeasement' rather than heightened altruism. There is little evidence, for example, that people are prepared to make significant sacrifices in either living standards or in free time for the sake of altruism. What is more likely is that we are witnessing a mixture of growing awareness of the negative impact of modern consumerism on the environment, and of guilt and maybe disillusion with the unrestrained consumerism of the 1980s. Some people, still a minority, have attempted to cope by turning to green consumerism, charity donations and ethical investment.

But such 'conscience appeasement' has clear limits. Ethical investments have to demonstrate they can perform as well as non-ethical ones for the great majority of potential clients. Despite the rise since 1984, the value of ethical unit trusts still only accounts for less than one per cent of total investment. One British survey has shown little evidence of any widespread sense of society's moral responsibility to give generously to charities, with as many as 60 per cent saying that 'it is *not* everyone's responsibility to give what they can to charity'.[176]

Figure 9.2 shows that the willingness to pay a premium for environmentally sound products declined between 1989 and 1991 as a result of the recession. The amount consumers are prepared to pay across a wide range of items fell from an average 4.5 per cent to 3.4 per cent premium. This suggests that 'conscience appeasement', like 'altruism', is a luxury commodity, the need for which declines in the face of other pressures on consumers' incomes. Perceived self-interest remains the overriding determinant of behaviour. The great majority of consumers are not prepared to buy products which are less effective or of a lower standard. Nor are they prepared to act in a way which really hurts.

There is, therefore, some, if limited, evidence supporting the post-materialist thesis. There is an increasing awareness of environmental problems and other social concerns, an acceptance of the need for greater personal responsibility and some willingness to adjust personal behaviour to protect the environment, even if this has only had a noticeable impact on a minority of consumers. Action, including 'green consumerism', is associated with both income and age, with higher income groups and younger people exhibiting the strongest support. While attitudes and action fluctuate in response to economic circumstances, this has been around a rising trend.

There is some reason in these findings to believe that rising affluence is associated with both a growing awareness and more decisive action. This will strengthen if the perceived threat continues to get worse. There is also evidence that the threshold of action has been lowering with rising awareness, probably the result of increasing concern about the perceived impact on people's own quality of life and health.

The insatiable, discerning or glutted consumer?

Central to the question of the future of consumerism and post-materialism is the issue of saturation. Is there a point at which the better off choose to step off the escalator of ever-rising consumption? Is there a limit to the volume of material possessions and activities that can be packed into already crowded homes and lives? One possibility is that no such point exists; that wants are essentially unlimited – that the history in modern societies of the creation of new wants as others have been satisfied is set to continue indefinitely. If so, today's luxuries will continue to become tomorrow's necessities with no end to the upward cycle. Alternatively, such a level may exist, but at what level of consumption?

There are reasons to believe that such a limit does exist, but that we are not yet close to it. That limit will be determined by two independent, but interlocking factors. First, by external social and physical constraints. Chapter 8 argued that for some items of consumption there is a desirable social or physical limit imposed at the point at which the extra marginal costs outweigh the extra benefits. This limit may continue to be exceeded, unless prevented by a change in personal behaviour or wider government intervention. Car use, for example, may continue to expand beyond the point at which the benefits continue to outweigh the costs. This will only be prevented if people choose to stop or reduce their use of

Figure 9.3: Exploding 'Needs and Wants'

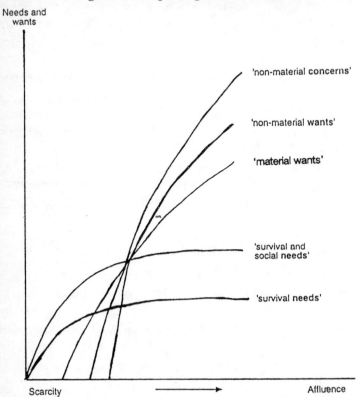

a car because it no longer provides the advantages it once did, *or* if they are persuaded or forced to do so because of government action such as higher taxation on use or physical bans.

Second, on the reality and nature of the hierarchy of wants identified earlier, and on whether a 'higher level' of non-material concerns exists beyond the satisfaction of physical and social needs and wants. This depends on whether these layers are substitutes or additives. A simple addition of each new layer of needs and wants to existing ones has very different implications for consumer behaviour than substitution, even if only at the margin. The more additive the new layers are, the more explosive the implications for social change. Figure 9.3 lays out the explosive thesis, in which limits exist for 'survival and social needs', but remain unlimited for 'desires and wants'.

Figure 9.4 presents an alternative 'saturation thesis' in which

Figure 9.4: A path to material saturation

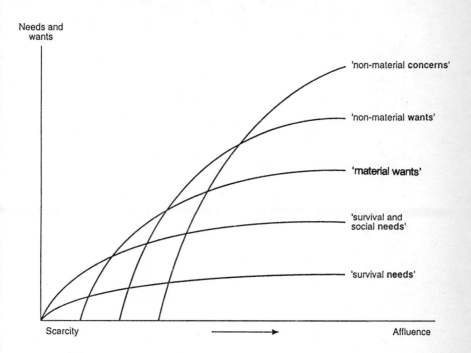

rising affluence brings continuous substitution between layers of the hierarchy. The figure assumes that survival needs reach a limit as societies move from scarcity to affluence, and that social needs also reach a limit at a higher stage of wealth. Material wants only become significant as societies move towards affluence and also reach a limit. Non-material wants emerge at a slightly higher stage and are also limited. Non-material concerns come later and are unlimited. Is this scenario realistic, and if so, are the limits reached before the problem of excess costs begins to bite?

The evidence on whether such limits exist is patchy. Table 9.2 shows that a minority of households (27 per cent) in Europe in 1990 believed that they are 'living comfortably on their present income', with big differences between countries, ranging from a low of 11 per cent in West Germany to a high of 59 per cent in the Netherlands, and not necessarily related to variations in per capita incomes. On the other hand, quite large percentages believed that they could

**Table 9.2: Attitudes to living on present income, 1990
(percentages)**

	Europe	West Germany	France	Italy	Great Britain	Neth-erlands	Belgium	Sweden
Living comfortably on present income	27	11	25	32	29	59	33	55
Coping on present income	48	62	50	41	46	30	47	34
Finding it difficult to cope on present income	17	18	20	21	16	6	10	8
Finding it very difficult to cope on present income	6	6	4	6	8	3	5	2
Don't know	2	4	2	1	1	3	6	1

Source: Readers Digest, 1991

cope, and only a minority (23 per cent) were finding it difficult or very difficult to cope.

Figure 9.5 shows the proportion of people in various countries who accept that they 'often buy things that they don't really need'. This suggests some awareness of the distinction between 'needs' and 'wants', between 'essential' and 'discretionary' spending. On the other hand, such awareness does not necessarily translate into action. Indeed, 'material desires' remain a dominating influence even among the better off whose spending patterns are concentrated among discretionary items. Affluence has led to people buying bigger houses than they need for shelter, faster cars than are needed for transport and the replacement of consumer durables long before they no longer serve their function.

This process has not reached anything like a peak. The demand for housing *space* is almost certainly unsaturated. In Europe, 11 per cent of households have second homes (table 2.1), and there is no evidence of a fall in the desire for more space. The average number of cars, televisions and other gadgets per household remains on a rising trend. The proportion of households in Europe with more than one car and more than one television has been steadily rising (table 2.1). Both are much higher in the United States. Henley Centre research has shown that the desire for replacement of a variety of consumer goods from hi-fi systems to microwaves remains high, with the prime motivation being not product failure but the desire for a new or better model – a TV with teletext or a hi-fi with a CD player.

Even if the trend towards multiple ownership and the replacement rate of existing products does slow down, the ingenuity

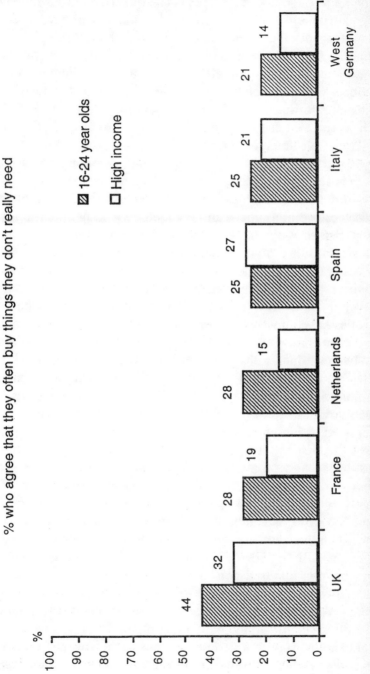

Figure 9.5: Consumer awareness, 1992

% who agree that they often buy things they don't really need

16-24 year olds

High income

Source: The Henley Centre, Frontiers Survey, 1992

of manufacturers means that new commodities will continue to come on to the market. The 1980s saw the arrival of a whole host of new consumer goods including the mobile phone, the home computer and the camcorder. The digital cassette player, high definition TV, the inter-active home video player and the speech operated computer are likely to be just a few of the new consumer products of the nineties. In the electronic goods industry, buzz-terms like 'format fatigue' are widely used to justify new products, such as the switch from vinyl to CD and now from CD to digital cassette. Consumer patterns have been, in the words of the Pope, the subject of both 'multiplication and continual replacement'. There is also little evidence that the demand for 'positional goods' – for more remote holidays, country cottages, cars – is fading.

To these commodities can be added a growing appetite for non-material desires or what could be termed 'experiential' consumption – leisure, relaxation, understanding, knowledge. Non-material desires can be divided into commercial and non-commercial activities, those that have wider resource implications and those that use minimal or no resources. There is little doubt that richer societies have chosen to substitute 'leisure' for work. The problem for the saturation thesis is that the leisure and knowledge industry has become increasingly commercialised. Sports centres, fitness activities, the pursuit of further qualifications is often expensive, as are financial advisers, therapists and private sports facilities.

Moreover, most of those interested in fitness and leisure are also interested in big cars, posh houses and fancy holidays. So even a move through the hierarchy does not necessarily imply consumer substitution and satiation as in figure 9.4. There is also a growing commercial market for services that have, since the war, been largely the preserve of public provision. At the moment, there seems no obvious ceiling to the number of new opportunities for more spending, and therefore for higher incomes to service those demands. Although there is some evidence of the existence of a fifth layer of 'non-material concerns' in the hierarchy of needs in the emergence of green consumerism and ethical investment, this remains relatively confined and weak, and reflects mixed motives.

Another factor that could encourage saturation would be a weakening of competitive individualism, the powerful tendency to measure ourselves against others. The main ways in which status has been secured has been through group affiliation and consumption patterns. The major driving force affecting consumer behaviour in affluent societies has been imitation, a desire to keep up with and move ahead of the Joneses. If societies were to begin to believe in the futility of this jostling for position and of the diminishing returns associated with a material culture, consumerism would begin to take on a different character. There are some signs that the obsession with status through possessions may be on the wane, that some people have grown weary of the acquisitive culture and feel less insecure with their status. There is some evidence of a disillusion with frivolous goods, and a slowing down of the speed of replacement and that people are turning to other sources of meaning and fulfilment such as knowledge and personal development. This does not mean that the need for power and status is waning, just that it can come from different sources.

Our own research has shown that between 1989 and 1992, the proportion of Britons 'who like the idea of buying things not many other people have' fell from 56 to 39 per cent. Yet, even if some of this represents a structural and not a short-term recessionary shift, it does not necessarily imply a weakening of 'competitive individualism'. For example, 'being knowledgeable or clever' may be slowly replacing 'being rich' as a currency of status, but this does not necessarily imply an end to competitiveness. Although it might bring a steady shift from material to non-material consumption, this might still require income if not possession competition, since knowledge and personal development can be expensive activities. If, on the other hand, it implied a shift in interest towards non-commercialised spiritual concerns, it would have the effect of weakening the grip of 'competitive individualism'.

Two broad scenarios can be inferred from this analysis. The first is that the demand for material desires and wants continues to expand indefinitely. Saturation exists only for basic material needs, not middle order wants and desires. If so, the problems associated with rising affluence are likely to persist, even intensify, with continuing consumer rivalry and inflationary pressure, a declining support for taxation and public spending, persistent unemployment and social instability. Saturation if it exists at all only comes at a point beyond which the environmental and social costs have become explosive.

The second scenario is less pessimistic. It accepts that the process of post-materialism is slow and marginal but remains a key dynamic. Acquisitive instincts remain but slow down sufficiently to allow a more rational and humane approach to decision-making. It may still be many years, perhaps another generation, before the impact is powerful and extensive enough to have a major influence on political management. Nevertheless, this second scenario opens up the possibility of an evolution in consumer behaviour in which individuals and societies move through three different phases – an insatiable phase, a more discerning phase and finally a saturated phase.

It is not possible to say which stage affluent societies have reached in this process. There are certainly some signs of the emergence of the *discerning* consumer – one more concerned with quality and with value-for-money than with emotional appeal and status, one with a higher awareness of environmental problems and an acceptance of the need for greater personal responsibility.

On the other hand, large proportions remain dissatisfied with their living standards. The persistence of unfulfilled expectations means that an improved material living standard is likely to remain a powerful motivation for a long time to come. Though Inglehart may be right about the direction of change, table 9.1 shows that the vast majority of the population of both Europe and the United States continue to display either materialist or mixed views. The process he describes is probably very slow. For the foreseeable future, the dominant value in advanced societies is likely to remain the perhaps slightly moderated consumerist values described in chapter 5.

Managing 'post-material affluence'

It may be many years, even decades, before we know whether the saturation scenario is likely to prove realistic. Certainly, the rise of a 'post-consumerist' ideology would open up the prospect of a very different way of organising societies, bringing the possibility of changing the priorities for the use of growing material wealth. A lower obsession with commodity-provided image and symbolism, a growing concern with social and individual health and a new sense of balance between public and social priorities could bring more moderate demands and expectations, with weaker inflationary pressures and a different approach to economic and political management.

Yet there is also a paradox involved. The thirst for higher levels of consumption has been a central motor of change in free-market societies, a critical ingredient of both growth and employment. In the poorer societies of the past, extravagant consumption by the rich sitting alongside widespread poverty may have brought moral indignation, but it also provided the employment that helped to alleviate that poverty.

In the period after the war, rising consumer demand, along with public investment, proved a key ingredient of full or near-full employment, as the incomes generated by an apparently insatiable demand were spent on items that created jobs. It contributed, in turn, to the growth of spending on public services. For twenty-five years after the war, this simple formula that translated high demand into rising living standards, jobs and services was a great success. High and unsatisfied consumer demand led to more production, more jobs, more resources for public spending and rising living standards all round. It underpinned the post-war boom that brought with it more secure and less divided societies.

The idea of insatiable human wants as a never-ending and benign force has a long lineage. The eighteenth-century liberal thinkers like Adam Smith and David Hume saw unlimited appetites, which had formerly been largely condemned as a source of instability and unhappiness, as the means to economic and social progress. The process of new wants emerging as old ones are met would lead to rising expectations, an indefinite expansion of productive capacity and the 'democratisation of consumption'. It was this central idea that became the driving force of the modern political economy for 200 years. It is only in the last twenty to thirty years that its message has been challenged, in part the product of the growing awareness of the physical, environmental and social limits to persistent growth, and in part a response to the effect that unquenched appetites are having on social cohesion.

Today, the simple formula that has guided the economic progress of the past does not work well – continued growth no longer guarantees anything like the full employment of the past and consumerism has come to play a very different role, contributing to the rise of material values, more competitive lifestyles and the erosion of social balance.

Despite this, unrestrained personal consumption is still widely seen as a panacea for economic problems. During the recession of the early nineties, economic slowdown was blamed on declining consumer confidence, and recovery was seen as dependent on consumers returning to the spendthrift days of the 1980s. In the United States, for example, Range Rover bought full-page advertisements in major periodicals urging Americans to 'Buy something. Our preference, of course, would be that you buy a Range Rover. But if that's not on the cards, buy a microwave. A basset hound. Theater tickets. A Tootsie Roll. Something.'[177]

Future trends now depend critically on the course of consumer behaviour. What are the implications for the management of affluence of a continuing, if slow, shift away from materialism to non-materialism? At first sight, this development might seem to carry the seeds of new economic problems with even slower growth and more unemployment. The rise of the 'glutted' or even the 'discerning consumer' might lead to a change in values, but wouldn't it simultaneously have the effect of bringing more unemployment?

This depends on the scale and character of a consumer slowdown. Suppose, for example, that consumer demand rises more slowly than productivity because some consumers choose to spend less. The impact depends on where the fall in demand is concentrated. Suppose it is concentrated among positional goods, as we would expect. Chapter 2 argued that the rising demand for those positional goods which are fixed or, in economic jargon, inelastic in supply, adds to the problems of running affluent economies as it creates inflationary pressures without creating jobs. The rising demand for housing as a form of investment is a classic example, and one that has done severe economic damage in the past. A slowing demand for those positional goods in fixed supply would have the effect of easing the inflationary pressures and economic turbulence that have contributed to rising unemployment.

On the other hand, a fall in demand for non-positional material goods such as consumer durables *would* mean a potential loss of jobs. A declining demand for cars, televisions or washing machines would cut jobs in these industries. The extent would depend on the cause of this fall and the impact of any compensatory policies. For example, assume that this fall is the product of a general slowing down in consumer spending caused by a rise in non-material concerns by the rich. If they simply forego spending to boost their saving, then job losses would arise in the areas where demand has slackened. But the rise of non-material values would also weaken competitive pressures and open up the possibility of compensatory policies. For example, it might make this group more sympathetic to higher taxation, or to policies aimed at reducing wage differentials or encouraging job-sharing.

If the effect was to permit higher taxation, this could be used to boost demand elsewhere. Investment in public infrastructure could be increased, or income redistributed to the unsatiated consumers on lower incomes. The effect would be a transfer of demand away from the marginal spending patterns of the rich to those of poorer groups, from larger homes and luxury cars to basic foodstuffs, clothes and household goods; and/or from private to public consumption, from more consumer durables and luxury holidays to more rented housing and better public transport. The effect would be similar to increasing progressive taxes in a recession and redistributing the proceeds to lower income groups such as the unemployed. This would have the joint effect of encouraging economic recovery and reducing inequalities. By reducing the income of the affluent, such redistribution would have the simultaneous impact of reducing their demand for positional goods, so easing inflationary pressure.

It would also reverse the trend of the last decade and a half towards greater inequality. The reduction of taxation on the better off, especially in Britain and the United States, seems to have failed to deliver the 'trickle down' effect promised by some politicians. The rise in retained profits over the 1980s also failed to increase investment and stimulate economic recovery as hoped. Instead, as Tibor Scitovsky has pointed out, 'What the increase in retained profits has done instead was to increase the number of takeovers, which are the business world's equivalent of the consumer's spending on positional goods. As such, they raised share prices but failed to stimulate the economy.'[178]

A second possibility arising from a fall in the demand for material goods is that those in work choose to accept a slower rise in their living standards in return for more spare time; that is, they choose to earn less. If this were to happen too rapidly, it would create problems for economic systems dependent on high demand for renewal. It could carry the risk of stagnation, of a slowing down of the process of innovation which has been the motor of change and dynamism.

This is an unlikely scenario. The alternative is that demand continues to increase but at a slower pace. If technology continues to offer improved productivity, these gains can then be taken in the form of more leisure, continuing or even accelerating the trend of the last 100 years. This has seen a gradual fall in working hours in mature economies, though with a short-term reversal in some countries over the last decade. One way of interpreting this trend is to attribute it to the steady rise of a post-material ideology, of an increasing demand for free time and relaxation. The dynamism that is needed for renewal could then be provided through routes other than more consumer products such as innovation in science, in health, in space and weather exploration, in environmental protection, in individual knowledge.

Of course, an alternative interpretation of the trend towards more 'leisure' is that people opt for shorter working times not for more leisure per se, but because they need more time to participate in higher levels of consumption. As one expert has put it, 'Consumption takes time; the more we produce, the more time we need for consumption. Working time reduction, in short, is a phenomenon of a deeply materialistic society.'[179] The waning of a materialist culture would therefore help to lessen the problem of time congestion noted in chapter 8. It would leave people with more free time for non-material pursuits.

It would also open up the possibility of lower unemployment through the redistribution of work. One of the ironies of the rise of affluence has been the co-existence of overwork and long overtime for some and enforced unemployment for others. The west is creating societies of workaholics and the involuntary idle. One of the central tasks of the management of affluence should be to improve the distribution between work and leisure which has become increasingly skewed.

Chapter 4 argued that there is limited scope for reducing unemployment through the traditional method of increasing the demand for labour. Attempts to date to reduce the supply of labour by encouraging early retirement and delaying entry into employment by the young have not been sufficient to prevent the steady rise of unemployment. Another alternative is to limit the time spent at work by some combination of a shorter working week, longer holidays or job-sharing alongside pro-rata reductions in pay.

Part of the problem of rising unemployment is attributable to rising real incomes of those in work, effectively a redistribution of income between those without to those with work. A slowing down of pay increases would have the effect of creating more jobs. Even during the recession, most people in work did remarkably well. When the whole economy is contracting, it would seem reasonable for everybody to accept a share of the burden. In Britain and elsewhere, real wages continued to rise even though output was falling. This contributed to higher unemployment as well as currency devaluation. Although 'incomes policy' is a discredited notion, a means of restricting pay increases in the early years of the 1990s could have led to significantly lower unemployment.

The theoretical potential for job creation through a shorter working week or year or more flexible hours is large provided it was accompanied by an equivalent reduction in pay. It has been estimated that shortening by just one hour the thirty-six hour average week in the United States would create 3 million extra jobs.[180] Many structural obstacles would have to be overcome before this theoretical possibility could be transferred into real work redistribution. Work-sharing is effectively about income-sharing, and its success in reducing unemployment would depend on changing attitudes of those already in work. It would not function effectively without wider social and aspirational changes. Several studies have shown widespread support for shorter working hours and more flexible working arrangements in both Europe and the United States, even if at the expense of pay. One reason why many people are unable to exercise a choice is that the option for shorter hours rarely exists.

Nevertheless, there is some evidence of successful experiments in 'work-sharing' in both Europe and the United States. In Germany during the 1980s, the metalworkers union, the IG Metall, initiated attempts to reduce standard weekly hours from forty to thirty-five. This proceeded in steps over the decade and was combined with moderations in pay settlements with the explicit aim of creating more jobs. This led to an extensive and controversial debate about whether redistributing work is an effective way of tackling unemployment. One study has claimed that the net effect of this policy of reduced hours was a reduction in unemployment of 600,000,[181] though this has been disputed by the employers, who always opposed the plan on the grounds that it undermines productivity. In Britain, there were some examples of groups of workers during the recession being willing to cut or moderate their wage demands in order to preserve jobs. The Sheffield and Southampton branches of the local government union, NALGO, voted in 1993 to forgo a pay rise in order to save jobs, though this was opposed by the national union.

There still remains widespread resistance to the idea, however. Most unions and employers, particularly in Britain, are hostile. So is the British Government, which long resisted the European Community Directive to introduce a maximum forty-eight hour working week and a minimum of four weeks' annual paid leave, despite extensive exemptions. The Government consistently argued that the measures are a threat to jobs, when one of the aims of the scheme is spreading work around by preventing excessive hours.

This alternative scenario of trading leisure for material goods opens up the possibility of at least a partial solution to three of the most intractable problems associated with today's two-track, affluent societies – high unemployment, deepening division, and environmental damage. But is it likely? This book has suggested that societies move through two distinct phases as they progress out of scarcity. In the first phase, the transition from scarcity to affluence enables large numbers of the population to move through a hierarchy of wants away from a predominant concern with survival needs to the satisfaction of first, social needs and then material desires and wants. This phase coincides with the beginnings and development of consumer societies. Phase two is associated with the arrival of majority affluence, bringing a change in consumer motivation and behaviour which puts increasing strain on the way societies function.

Whether this phase persists and for how long, or whether it ushers in a different phase is a matter of speculation. There are several alternative paths that could be followed. Which will depend partly on the pattern of external events – on the course of the international economy, on technology and on the global pattern of success and failure. But it will depend too on the course of consumer behaviour and personal ambition, and on the development of political ideology. The possible scenarios are explored in the final chapter.

10. A New Dawn?

. . . a society dedicated to the enrichment and enhancement of the self will only survive and certainly will only prosper if the dominant ethic is the support and encouragement of others. Proper selfishness is rooted in unselfishness.

(Charles Handy)1[82]

Let's put the public interest before the personal interest and keep it there for the next four years to turn this country around . . . We need a new spirit of community, a sense that we are all in this together, or the American dream will continue to wither.

(Bill Clinton)[183]

The Prime Minister should state, as boldly as he can, that it is his government's intention to turn Britain into the Hong Kong of Western Europe . . . a low-cost, high productivity, low tax, high-technology, off-shore island.

(*Sunday Times*)[184]

Today's most economically advanced nations have reached another crossroads in post-war history. In the first twenty-year period after the war, a unique set of economic, social and political circumstances brought consensus, economic stability and social cohesion. The arrival of mass prosperity, however, undermined the conditions that had created it. This very success set in train the changes that led to a second phase of greater economic turbulence, political discord and growing fragmentation. The central question now is the permanence of this second era. Are societies locking themselves into a more turbulent and unstable future? Or will this new phase prove short-lived and give way to a second turning point in post-war history with a new and more successful approach to political management?

The world's leading nations are approaching the end of the century in economic, social and ideological uncertainty. There are real fears that global economic recovery will prove too fragile to bring stable and continued growth and significantly lower unemployment. There are severe doubts too over the future course of social stability. In Britain, much of the old institutional order – Parliament, the civil service, local government, the judiciary, the education system – is suffering a crisis of credibility and authority, a problem of legitimacy which has also affected other parts of Europe. This malaise has also infected the world's major political parties which are facing an increasingly sceptical public mood.

Modern societies are going through a period of upheaval from which the status quo is unlikely to survive. The world's leaders are only too conscious of the fragile state of their own national governments and those of the rest of the globe. But while there is no lack of awareness of the contemporary predicament, what is missing is a solution. The past has little to offer. The most successful models of the post-war era – Germany's social market economy, Sweden's welfare socialism, Japan's developmental state – are all facing their own problems of identity and inevitable evolution.

The collapse of welfare capitalism has brought a new, deregulated approach to governance, but, at least to date, this has been unable to handle the problems of international and domestic change. The economic success of the developing nations of South East Asia offers only limited lessons for the more mature economies of the north. Their combination of interventionist but authoritarian government and a culture of co-operation and self-restraint proved the right ingredients for economic take-off, but that combination may prove difficult to sustain during the next stage of development. Something, sooner or later, is going to have to give. Either societies will plunge into a further period of turmoil and upheaval *or* this very instability will create the conditions for a change in direction.

'Decline'

One possibility is that the malaise and slow decline of recent years continues and even accelerates. Decline would be the product of deepening economic problems, a continuing crisis of government, politics and the traditional institutions and a brooding public mood. In this scenario, the 'hands-off' approach to government continues but proves no match for the wider forces at work. The lifting of economic controls and the ideology of weakened government brings a harsher, meaner and more insecure social climate but fails to create the economic dynamism promised.

It is possible, too, that a new period of history is in the making which will mark the end of the dominance of western Europe and the United States – economically, culturally and politically; that these blocs are caught in a spiral of irresistible decline which they will find it increasingly difficult to reverse. Extreme versions of declinism abound, especially in the United States. Paul Kennedy's study of 'imperial over-stretch' – *The Rise and Fall of the Great Powers*[185] – predicted that the United States is on the edge of losing its status as the last great superpower. He argued that it was about to enter a period of relative economic decline as a result of its global military commitments.

Others have also argued that America is entering a period when it will fail to keep pace with its competitors, old and new, and that America's decline will soon be followed by Europe. This thesis points to the power of Japan and of the rise of South East Asia and China which have enjoyed extraordinary growth rates over the last decade. Political and economic failure combine to reduce the relative status of the former powers which gradually slide to second class status, replaced by China, India, South East Asia and even parts of the former Soviet Bloc as the dynamic nations of the next century and the new focus of economic, political and cultural change.

A handful of 'developing nations' including South Korea, Taiwan, Singapore, Hong Kong and parts of China already have income levels that are on a par with parts of Europe. China already has a 57-million 'middle-class' population and the 'Asian Tigers' 40 million, compared with 322 million in western Europe, 223 million in North America and 118 million in Japan. Parts of India have developed highly sophisticated economic bases such as in accounting and computer systems that are attracting western companies. Between 1989 and 1993, the developing nations' share of world exports jumped three percentage points to 20 per cent. The west is beginning to lose its traditional vital lead in brainpower. In the short term, this new and brutally competitive world economic order is changing the economic facts of life and contributing to job losses in the west. Some believe that it is signalling a more permanent decline.

In a more recent book,[186] Paul Kennedy has predicted a grim new century of instability from other sources – a combination of technological, demographic and ecological shocks. His thesis is that the potential catastrophe of population outstripping resources originally predicted by Malthus two centuries ago is finally happening in the developing world of today. This will create new divisions and demands for migration that will prove unsustainable. Some western strategists have also been predicting new North-South conflicts to replace old East-West tensions. This is based on the prospect of an ever-widening gap between rich and poor countries leading to new instabilities, conflicts over resources and the dislocation of millions of people fleeing war, famine, disease and environmental disaster.

The reality of declinism may be less dramatic – a slower and less convulsive descent, triggered by continuing economic difficulties during the nineties, weak economic recovery, slow growth and persistent unemployment. The last twenty years has seen three global recessions, one a decade, each more serious than the last. The long post-war boom may well prove to be the aberration rather than the more recent pattern of slow and unstable growth. If so, the western world may be in for a long era of economic volatility and uncertainty.

Several factors could contribute to continuing economic turmoil and slow growth, with the impact varying between nations. The process of technological change and industrial restructuring that began in the 1980s is likely to continue to bring disruption. Some of the most successful nations such as Germany have a relatively distorted industrial pattern, with too high a dependence on the older industries of the past and not enough investment in the likely winners of the future. German productivity has been rising more slowly than elsewhere, and with its high wages and, according to Helmut Kohl, propensity for 'soft living', may find it difficult to recover its competitive edge. With Germany still critical to the economic performance of Europe, its relative decline would reverberate around the continent. Some analysts have argued that large areas of European industry are insufficiently lean to compete effectively with their Japanese and American rivals, and that Europe therefore needs to go through a further period of painful restructuring if it is to avoid relative decline.

What is most likely to emerge out of these trends is a changing pattern of regional and national success, continuing upheaval in employment opportunities and a new generation of winners and losers. Some countries will find their historical legacies less suitable to survival in a rapidly changing economic climate. The continuing success of the new developing nations will contribute to a changing global pattern. Within nations, the effect on some regions and groups could be acute. In France, for example, a new gulf has emerged between a prosperous, largely urban, entrepreneurial class of winners, and an 'old France' of small shopkeepers and rebellious farmers and fishermen. Existing divisions are likely to continue to widen with what one commentator has described as the likely emergence of a 'prosperous golden triangle based on Frankfurt, Paris and Milan, and, on the other hand, a brown banana or doughnut of more disadvantaged regions on the periphery – including much of the UK, Ireland, Spain, Portugal, Southern Italy and Greece'.[187]

These problems of growing divisions arising from economic and industrial change would be reinforced with hardening public attitudes. During the early 1990s, the public mood throughout most developed nations turned from contentment to anxiety and resentment. The aspirant middle majority grew increasingly restive, mainly over jobs, but also over schooling, health and crime. A growing sense of impotence and insecurity helped to produce an indifference and even hostility towards more disadvantaged groups. Failure to restore the growth of prosperity is likely to leave this group increasingly frustrated, apprehensive and more inward-looking. They would then be less willing to make the sacrifices that are needed to spread the benefits of technological change and to reverse the anti-investment, short-term and pro-consumption ethos that has contributed to economic and political malaise.

The risk is that the affluent majority will then be driven into a defensive mood with new attempts to protect their position against those seen as a potential threat. Chapter 6 argued that the dominant source of personal motivation is one of pragmatic self-interest, promoted either by collectivism or individualism. A more apprehensive and resentful public mood could then lead to a further swing of the pendulum between the cells shown in figure 6.1 from the bottom to the top row and from the left to the right hand column, in the direction of less generosity and greater dependence on self-reliance. This would further weaken any remaining sense of civic culture and of common purpose.

The first half of the 1990s brought a hardening of attitudes towards some groups. There was a rise of intolerance towards migrant workers and refugee communities across much of Europe. There were also signs of a selective backlash against other social groups such as single parents, travellers and certain sections of the unemployed and homeless. These hardening attitudes led to tougher immigration controls and attacks on some social benefits in Europe, and in Britain, attempts to restrict the movement of travelling people, the growth of vigilantes, and calls for tougher sentencing and harsher prison regimes. A persistently more uncertain economic environment could lead to an increasingly authoritarian and intolerant moral climate.

Persistent and rising instability together with a less permissive social climate could also spur the movement towards increasing social and geographical polarisation with the better off abandoning certain inner city areas and opting out of state education and health services. This would reinforce the process of regional and social concentration of winners and losers. There are risks too that continuing economic problems would lead Europe to retreat behind new economic and social barriers aimed at weakening Asian competition and reducing immigration flows from Eastern Europe and the third world still further. Building a 'Fortress Europe' and reversing the trend towards free trade might provide a temporary respite from industrial and economic decline, but it would carry heavy risks of delayed economic recovery and self-defeating retaliation.

Hardening public attitudes, persistent unemployment and faltering economic recovery would also escalate the process of welfare dismantling that has been spreading from Britain to the mainland. The victims of economic and social change in Europe have been at least partially cushioned from the changes of the last twenty years by relatively generous welfare and social policies which have provided minimum benefits, employment rights and wages. A degree of protection has also been provided by European Community programmes that have redistributed resources from the more to the less successful nations and regions. These policies have been under increasing strain during the 1990s and further weakening would hasten the process of deepening division. It is not inconceivable that the European project, the grand plan of Jacques Delors and other leaders, could not merely falter during the nineties, but go into reverse with the steady dismantling of the European social chapter, and the abandonment of plans for further economic and political integration.

Decline would also be promoted by continuing political weakness. Political stability has been associated with flexibility and adaptability, instability with short-termism and reactive politics. The early 1990s was marked by a new impotence in political and economic leadership. This was partly a product of the new hands-off, pro-market ideology. But it also reflected a lack of national and global political confidence that hindered effective economic management during the recession. Expressions of concern by national leaders, both individually and collectively, about rising unemployment, deepening recession and industrial dislocation were never translated into effective policies. A persistence of economic problems throughout the 1990s would continue to undermine political popularity and accentuate the problems of economic management.

The threat of further decline would also be increased by the failure of Bill Clinton to secure the new approach to politics which he has attempted to pioneer. His aims of a 'new spirit of community' and 'willingness to sacrifice' have proved increasingly difficult to achieve. Invested with so much hope, both in the United States and around the world, his administration has found it difficult to implement the economic and social programmes that he hoped would build a more united nation. Far from initiating a new ideological politics, his administration has been rocked by the demands of coalition partners and the power of minority interests, forcing an increasingly pragmatic, pick 'n' mix approach to governing. It is further evidence of the increasingly intractable problems facing modern political leaders.

This pessimistic scenario is all too plausible. The developed world may well be on the brink of a downward spiral which proves increasingly difficult to resist. It is a course that would be encouraged by hesitant political leadership, weak government, growing protectionism and isolationism, and a hardening public mood. On the other hand, it may be that the gloomier scenario of a Europe and North America in long term and irreversible structural decline proves to be exaggerated but that problems of adjustment and political transition still usher in an era of prolonged tension, upheaval, instability and ever-widening divisions.

Critics might argue that decline will be prevented by political adjustment and at least a partial return to 'managed government'. This would involve a modest retreat from full-blooded neo-liberalism but not a reversal to highly interventionist and redistributive government. What could then emerge is a modest recovery and a new political realignment with continental Europe retreating slowly from its more interventionist government and Britain from its more market dominated approach.

This could usher in not just a 'post-socialist' but a 'post-market' era as well, an era dominated not by ideological but by managerial and pragmatic politics. Such an era would be inclined to follow rather than lead public opinion. It would not tolerate higher levels of taxation or public spending and would move slowly towards a more residual model of welfare. It would be dominated by a persistence of individualism but one which is less competitive than in the past.

This alternative would amount to muddling on with a modest tinkering with political institutions and the tools of management. Such drift might slow down, but would be unlikely to prevent, continued decline. The problems facing modern societies are too difficult to be resolved by a continuation or a mild modification of the status quo. It would not provide the social and economic renewal required to make a real difference to the deep-seated problems of long term unemployment and social polarisation, which would require a very different set of political and social attitudes.

'Market triumphalism'

An alternative scenario could see steady economic progress led by non-inflationary growth out of the recession, built on the pro-market foundations laid during the 1980s. Ironically, this could be a course that begins in Britain and then spreads to Europe. Britain is, arguably, more deeply entrenched in malaise than the rest of Europe, but is also closest to a new revolution. Success, if it came, would represent a vindication of the Thatcherite revolution and, at least in part, of Fukuyama's claims of the end of history. It would see a re-run of the long post-war boom this time triggered by the freeing of markets, the rise of the developing world through its embracement of structural adjustment, the reconstruction of the former Soviet Bloc and a boost to trade in services.

In this scenario, the reforms of the 1980s would finally bear fruit, with the recession proving to be a short term blip on route to higher productivity, greater efficiency and a more enduring recovery. The combination of a harsh industrial restructuring, the weakening of trade unions and other labour market controls, cuts in direct taxation and the reform of outdated institutions would eventually unleash the entrepreneurial and creative spirit that had been held back by excessive state interference. This success would help to restore at least some public faith in the political process.

Economic success would be encouraged too if the harsh anti-inflationary policies of the 1980s bring a more permanent period of weakened inflationary pressure. Trade union and labour market reforms, the weakening power of the oil producing nations, and tightening international competition all contributed to the downward pressure on prices and the lower inflation of the early 1990s. To date, this lower inflation has not been translated into an alternative approach to economic management. If it represents a sustained and structural shift, it would mean that economies could be run at a higher level of employment and growth.

Success would also be more assured if the rise of the developing world through freer trade and intensified competition brought new markets and new economic opportunities for the west rather than relative economic decline. It may simply be that the west needs a little more patience before the boom in Asia, parts of Latin America and elsewhere is translated into rising demand for goods and services from the 'First World'.

Recovery might also see a transformation in the character of industrial organisation, bringing a major role for a whole raft of new small businesses, a renewal of enterprise and a more freely operating labour market. As some manufacturing continued to move to the newly industrialising nations, western Europe would develop new product lines in which mature economies have a comparative advantage. This might include the arts, culture, music, knowledge, education, certain forms of craft production, fashion goods, design.

If the market experiment is going to work anywhere, it will be in Britain which has gone furthest in dismantling the old interventionist and welfarist model. Some commentators have talked of the UK as the potential Hong Kong of Europe, a satellite of success and a magnet for investment created by low employment costs and personal taxes and a relatively free labour market. Britain is now one of the best tax havens in the world, and in the early 1990s attracted a large number of rich foreigners. Between a half and two-thirds of the buyers of country houses worth more than £750,000 in the early 1990s were foreigners. A study by Guinness Flight, the City fund managers, suggested that the mobile rich brought in as much as £5 billion a year in foreign exchange in this period. This is five times as much as Britain gained from Japanese investment in its car industry in 1992, and covered more than a third of its current-account deficit.

The success of the market model could trigger a similar process in the rest of Europe. It could encourage the weakening of the social chapter of the Maastricht treaty and lead to further steps to dismantle existing welfare and social controls with the aim of following the market lead given by Britain. Indeed, some commentators would argue that continued economic success would depend on it, that the preservation of an all embracing welfare state is incompatible with a Europe lean enough to compete with the more efficient economies elsewhere.

This scenario would put Britain, either on its own or with the rest of Europe, on course for the American political and social model, which was Mrs Thatcher's ultimate objective. It would produce more vigorous and opportunistic but fragile and unequal societies, just at the point when Bill Clinton is attempting to steer his country in a different direction. As in the United States, it would not solve all the problems inflicting modern societies. It would be largely good news for the affluent majority and would bring restored contentment. It would bring fewer, though some potential, gains for the poorest third. Higher growth might reduce the problem of unemployment but do little to help the more stubborn problem of long term unemployment, especially among young, urban unskilled males.

As in the 'declinist' scenario, there would be a different pattern of winners and losers and deepening divisions between them. Personal success would depend on individual skill and experience, on knowledge, flexibility and imagination, and on the willingness and ability to take advantage of what would become an even more competitive and self-dependent environment. Success, however, would be far from evenly shared and there would be fewer mechanisms to protect the losers, both individuals and regions. Markets might succeed in promoting faster growth but can do little to prevent the community devastation that can accompany market freedom and jobless growth.

The public mood in this new environment would be likely to remain schizophrenic. More wealth might bring a more generous mood among the winners, though not enough to prevent a further erosion of welfare protection which would be seen as crucial to continued economic success. There might be some, though minimal, realignment of the pattern of public attitudes shown hypothetically in figure 6.1, with maybe some switch from the top to the bottom row.

The durability of this otherwise optimistic scenario would depend on the reaction of the losers. Deepening divisions could bring rising instability and further attempts at protection by the winners. This would therefore carry the same risk as in the declinist scenario of a more authoritarian and intolerant climate. This could be characterised by growing antagonism to outsiders and social dissidents, and increased intolerance to those not seen as conforming. Conventional families might find a higher acceptability than single parents or gay couples. Criminals and drug users and pushers might be dealt with increasingly harshly. Smokers or dangerous drivers might find themselves denied state medical care and private insurance. Unemployment and poverty might be increasingly viewed as self-induced, the product of laziness or lack of willpower rather than injustice. It would be a harsher world, one with high rewards for the successful but few for the failures. Its acceptability to the majority would depend on their willingness to accept more instability in return for higher living standards.

Success would also be threatened if initial recovery simply led to a return to the whetted appetites and consumerist goals of the 1980s. This would encourage renewed inflation and a distorted distribution of the gains of growth. Sustained recovery would depend on the holding of consumption and dividends in check in order to encourage a higher level of investment in both technology and human capital. It would therefore require a modification of 1980s' consumer capitalism, and the development of a different pattern of the symbols of performance and achievement that rested less heavily on material wealth and conspicuous consumption. Failure to secure this would mean that this model would prove no more sustainable than the welfarist models of the past, with the risk of a new political vacuum filled by increasingly extreme reactions.

'Post-consumerism'

The central problem with this second option is that economic dynamism carries the price of continued social inequality and therefore of the risk of persistent social instability. So is there an alternative which offers economic success *and* a sense of social solidarity? Is there a possibility of a third, distinctive phase of post-war history combining the principles of opportunity and individuality *and* a deeper sense of community and of common purpose?

Going backwards is not a serious option. Western societies have reached and passed the limits of welfare capitalism which found expression in the long post-war economic and social boom. The days of revisionist socialism which reached its peak in Sweden in the 1970s and 1980s are almost certainly over. Modified collectivism and limited state planning may yet come back into fashion, but this would not be enough on its own to avoid the instability inherent in contemporary economic and social change.

The possibility of a new way of running societies would depend on the course of social behaviour and political culture. The present crisis has been exacerbated by the excessive expectations created by the dynamics of affluent societies. Its solution depends on bringing aspirations and economic capacity back into line, and hence on the development of a new politics built around the idea of restraint.

As shown in chapter 9, a new moderation by the affluent majorities of the world's most developed nations would enable a very different approach to managing affluence. It would lessen the problem of 'over-consumption', enable a redirection of resources towards investment and redistribution, and allow for the option of greater work sharing and leisure. It would make it easier to tackle the three main problems of modern societies – high unemployment, deepening inequality and a deteriorating environment. Moderation by the world's richest nations is also critical to solving the intractable problems of stagnation and decline in the world's poorest.

A 'new politics of moderation' would depend heavily on a shift in public attitudes. It would be encouraged, for example, by a growing frustration with the stress associated with more harried and congested lives and a growing interest in relaxation and health. A growing awareness of the futility of 'competitive individualism' and of the growing social costs and the decreasing returns associated with ever rising consumption would also weaken the constant jostling for position. Disillusion with the use of possessions as a source of wider meaning would also weaken the power of consumer and material values. This could be reinforced by a new sense that there are other more important and sustainable routes to happiness than material wealth, that conspicuous consumption may be less a sign of success than of a moral vacuum.

The emergence of what might be called a 'post-consumerist culture' would not mean the end of image or symbolism. These would simply take different forms, ones based less on material possessions. The consumer in this somewhat utopian scenario would gradually become more mature and more discerning. New and ultimately more tangible and less ephemeral images based on personal qualities such as knowledge, health, generosity and political awareness would gain currency. These would be less crude and grasping than those of the 1980s. They would be reinforced by new values which downgraded the importance of the pursuit of material self-interest and relative performance and which gave greater emphasis to the virtues and benefits of public co-operation, group loyalty and consensus building.

Changing attitudes along these lines could bring a growing concern with individual and national health and a new sense of balance between public and private priorities. This could produce a very different era with more moderate demands and expectations, with weaker inflationary pressure and a different approach to economic and political management. It would open up the possibility of another shift in the pattern of public motivation represented in figure 6.1. The combination of greater generosity and a different interpretation of self-interest with less self-preoccupation and a greater awareness of mutual dependency would lead to a downward and leftward shift between the cells.

This scenario would be more likely with a changing political climate in which electorates are made more aware of the limitations of ever-rising material gains, the growing constraints and costs associated with consumption-led growth, and the social and economic trade-offs involved. Given the constraints at work, western populations may no longer be able to enjoy permanently rising consumption at the growth rates of the past. If such rises are confined to only the affluent majority both within and between nations, they may also threaten social and economic stability.

Although societies have been prepared to tolerate higher levels of crime, social disorder, poverty and congestion than in the past, this tolerance has a limit. If the public became more aware of the costs of growing instability they might be more prepared to accept tougher policies even at the price of lower material living standards. 'Post-consumerism' might then be inspired not by any moral revival but by a more developed sense of self-interest, or even of social survival.

A politics aimed at creating greater restraint would require a very different role for political parties. The western electoral system has been built around a process of competitive bidding for votes on the basis of a largely material agenda. The winners have been those seen as bringing economic success and higher material living standards. A multiple system with a variety of parties is an essential ingredient of healthy democracy. The problem is that with the exception of a few small, minority parties such as the Greens, none have been willing and able to depart from the promise of delivering a faster growth of material well-being. Advocating a more rational approach to the use of material resources would carry high political risks. Promising less is unlikely to have proved a successful electoral strategy. It is this which has contributed to the rise of reactive and the decline of proactive politics, to the domination of managerialism and the lack of alternative ideologies and political ideas. Ideology has become dangerous territory if not rooted in the status quo.

This approach to politics may have been appropriate for much of the post-war period when the management of scarcity demanded rapid growth and rising consumption. While it is much less relevant today, the competitive character of western political systems has thwarted the necessary adjustment. This helps to account, too, for the malaise facing politics, governments and the institutions of government. Electorates have grown weary of parties offering promises that can no longer be delivered, yet they have not been prepared to accept the painful side-effects of the alternatives. This process of over-promising and under-achieving needs to be reversed if the political system is to progress out of its present debility.

Achieving this would depend on creating a new sense of social responsibility and mutual respect that was undermined by the political culture of the 1980s. A more successful politics would depend on a greater understanding of the social consequences – both costs and benefits – of different kinds of individual behaviour. This could be achieved without a return to state-organised collectivism. A highly developed individualism is not necessarily at odds with a strong sense of social responsibility and citizenship, but the competitive individualism that has evolved with growing affluence is. For societies to use the benefits of affluence more wisely, competitive individualism needs to be replaced by a more developed awareness of the mutual advantages of a more co-operative approach to management. This would mean a new emphasis on community as well as individual success and achievement.

Creating such a culture would depend on a greater understanding of the importance of mutual interdependence, and an acceptance of the limitations of the pursuit of pure self-interest. It would mean less short-termism and a greater emphasis on the importance of interaction, of mutual support and encouragement, of the negative and positive effects of individual and social behaviour. Creating a new emphasis on co-operation therefore depends on developing a more heightened awareness of self-interest, and that it is not always best served by short-term personal gains.

In particular, it would require a greater perception of the relationship between excessive inequality and instability; between long-term unemployment and social exclusion, drug abuse and crime; between over-consumption and environmental damage;

between social segregation and stability; between economic performance and social values. Acceptance of social obligations is not just a matter of duty, it is also a matter of social harmony, security and ultimately even survival. A co-operative individualism is therefore quite consistent with that of self-interest.

The emergence of a more discerning consumer would make this adjustment easier, and would offer the possibility of a benign inter-relation between public opinion and politics. A declining obsession with the symbolic importance of consumerism would weaken the competitive character of societies and hence of the political process. It would encourage greater plurality and the development of new and more participatory political forms, more in tune with the real rather than the politically distorted choices facing modern societies.

The importance of mutual dependency is also no longer confined to national boundaries. Individual decisions rebound not just on the local community and the nation but internationally too. A new politics would therefore require an increasing emphasis on international co-operation. After the war, economic success in Europe was crucially linked to international arrangements. The Marshall Plan aid programme directed against 'human poverty, desperation and chaos' was inspired not primarily by the altruism implied by the rhetoric. It was a self-interested act of international diplomacy, geared, above all, to preventing the rise of communism on the continent. It was simultaneously a generous and selfish act which also contributed to post-war recovery. In the more turbulent and interdependent economic climate of today, global co-operation is even more vital to the achievement of economic and social stability.

Which path?

There are therefore three broad routes that societies could follow. They could end up facing persistent economic and social decline. They could find that the market revolution initiated in Britain finally begins to bring economic success but at the price of an increasingly competitive environment that takes its toll of the softer social values. Or they could follow a different approach to government around the ideas of more moderate expectations, mutual dependency and shared purpose.

Each of these scenarios is possible. The signs are mixed as to which is the most likely outcome. The global economic situation remains deeply uncertain. Faltering growth would bring continued instability. Even rising world demand would have a differential impact, with some countries likely to prove much better placed to take advantage than others. Even in the era of market dominance, some countries have retained much more active governments than others, and the relative merits of market and interventionist approaches for economic performance remain a matter of uncertainty.

The path of public opinion is also unclear. Even sustained economic recovery is likely to leave a legacy of uncertainty and ambiguity. The end of the recession is likely to bring some optimism and a growing generosity, but with a residue of anxiety and insecurity. The weaker the recovery, the greater the risk of more authoritarian and unsympathetic attitudes. Societies are also likely to be heading towards a less passive climate, more intolerant of corrupt and self-serving politics and business, and more hostile to crime and those unwilling to conform.

Politics, too, is in a state of drift. Both sides of the political divide are struggling for an answer to modern problems. For the Left, there is a new awareness of the limits of government. State-centred politics is no longer tenable in the new individualistic and interdependent world. The painful message for the Left in the nineties is that modern societies have reached, and passed, the limits of public spending and taxation. As recent elections have confirmed, it has, as yet, found no alternative for creating fairer societies.

In the British general election of 1992, Labour attempted to win support for a fairer society through an appeal to altruism, effectively to the consciences of the better off. It offered a modest degree of redistribution through a tax increase restricted to the top fifth of earners. It was not particularly radical and would have done little to reverse the rise of inequality of the previous decade. Yet it was rejected not merely by the better off but also by those on middle and lower incomes who saw it as a cap on their aspirations.

In France, the Socialists were routed in the 1993 elections for different reasons. They followed tight economic policies of fiscal and monetary discipline that brought low inflation, a strong franc, a relatively modest budget deficit and a healthy balance of payments.

Yet these achievements were unable to prevent soaring unemployment to over 3 million, despite a threefold increase in spending on training. They also failed to bring electoral popularity.

The problem for the Right is that individualism has, at least to date, failed to deliver the more enterprising, opportunistic and dynamic economies that were promised. This may yet come, but it has left the Right in a similar state of ideological uncertainty. In Britain, John Major's response to the Thatcherite decade has been an attempt to build a gentler and more caring image, 'a nation at ease with itself'. His policies, however, have continued the process of deregulation begun by Mrs Thatcher. They have done little to reverse the problem of deepening inequality and high unemployment. They have been marked by continued opposition to the social policies of the European Community, by attempts to reduce public spending, and by harsher welfare policies. The market is still seen as the principal mechanism for tackling the problems of slow growth and high unemployment.

Bill Clinton attempted to break the political deadlock with calls for a new spirit of 'sacrifice', and for new responsibilities based on 'a new covenant' between state and people. He challenged the 'supply-side, trickle-down' Reaganomics that the poor could be helped by the enrichment of the few, and has attempted to restore the idea that the rich should bear a higher burden of the costs of revival. Like Labour's programme, none of this has been especially ambitious.

Despite this, Clinton has had great difficulty in implementing even his modest plans. With only 43 per cent of the vote, he has lacked a real mandate. A large majority voted against the 'mandate for change' that Clinton sought and claimed. Without the sacrifices he sought, he has found it impossible to reconcile the variety of conflicting pledges and demands – to halve the deficit, increase public investment, help the poor and reduce middle class taxes. Clinton has had to live within the new electoral requirements of the politics of affluence and the constraint of the budget deficit which has precluded anything other than a modest redistribution. His policies will do little more than dent the rising inequality and growing poverty of the last decade.

To date, the only place where a new political order is emerging is Italy. After decades of corruption and a new crisis of legitimacy, the old establishment has been washed away on a tide of public hostility and national rebellion. Italy is in the throes of a political revolution that is as yet incomplete. In Japan a similar discontent with corruption and the old establishment ended the forty-year rule of the Liberal Democrats. Japan is entering a period of transition but with a much more uncertain outcome. As yet, disillusion with the old institutions has not led to such convulsive change elsewhere. Nevertheless, politics and societies are in a process of transition. The old models are no longer sustainable.

The most pessimistic outcome of these changes is a continuation of the decline that set in at the end of the 1980s from the seeds of change planted in earlier years. A more optimistic possibility is that the market solutions tried in the eighties may yet emerge in triumph from the recession.

The most optimistic, even utopian, of the scenarios presented above is also the least likely. A post-consumerist world offers the best prospect of building more stable societies. Post-consumerism may never happen. On the other hand, it may come eventually, but still be a long way off. It may be that the affluent majorities around the world will eventually accept some moderation in their aspirations, but will demand at least another generation of improved material living standards first. If so, societies will have to continue to live with the contradictions of affluence and the lost potential of prosperity for many decades to come.

Notes

Chapter 1

1. From the film *Up The Junction*, 1967.
2. C.A.R. Crosland, *The Future of Socialism*, Cape, London, 1956.

Chapter 2

3. F. Hirsch, *The Social Limits to Growth*, Routledge & Kegan Paul, London, 1977, p 9.
4. J.K. Galbraith, *The Culture of Contentment*, Sinclair-Stevenson, London, 1992, p 15.
5. A. Maddison, *The World Economy in the Twentieth century*, OECD, Paris, 1989, table 1.3.
6. F. Hirsch, *The Social Limits to Growth*, Routledge & Kegan Paul, London, 1977.
7. W.G. Runciman, *Relative Deprivation and Social Justice*, Routledge & Kegan Paul, London, 1966.
8. Thornstein Veblen, *The Theory of the Leisure Class*, Allen and Unwin, London, 1949.
9. D. Reisman, *Thornstein Veblen*, Scribner's, New York, 1953.
10. Abraham Maslow, *Motivation and Personality*, Harper & Row, New York, 1954.
11. J.K. Galbraith, *The Culture of Contentment*, Sinclair-Stevenson, London, 1992.
12. J. Mack and S. Lansley, *Poor Britain*, Allen and Unwin, London, 1985.
13. J.K. Galbraith, *The Culture of Contentment*, Sinclair-Stevenson, London, 1992.

Chapter 3

14. William Whitelaw (1978), quoted in A. Travis and S. Milne, 'Jobs and youth crime linked by Whitelaw', *The Guardian*, 25 February, 1993.
15. BBC, *Panorama*, on the Meadow Well riots, 4 November, 1991.
16. P. Burton, R. Forrest and M. Stewart, *Accommodation and Social Cohesion in the Urban Environment*, European Foundation for the Impact of Living and Working Conditions, Dublin, 1989.
17. C.A.R. Crosland, *The Future of Socialism*, Cape, London, 1956.
18. Quoted in V. George and I. Howards, *Poverty Amidst Affluence*, Edward Elgar, Aldershot, 1991.

Notes

19. M. O'Higgins and S. Jenkins, *Poverty in Europe*, Paper to European Commission Conference on Poverty, Noordwijke, Netherlands, 1989; Commission of the European Community, *Social Europe: Towards a Europe of Solidarity in Housing*, 1992 (a).
20. Department of Social Security, *Households Below Average Incomes, 1979-1990/91*, HMSO, London, 1993.
21. V. George and I. Howards, *Poverty Amidst Affluence*, Edward Elgar, Aldershot, 1991.
22. G. Room et al, *Observatory on National Policies to Combat Social Exclusion, Second Annual report*, Commission of European Community, Brussels, 1992, p 101.
23. D.W. Urwin and W.E. Paterson (eds), *Politics in Western Europe*, Longman, London, 1990, ch 12.
24. P. Ormerod and J. Rigg, *Economic and Social Cohesion in Europe*, The Henley Centre, London, 1991.
25. R.B. Reich, *The Work of Nations*, Alfred A. Knopf, New York, 1991, p 203.
26. M. Jahoda, 'Unemployment: Facts, Experiences and Social Consequences' in C. Freeman and L. Soete (eds), *Technical Change and Full Employment*, Basil Blackwell, Oxford, 1987, p 20.
27. G. Room et al, *Observatory on National Policies to Combat Social Exclusion, Second Annual Report*, Commission of European Community, Brussels, 1992, p 25.
28. N. Buck, 'Labour Market Inactivity and Polarisation', in D.J. Smith (ed), *Understanding the Underclass*, Policy Studies Institute, London, 1992.
29. R. Dahrendorf, *The Underclass and the Future of Britain*, Paper delivered at Windsor Castle, 27 April, 1987.
30. C. Murray, *Losing Ground: American Social Policy 1950-1980*, Basic Books, New York, 1984.
31. Quoted in T.R. Marmore and W. Plowden, 'Spreading the Sickness', *Times Higher Educational Supplement*, 25 October, 1991.
32. R.B. Reich, *The Work of Nations*, Alfred A. Knopf, New York, 1991, p 206.
33. Commission of the European Community, *Employment in Europe*, Brussels, 1991(a).
34. W.J. Wilson, *The Truly Disadvantaged*, The University of Chicago Press, Chicago, 1987.
35. M. Bane and D. Ellwood, 'Slipping Into and Out of Poverty: The Dynamics of Spells', *The Journal of Human Resources*, vol 21, no 1, 1986.
36. M. Prowse, 'The Not So Great Society', *Financial Times*, 10 April, 1991.
37. United Nations, *Human Development Report*, 1993 (a).
38. P. Burton, R. Forrest and M. Stewart, *Accommodation and Social Cohesion in the Urban Environment*, European Foundation for the Impact of Living and Working Conditions, Dublin, 1989, p 93.
39. Commission of the European Community, *Employment in Europe*, Brussels, 1991(a), p 8.
40. M. Di Palma et al, *Urban Environment, Social Cohesion, Accommodation: The Implications for Young People in Italy*, The European Foundation for the Improvement of Living and Working Conditions, Dublin, 1987.
41. G. Room et al, *Observatory on National Policies to Combat Social Exclusion,*

Second Annual Report, Commission of European Community, Brussels, 1992, p 87.

42. P. Burton, R. Forrest and M. Stewart, *Accommodation and Social Cohesion in the Urban Environment*, European Foundation for the Impact of Living and Working Conditions, Dublin, 1989, p 25.
43. Commission of the European Community, *Social Europe: Towards a Europe of Solidarity in Housing*, Brussels, 1992(a), p 16.
44. *Ibid*. p 8.
45. W.J. Wilson, *The Truly Disadvantaged*, The University of Chicago Press, Chicago, 1987, p 3.
46. *Ibid*. p 144.
47. S. Field, *Trends in Crime and Their Interpretation*, Home Office Research Study 119, HMSO, London, 1990.
48. S. Box, *Recession, Crime and Punishment*, Macmillan, Basingstoke, 1987, p 96.
49. J. Lea and J. Young, *What Is To Be Done About Law and Order?*, Penguin, Harmondsworth, 1984, p 88.
50. Association of Chief Officers of Probation, *Social Circumstances of Young Offenders Under Supervision*, 1993.
51. T. Ronayne, *The Social and Economic Position of Young People in Ireland*, European Foundation for the Improvement of Living and Working Conditions, Dublin, 1987, p 31.
52. Commission of the European Community, *Urban Social Development: Social Europe Supplement*, 1/92, Brussels, 1992(b), p 19.
53. P. Burton, R. Forrest and M. Stewart, *Accommodation and Social Cohesion in the Urban Environment*, European Foundation for the Impact of Living and Working Conditions, Dublin, 1989, p 9.

Chapter 4

54. M. Heseltine, *Where There's a Will*, Hutchinson, London, 1987.
55. N. Lamont, House of Commons, February, 1992.
56. Jacques Delors, Speech to the European Parliament, June, 1993.
57. OECD, *Employment Outlook*, July, 1991, p 40.
58. E. Balls, 'No Jobs for the Boys', *New Statesman and Society*, 28 August, 1992.
59. A. Maddison, *Phases of Economic Development*, Oxford University Press, 1982, p 133.
60. V. Keegan, 'Servicing the Wealth Machine', *New Statesman and Society*, 25 September, 1992.
61. OECD, *Economic Outlook*, December, 1992(b), p 12.
62. *Ibid*. p 7
63. R.D. Hershey, 'High Joblessness Gaining Acceptance', *New York Times*, 14 October, 1986.
64. H.L. Schiller, *Culture Inc: The Corporate Takeover of Public Expression*, Oxford University Press, 1989, p 8.
65. See for example C. Breakwell et al, 'Attitudes Towards the Unemployed', *British Journal of Social Psychology*, 23, 1984.
66. B. Rowthorn and A. Glyn, 'The Diversity of Unemployment Experience Since 1973', *Structural Change and Economic Dynamics*, vol 1, no 1, 1990, p 80.

67. J. Whitley and R.A. Wilson, 'Quantifying the Employment Effects of Micro-electronics', *Futures*, December, 1982.
68. I. Christie, J. Northcott and A. Walling, *Employment Effects Of New Technology in Manufacturing*, Policy Studies Institute, 1990.
69. C. Freeman and L. Soete, *Technical Change and Full Employment*, Blackwell, Oxford, 1987.
70. *Ibid*.
71. P. Ormerod and J. Rigg, *Economic and Social Cohesion in Europe*, The Henley Centre, London, 1991, p 13.
72. C. Freeman and L. Soete, *Technical Change and Full Employment*, Blackwell, Oxford, 1987, p 115.
73. I. Christie, J. Northcott and A. Walling, *Employment Effects of New Technology in Manufacturing*, Policy Studies Institute, 1990, p 111.
74. M. White, *Long Term Unemployment and the Labour Market*, Policy Studies Institute, 1984.
75. D. Bell, *The Coming of Post-Industrial Society*, Basic Books, New York, 1973.

Chapter 5

76. 'Material Girl', Madonna, 1984.
77. Pope John Paul II, Solicitudo Rei Socialis, Holy See, 1988.
78. A. Durning, *How Much Is Enough?*, Norton & Co, New York, 1992, p 131.
79. A. Miller, *The Price*, Act 1, 1985.
80. R. Leiby, 'The Junk Mail Plague', *Washington Post*, 22 April, 1991.
81. E. Linke, 'New-Home Shopping Technologies', *OECD Observer*, 178, October/November, 1992, p 17.
82. C. Gardiner and J. Sheppard, *Consuming Passion*, Unwin Hyman, London, 1989, p 63.
83. J. Schor, *The Overworked American*, Basic Books, New York, 1991, p 107.
84. *Ibid*. p 108.
85. F. Mort, 'The Politics of Consumption', in S. Hall and M. Jacques (eds), *New Times*, Lawrence & Wishart, London, 1989, p 160.
86. J. Woudhuysen, *Forecasting the Future of Design*, Design Council, 1993.
87. V. Packard, *The Hidden Persuaders*, Longmans, London, 1957; J.K. Galbraith, *The Affluent Society*, Houghton Mifflin, Boston, 1958 and *The New Industrial State*, Hamish Hamilton, London, 1967; H. Marcuse, *One Dimensional Man*, Routledge & Kegan Paul, London, 1964; P. Baran and P. Sweezy, *Monopoly Capital*, Pelican, London, 1968.
88. Quoted in S. Ewan, *All Consuming Images*, Basic Books, New York, 1988, p 243.
89. H.L. Schiller, *Culture Inc: The Corporate Takeover of Public Expression*, Oxford University Press, 1989.
90. *Ibid*. (quoted in).
91. D. Baldwin, 'The Hard Sell', *Common Cause Magazine*, May/June, 1991.
92. Quoted in A. Durning, *How Much Is Enough?*, Norton & Co, New York, 1992, p 120.
93. W. Leith, 'These Foolish Things', *The Independent on Sunday Magazine*, 3 November, 1991.
94. J. Baudrillard, 'Consumer Culture' in M. Poster (ed), *Jean Baudrillard: Selected Writings*, Polity Press, Cambridge, 1988.

95. S. Bate, 'Wrap Artistes Get Their Act Together', *Marketing Week*, 25 October, 1991.
96. A. Tomlinson, 'Introduction', in A. Tomlinson (ed), *Consumption, Identity and Styles*, Routledge, London, 1990, p 13.
97. F. Mort, 'The Politics of Consumption', in S. Hall and M. Jacques (eds), *New Times*, Lawrence & Wishart, London, 1989.
98. S. Hall, 'The Meaning of New Times', in S. Hall and M. Jacques (eds), *New Times*, Lawrence & Wishart, London, 1989, p 131.
99. C. Lasch, *The True and Only Heaven*, Norton, New York, 1991, p 520.

Chapter 6

100. M. Lewis, *Liar's Poker*, Hodder and Stoughton, London, 1989, p 11.
101. *Fortune*, 27 January, 1992.
102. *Le Monde*, July, 1992, on the French lorry drivers' dispute.
103. *Fortune*, 27 January, 1992, p 47.
104. S.B. Wolinetz (ed), *Parties and Party Systems in Liberal Democracies*, Routledge, London, 1988, p 171.
105. *Ibid.* p 60.
106. R.J. Dalton, *Citizen Politics in Western Democracies*, Chatham House, New Jersey, 1988, p 231.
107. R.J. Whybrow, *Britain Speaks Out, 1937-87*, Macmillan, Basingstoke, 1989, p 101.
108. P. Golding and S. Middleton, *Images of Welfare*, Martin Robertson, Oxford, 1982, p 59.
109. Quoted in J. Rentoul, *Me and Mine*, Unwin Hyman, London, 1989.
110. Commission of the European Community, *Social Europe: Towards a Europe of Solidarity in Housing*, Brussels, 1992(a).
111. S.B. Wolinetz (ed), *Parties and Party Systems in Liberal Democracies*, Routledge, London, 1988, p 173.
112. *Ibid.* p 180.
113. E.J. Dionne, *Why Americans Hate Politics*, Simon & Schuster, New York, 1991, p 53.
114. A. Sampson, *The Midas Touch*, Hodder and Stoughton, London 1989, p 21.
115. *Ibid.* p 24.
116. Quoted in J. Chancellor, *Peril and Promise*, Harper Perennial, New York, 1990, p 115.
117. OECD, *Economic Outlook*, December 1992, table 35.
118. R. Jowell et al (eds), *British Social Attitudes, The 8th Report*, Dartmouth, Aldershot, 1991, p 25.
119. P. Taylor-Gooby, 'Social Welfare: The Unkindest Cuts', in R. Jowell et al (eds), *British Social Attitudes, The 7th Report*, Gower, Aldershot, 1990.
120. R. Harris and A. Seldon, *Welfare Without the State*, Institute of Economic Affairs, 1987.
121. P. Taylor-Gooby, 'Citizenship and Welfare', in R. Jowell et al (eds), *British Social Attitudes, The 1987 Report*, Gower, Aldershot, 1987, p 12.
122. P. Saunders and C. Harris, *Popular Attitudes to State Welfare Services*, The Social Affairs Unit, London, 1990, p 8.

Notes

123. P. Taylor-Gooby, 'Social Welfare: The Unkindest Cuts', in R. Jowell et al (eds), *British Social Attitudes, The 7th Report*, Gower, Aldershot, 1990, p 13.
124. R. J. Dalton, *Citizen Politics in Western Democracies*, Chatham House, New Jersey, 1988, p. 102.
125. P. Saunders and C. Harris, *Popular Attitudes to State Welfare Services*, The Social Affairs Unit, London, 1990, p 27.
126. R.J. Dalton, *Citizen Politics in Western Democracies*, Chatham House, New Jersey, 1988, p 102.
127. B.G. Peters, *European Politics Reconsidered*, Holmes Meier, New York, 1991, p 124.
128. B. Williamson, *The Temper of the Times*, Blackwell, Oxford, 1990, p 231.
129. R.J. Dalton, *Citizen Politics in Western Democracies*, Chatham House, New Jersey, 1988, p 162.
130. *Ibid*. p 230.
131. A. Durning, *How Much Is Enough?*, Norton & Co, New York, 1992, p 132.
132. *The Independent*, 14 May, 1992, p 1.
133. A. Durning, *How Much Is Enough?*, Norton & Co, New York, 1992, p 34.
134. P. Kellner, *The Independent*, 2 May, 1989.
135. Readers Digest, *Eurodata*, R.D. Associates, London, 1991.

Chapter 7

136. James Callaghan, Labour Party Conference, October, 1976.
137. Ronald Reagan, January, 1982.
138. Michael Dukakis, 1988.
139. H. Glennerster, 'Social Policy Since the Second World War', in J. Hills (ed), *The State of Welfare*, Oxford University Press, Oxford, 1990, p 12.
140. D. Bell, *The End of Ideology: On the Exhaustion of Political Ideas in the Fifties*, Free Press of Glencoe, 1960.
141. D. Bell, *The Cultural Contradictions of Capitalism*, Basic Books, New York, 1976.
142. W. Robson, *Welfare State and Welfare Society*, Allen and Unwin, London, 1976.
143. S. Holland (ed), *Out of Crisis*, Spokesman, Nottingham, 1982.
144. G. Vickery, 'Global Industries and National Policies', *OECD Observer*, 179, December, 1992.
145. United Nations, *World Investment Report, 1993: Transnational Corporations and Integrated Interactive Production*, 1993 (b).
146. D. Julius, *Global Companies and Public Policy*, Pinter, London, 1990, p 106.
147. R.J. Dalton, *Citizen Politics in Western Democracies*, Chatham House, New Jersey, 1988, p 188.
148. W. Schneider, 'The Suburban Century Begins', *The Atlantic Monthly*, July, 1992.
149. F. Fukuyama, *The End of History and the Last Man*, Penguin, Harmondsworth, 1992.

Chapter 8

150. A. Gore, *Earth in the Balance*, Earthscan, London, 1992, p 221.
151. E. Childers, *In a Time Beyond Warnings*, Catholic Institute for International Relations, London, 1993.

152. J. Gershuny, 'Are We Running Out of Time?', *Futures*, January/February, 1992.
153. J. Schor, *The Overworked American*, Basic Books, New York, 1991.
154. *Ibid*. p 11-13.
155. G. Becker, 'A Theory of the Allocation of Time', *The Economic Journal*, 493, September 1965; S. Linder, *The Harried Leisure Class*, Columbia University Press, 1970.
156. F. Hirsch, *The Social Limits to Growth*, Routledge & Kegan Paul, London, 1977.
157. R.E. Levine, 'The Pace of Life', *American Scientist*, September/October, 1990.
158. E. Cahn and J. Rowe, *Time Dollars*, Rodale Press, Emmaus, 1992, p 22.
159. D. Meadows et al, *The Limits to Growth*, Earth Island, London, 1972; D. Meadows, D.L. Meadows and J. Randers, *Beyond the Limits*, Earthscan, London, 1992.
160. Policy Studies Institute, *Children, Transport and the Quality of Life*, 1993.
161. R.B. Reich, *The Work of Nations*, Alfred A. Knopf, New York, 1991.
162. D. Pearce et al, *Blueprint for Survival*, Earthscan, London, 1989.
163. E. Mishan, *The Costs of Economic Growth*, Penguin, Harmondsworth, 1969.
164. C.A.R. Crosland, *Socialism Now*, Cape, London, 1974, p 79.
165. J. Pezzy, 'Greens and Growth – a Reply', *UK Centre for the Economic and Environment Development Bulletin*, no 22, 1989.

Chapter 9

166. Lands' End, Direct Retailing Advertisement, 1992.
167. C. Lasch, *The True and Only Heaven*, Norton, New York, 1991, p 532.
168. Noriko Hama, 'Too far from the bottom line', *The Japan Times*, 24 May, 1992.
169. Quoted in B. Durr, 'Little Luxuries You can no Longer Afford', *Financial Times*, 12 December, 1991.
170. *Ibid*.
171. R. Inglehart, *Culture Shift in Advanced Urban Societies*, Princeton University Press, 1990, p 68.
172. S. Harding et al, *Contrasting Values in Western Europe*, Macmillan, Basingstoke, 1986, p 104.
173. R.J. Dalton, *Citizen Politics in Western Democracies*, Chatham House, New Jersey, 1988, p 84.
174. S. Harding et al, *Contrasting Values in Western Europe*, Macmillan, Basingstoke, 1986, p 107.
175. D.G. Barker, 'Changing Social Values in Europe', Paper presented to an International Symposium on the Unexpected Europe, University of Maryland, 1991.
176. S. Barnett and S. Saxob-Harrold, 'Interim Report: Charitable Giving', in R. Jowell (ed), *British Social Attitudes: the 9th Report*, Dartmouth, Aldershot, 1992, p 203.
177. Quoted in A. Durning, *How Much Is Enough?*, Norton & Co, New York, 1992, p 105.
178. T. Scitovsky, 'Growth in the Affluent Society', *Lloyds Bank Review*, January, 1987.

179. J. Gershuny, 'Are We Running Out of Time?', *Futures*, January/February, 1992.

180. T. Scitovsky, 'Growth in the Affluent Society', *Lloyds Bank Review*, January, 1987.

181. M. Seifert, 'Employment Effects of Working Time Reduction in the Former Federal Republic of Germany', *International Labour Review*, vol 130, no 4, 1991, p 495.

Chapter 10

182. C. Handy, *The Age of Unreason*, Business Books, London, 1991, p 205.

183. Bill Clinton, November, 1992.

184. *Sunday Times* leader, 6 June, 1993.

185. P. Kennedy, *The Rise and Fall of the Great Powers*, Unwin Hyman, London, 1988.

186. P. Kennedy, *Preparing for the Twenty-First Century*, HarperCollins, London, 1993.

187. J. Benington and M. Taylor, 'Change and Challenges Facing the UK Welfare State in the Europe of the 1990s', *Policy and Politics*, vol 21, no 2, 1993.

Bibliography

Association of Chief Officers of Probation, *Social Circumstances of Young Offenders Under Supervision*, 1993.

D. Baldwin, 'The Hard Sell', *Common Cause Magazine*, May/June, 1991.

M. Ball, F. Gray & L. McDowell, *The Transformation of Britain*, Fontana, London, 1989.

E. Balls, 'No Jobs for the Boys', *New Statesman and Society*, 28 August, 1992.

M. Bane & D. Ellwood, 'Slipping Into and Out of Poverty: The Dynamics of Spells', *The Journal of Human Resources*, vol 21, no 1, 1986.

Bank for International Settlements, *Annual Report, 1993*.

P. Baran and P. Sweezy, *Monopoly Capital*, Pelican, London, 1968.

D.G. Barker, 'Changing Social Values in Europe', Paper presented to an International Symposium on the Unexpected Europe, University of Maryland, 1991.

S. Barnett and S. Saxob-Harrold, 'Interim Report: Charitable Giving', in R. Jowell (ed), *British Social Attitudes: the 9th Report*, Dartmouth, Aldershot, 1992.

S. Bate, 'Wrap Artistes Get Their Act Together', *Marketing Week*, 25 October, 1991.

J. Baudrillard, 'Consumer Culture' in M. Poster (ed), *Jean Baudrillard: Selected Writings*, Polity Press, Cambridge, 1988.

G. Becker, 'A Theory of the Allocation of Time', *The Economic Journal*, 493, September, 1965.

D. Bell, *The End of Ideology: On the Exhaustion of Political Ideas in the Fifties*, Free Press of Glencoe, 1960.

D. Bell, *The Coming of Post-Industrial Society*, Basic Books, New York, 1973.

Bibliography

D. Bell, *The Cultural Contradictions of Capitalism*, Basic Books, New York, 1976.

J. Benington and M. Taylor, 'Change and Challenges Facing the UK Welfare State in the Europe of the 1990s', *Policy and Politics*, vol 21, no 2, 1993.

S. Box, *Recession, Crime and Punishment*, Macmillan, Basingstoke, 1987.

C. Breakwell et al, 'Attitudes Towards the Unemployed', *British Journal of Social Psychology*, 23, 1984.

N. Buck, 'Labour Market Inactivity and Polarisation', in D.J. Smith (ed), *Understanding the Underclass*, Policy Studies Institute, London, 1992.

P. Burton, R. Forrest and M. Stewart, *Accommodation and Social Cohesion in the Urban Environment*, European Foundation for the Impact of Living and Working Conditions, Dublin, 1989.

E. Cahn and J. Rowe, *Time Dollars*, Rodale Press, Emmaus, 1992.

Central Statistical Office, *Social Trends, 21*, HMSO, London, 1990.

Central Statistical Office, *Social Trends, 22*, HMSO, London, 1992.

J. Chancellor, *Peril and Promise*, Harper Perennial, New York, 1990.

E. Childers, *In a Time Beyond Warnings*, Catholic Institute for International Relations, London, 1993.

I. Christie, J. Northcott and A. Walling, *Employment Effects of New Technology in Manufacturing*, Policy Studies Institute, London, 1990.

Commission of the European Community, *Employment in Europe*, Brussels, 1991(a).

Commission of the European Community, *Eurobarometer Trends, 1974-1990*, Brussels, 1991(b).

Commission of the European Community, *Final Report on the Second European Poverty Programme, 1985-1989*, COM (91) 29, Brussels, 1991(c).

Commission of the European Community, *Social Europe: Towards a Europe of Solidarity in Housing*, Brussels, 1992(a).

Commission of the European Community, *Urban Social Development: Social Europe Supplement*, 1/92, Brussels, 1992(b).

C.A.R. Crosland, *The Future of Socialism*, Cape, London, 1956.

C.A.R. Crosland, *Socialism Now*, Cape, London, 1974.

R. Dahrendorf, *The Underclass and the Future of Britain*, Paper delivered at Windsor Castle, 27 April, 1987.

R.J. Dalton, *Citizen Politics in Western Democracies*, Chatham House, New Jersey, 1988.

H. Daly & J. Cobb, *For the Common Good*, Green Print, London, 1989.

N. Deakin, 'In Search of Post-War Consensus', *LSE Quarterly*, 3, no 1, 1989.

Department of Social Security, *Households Below Average Incomes, 1979-1990/91*, HMSO, London, 1993.

E.J. Dionne, *Why Americans Hate Politics*, Simon & Schuster, New York, 1991.

M. Di Palma et al, *Urban Environment, Social Cohesion, Accommodation: The Implications for Young People in Italy*, The European Foundation for the Improvement of Living and Working Conditions, Dublin, 1987.

A. Durning, *How Much Is Enough?*, Norton & Co, New York, 1992.

B. Durr, 'Little Luxuries You can no Longer Afford', *Financial Times*, 12 December, 1991.

S. Ewan, *All Consuming Images*, Basic Books, New York, 1988.

S.Field, *Trends in Crime and Their Interpretation*, Home Office Research Study 119, HMSO, London, 1990.

H. Frayman, *Breadline Britain, 1990*, Domino Films/LWT, 1991.

C. Freeman and L. Soete, *Technical Change and Full Employment*, Blackwell, Oxford, 1987.

F. Fukuyama, *The End of History and the Last Man*, Penguin, Harmondsworth, 1992.

J.K. Galbraith, *The Affluent Society*, Houghton Mifflin, Boston, 1958.

J.K. Galbraith, *The New Industrial State*, Hamish Hamilton, London, 1967.

J.K. Galbraith, *The Culture of Contentment*, Sinclair-Stevenson, London, 1992.

C. Gardiner and J. Sheppard, *Consuming Passion*, Unwin Hyman, 1989.

V. George & I. Howards, *Poverty Amidst Affluence*, Edward Elgar, Aldershot, 1991.

J. Gershuny, 'Are We Running Out of Time?', *Futures*, January/February, 1992.

H. Glennerster, 'Social Policy Since the Second World War', in J.

Hills (ed), *The State of Welfare*, Oxford University Press, Oxford, 1990.

A. Glyn, 'The Costs of Stability: The Advanced Capitalist Countries in the 1980s', *New Left Review*, no 195, September/October, 1992.

P. Golding & S. Middleton, *Images of Welfare*, Martin Robertson, Oxford, 1982.

A. Gore, *Earth in the Balance*, Earthscan, London, 1992.

S. Hall, 'The Meaning of New Times', in S. Hall & M. Jacques (eds), *New Times*, Lawrence & Wishart, London, 1989.

C. Handy, *The Age of Unreason*, Business Books, London, 1991.

S. Harding et al, *Contrasting Values in Western Europe*, Macmillan, Basingstoke, 1986.

R. Harris & A. Seldon, *Welfare without the State*, Institute of Economic Affairs, 1987.

H. Heclo, A.J. Heidenheimer and C.T. Adams, *Comparative Public Policy*, Third Edition, St Martins Press, New York, 1990.

R.D. Hershey, 'High Joblessness Gaining Acceptance', *New York Times*, 14 October, 1986.

M. Heseltine, *Where There's a Will*, Hutchinson, London, 1987.

F. Hirsch, *The Social Limits to Growth*, Routledge & Kegan Paul, London, 1977.

S. Holland (ed), *Out of Crisis*, Spokesman, Nottingham, 1982.

R. Inglehart, *Culture Shift in Advanced Urban Societies*, Princeton University Press, Princeton, 1990.

M. Jahoda, 'Unemployment: Facts, Experience and Social Consequences' in C. Freeman & L. Soete, (eds), *Technical Change and Full Employment*, Basil Blackwell, Oxford, 1987.

R. Jowell et al (eds), *British Social Attitudes, The 8th Report*, Dartmouth, Aldershot, 1991.

D. Julius, *Global Companies and Public Policy*, Pinter, London, 1990.

V. Keegan, 'Servicing the Wealth Machine', *New Statesman and Society*, 25 September, 1992.

P. Kellner, *The Independent*, 2 May, 1989.

P. Kennedy, *The Rise and Fall of the Great Powers*, Unwin Hyman, London, 1988.

P. Kennedy, *Preparing for the Twenty-First Century*, HarperCollins, London, 1993.

C. Lasch, *The True and Only Heaven*, Norton, New York, 1991.

J. Lea & J. Young, *What Is To Be Done About Law and Order?*, Penguin, Harmondsworth, 1984.

R. Leiby, 'The Junk Mail Plague', *Washington Post*, 22 April, 1991.

W. Leith, 'These Foolish Things', *The Independent on Sunday Magazine*, 3 November, 1991.

R.E. Levine, 'The Pace of Life', *American Scientist*, September/October, 1990.

M. Lewis, *Liar's Poker*, Hodder and Stoughton, London, 1989.

S. Linder, *The Harried Leisure Class*, Columbia University Press, 1970.

E. Linke, 'New-Home Shopping Technologies', *OECD Observer*, 178, October/November, 1992.

J. Mack and S. Lansley, *Poor Britain*, Allen and Unwin, London, 1985.

A. Maddison, *Phases of Economic Development*, Oxford University Press, 1982.

A. Maddison, *The World Economy in the Twentieth Century*, OECD, Paris, 1989.

H. Marcuse, *One Dimensional Man*, Routledge & Kegan Paul, London, 1964.

T.R. Marmore & W. Plowden, 'Spreading the Sickness', *Times Higher Educational Supplement*, 25 October, 1991.

D. Marquand, *The Unprincipled Society*, Jonathan Cape, London, 1988.

A. Maslow, *Motivation and Personality*, Harper & Row, New York, 1954.

D. McGahey, 'Economic Conditions, Neighbourhood Organisation and Urban Crime', in A. Reiss and M. Tonry (eds), *Communities and Crime*, Chicago University Press, Chicago, 1986.

D. Meadows et al, *The Limits to Growth*, Earth Island, London, 1972.

D. Meadows, D.L. Meadows & J. Randers, *Beyond the Limits*, Earthscan, London, 1992.

A. Miller, *The Price*, Methuen, London, 1985.

E. Mishan, *The Costs of Economic Growth*, Penguin, Harmondsworth, 1969.

F. Mort, 'The Politics of Consumption' in S. Hall & M. Jacques (eds), *New Times*, Lawrence & Wishart, London, 1989.

C. Murray, *Losing Ground: American Social Policy 1950-1980*, Basic Books, New York, 1984.

OECD, *Employment Outlook*, July, 1990.

OECD, *Employment Outlook*, July, 1991.

OECD, *Employment Outlook*, July, 1992 (a).

OECD, *Economic Outlook*, December, 1992 (b).

M. O'Higgins and S. Jenkins, *Poverty in Europe*, Paper to European Commission Conference on Poverty, Noordwijke, Netherlands, 1989.

P. Ormerod & J. Rigg, *Economic and Social Cohesion in Europe*, The Henley Centre, London, 1991.

V. Packard, *The Hidden Persuaders*, Longmans, London, 1957.

D. Pearce et al, *Blueprint for Survival*, Earthscan, London, 1989.

B.G. Peters, *European Politics Reconsidered*, Holmes Meier, New York, 1991.

J. Pezzy, 'Greens and Growth – a Reply', *UK Centre for the Economic and Environment Development Bulletin*, no 22, 1989.

Policy Studies Institute, *Children, Transport and the Quality of Life*, 1993.

M. Prowse, 'The Not So Great Society', *Financial Times*, 10 April, 1991.

Readers Digest, *Eurodata*, R.D. Associates, London, 1991.

R.B. Reich, *The Work of Nations*, Alfred A. Knopf, New York, 1991.

J. Rentoul, *Me and Mine*, Unwin Hyman, London, 1989.

D. Riesman, *Thornstein Veblen*, Scribner's, New York, 1953.

W. Robson, *Welfare State and Welfare Society*, Allen and Unwin, London, 1976.

T. Ronayne, *The Social and Economic Position of Young People in Ireland*, European Foundation for the Improvement of Living and Working Conditions, Dublin, 1987.

G. Room et al, *Observatory on National Policies to Combat Social Exclusion, Second Annual report*, Commission of European Community, Brussels, 1992.

B. Rowthorn and A. Glyn, 'The Diversity of Unemployment Experience Since 1973', *Structural Change and Economic Dynamics*, vol 1, no 1, 1990.

W.G. Runciman, *Relative Deprivation and Social Justice*, Routledge & Kegan Paul, London, 1966.

A. Sampson, *The Midas Touch*, Hodder and Stoughton, London, 1989.

P. Saunders and C. Harris, *Popular Attitudes to State Welfare Services*, The Social Affairs Unit, London, 1990.

H.L. Schiller, *Culture Inc: The Corporate Takeover of Public Expression*, Oxford University Press, 1989.

W. Schneider, 'The Suburban Century Begins', *The Atlantic Monthly*, July, 1992.

J. Schor, *The Overworked American*, Basic Books, New York, 1991.

T. Scitovsky, 'Growth in the Affluent Society', *Lloyds Bank Review*, January 1987.

M. Seifert, 'Employment Effects of Working Time Reduction in the Former Federal Republic of Germany', *International Labour Review*, vol 130, no 4, 1991.

T.W. Smith, 'Inequality and Welfare' in R. Jowell (ed), *British Social Attitudes: Special International Report*, Gower, Aldershot, 1989.

P. Taylor-Gooby, 'Citizenship and Welfare', in R. Jowell et al (eds), *British Social Attitudes, The 1987 Report*, Gower, Aldershot, 1987.

P. Taylor-Gooby, 'Social Welfare: The Unkindest Cuts', in R. Jowell et al (eds), *British Social Attitudes, The 7th Report*, Gower, Aldershot, 1990.

N. Timms & S. Ashford, *What Europe Thinks: A Study of Western European Values*, Dartmouth, Aldershot, 1992.

A. Tomlinson, 'Introduction' in A. Tomlinson (ed), *Consumption, Identity and Styles*, Routledge, London, 1990.

United Nations, *Human Development Report*, 1993 (a).

United Nations, *World Investment Report, 1993: Transnational Corporations and Integrated Interactive Production*, 1993 (b).

D.W. Urwin and W.E. Paterson (ed), *Politics in Western Europe*, Longman, London, 1990.

Thornstein Veblen, *The Theory of the Leisure Class*, Allen and Unwin, London, 1949.

G. Vickery, 'Global Industries and National Policies', *OECD Observer*, 179, December, 1992.

M. White, *Long Term Unemployment and the Labour Market*, Policy Studies Institute, 1984.

J. Whitley and R.A. Wilson, 'Quantifying the Employment Effects of Micro-electronics', *Futures*, December, 1982.

Bibliography

R.J. Whybrow, *Britain Speaks Out, 1937-87*, Macmillan, Basingstoke, 1989.

B. Williamson, *The Temper of the Times*, Blackwell, Oxford, 1990.

W.J. Wilson, *The Truly Disadvantaged*, The University of Chicago Press, Chicago, 1987.

S.B. Wolinetz (ed), *Parties and Party Systems in Liberal Democracies*, Routledge, London, 1988.

J. Woudhuysen, *Forecasting the Future of Design*, Design Council, London, 1993.

K. Young, 'Shades of Green' in R. Jowell et al (eds), *British Social Attitudes: the 8th Report*, Dartmouth, Aldershot, 1991.

Index

Adenauer, Konrad 111, 142
advertising 86, 93-100, 173
affluence, 'affluence effect' 16-28,
  199; change 101, 147, 156-7, 196;
  competitive individualism 110;
  consumerism 85, 170, 212-3;
  contradictions 4-5, 11, 241; cost
  of 176-82, 191, 193; defensiveness
  227; expectations 50; growth 59;
  inflation 59, 79; ideology 92;
  instability 55; isolation 132; the
  Left 91; lifestyle fashions 94;
  management of 220, 235; mass
  13, 139; migration 52;
  opportunities 102; political
  apathy 67; post-materialism
  216-22; restraint 234; rise of 4-6,
  38, 203-4, 215; scarcity and, 9,
  11, 137; social polarisation 45,
  222; social welfare 108-9;
  taxation 124-5; unease 30; youth
  market 86-7
Africa, North 44, 51
agriculture 80, 184
aid 146
AIDS 30
American Economic Association
  31
American Express 99
Asia 20, 146, 155, 228, 231; South
  East Asia 3, 224-5

Audi 197
Australia 36, 126, 146, 154, 196
Austria 39, 51, 69-71, 81, 154
Avis 96

Bahamas 43
Barcelona 45
balance of payments 144, 152, 239
Balladur, Edouard 162
Bartle, Bogle and Hegerty 99-100
Baudrillard, Jean 99
BBC 29, 95, 130; Panorama 29
Beamish Stout 95
Beer, Samuel 103
begging 30, 35
Belgium 34-6, 51, 62, 69, 76, 113,
  140, 154, 156, 212
Bell, Daniel 83, 143-4, 148
Benetton 93
Beregovoy, Pierre 162
Beveridge, Sir William 54
Biba 86
Bildt, Karl 160
bio-diversity 186
black people 40-2, 46-7
Blue Arrow 117
BMW 75, 104, 197
Bolivia 42
Bombay 155
Boots 97
Bosnia 3

Boston 41, 116
Bow Group 66
Brandt, Willy 144
Bristol 187
Britain, 1950s 86; boom 65, 159; business failures 69; centre-right in power 62; church attendance 127, 131; Communist Party 92; community involvement 131; competitive individualism 110, 115; Conservative Party 33-4, 124, 145; consumerism 11, 16, 97, 212-3; confidence in institutions 129-30, 224; crime 47; debts 118, 196; decline 227; deregulation 37; drugs 43; education 40, 165, 224; electronics 74; end of consensus 111; Eurocommunists 87; FTSE index 116; growth 58, 63, 78; health 138-9, 165; home ownership 114; Hong Kong of Europe 223, 232; industrial bargaining 64, 222; inner cities 30; investment, 153-4, 156, 232; labour market 82, 232; Labour Party 17, 62, 111, 124-5, 144, 155, 159, 162; Left, the 145; leisure 180; manufacturing 78; materialism 216; migration 52; privatisation 113; recession 159, 222; services 77; social attitudes 24, 140, 174, 207; social legislation 142; social polarisation 45; state employment 71; taxation 126, 232; Thatcherism 112, 231; underclass 38; unemployment 56-7, 65-6, 68-9, 76, 78-9, 221-2; working hours 177
British Airways 117
British Rail 133
British Social Attitudes Survey 67, 119, 122-3

British Telecom 66, 75
Brixton 187
Brundtland Report 185
Bulger, James 164
bureaucracy 114, 143
Burger King 97
Bush, George 124, 160

C&A 92
California 125
Calkins, Ernest Elmo 94
Callaghan, James 141, 152
Camorra 43
Canada 36, 42, 65, 154, 196
capitalism 143, 146; 1980s 88; consumer capitalism 10-11, 85, 88, 93, 169, 234; deregulated 158; final triumph of 2; welfare capitalism 9, 10, 31, 85, 88, 108, 143, 169, 224
car crime 47, 50
car usage 13, 22, 85-6, 88, 50-1, 98, 155, 182, 193-4, 209, 212, 218-9
Caribbean 183
Carter, Jimmy 62, 125, 144
Catholicism 45
Channel 4 95
charity 17
Chicago 42, 116
Childers, Erskine 173
children 96-7; 187
China 3, 20, 146, 225
choice 91-2, 102, 137
Christianity 164, 204
churches 101, 127-31
Churchill, Caryl 116
Citizen's Charter 137
Clinton, Bill 124, 160, 194, 223, 229, 232, 240
Coca-Cola 93
cold war 3
collectivism 112-4, 118-23, 148, 162, 228, 234, 237

command economies 146, 152
communism 3, 20, 143, 146, 238
community 45, 47, 50, 52, 107-9,
127, 130, 132-3, 137, 139, 181,
188, 223, 229, 234, 237
competition 3-5, 28, 36-7, 65, 74-5,
77, 79-81, 146-7, 151, 155, 170-1,
177, 179, 182, 219, 226, 230, 233,
237-8, *see also* competitive
individualism
competitive individualism 5, 11, 19,
53, 107-40, 170, 179, 192, 199-
200, 214, 235, 237
Conran, Terence 86
consumerism, abstinence 195-222;
blurs culture and commercialism
96, 130; 'caring' 1990s 201;
children 96-7; conspicuous
consumption 20, 234; consumer
capitalism 10-1, 85, 88, 93;
consumer confidence 196-8, 218;
consumer goods table 14;
consumer satisfaction 175-82;
consumer society 59, 84-8; 91-2,
132-3, 179; consumer sovereignty
91-8; culture of constraint 80;
deconsumption 200; 'defensive'
189; democratisation of
consumption 85, 217;
dependence on 104; discerning
209-16, 218, 235, 238;
dismantling of society 133, 181;
disposable age 104-5;
empowerment 93; environment
205-9; experiental 214; future
173-94; Germany 79; hierarchy
of needs 20-2; hierarchy of
wants 23-7, 204, 210-1, 214, 222;
identity through 98-100, 103;
imitative consumerism 86, 93,
170; immediate gratification 84,
105; individualism 100;
investment 149, 192; isolation

132; Japan 79; keeping up with
the Joneses 16-7, 101, 215;
keeping away from the Joneses
102; language of consumption
99, 101; lifestyle 26; malls 132;
manipulation 91-8; mass
consumption 10, 50, 59, 86, 91,
105, 148; morally repugnant
201-2; over-consumption 15-6,
85, 235; planned obsolescence
94; post-consumerism 234-8,
241; post-material 202-5, 207-8,
216-22; post-war boom 10;
relativity of 16-18, 20, 23, 175,
186, 188, 194, 200; shallowness
104; social welfare 151;
superstores 132-3; symbolic
consumption 98; table of
necessities 25; trend to quality
not status 197-202, 216;
unsustainable 14, 20, 59-60,
105-6, 184, 192, 201; upward
cycle 192, 209; values 11, 103,
202-5, 219, 235; youth culture
86-8, 98
Colouche 118
contentment, culture of 13, 22, 27,
227, 232
Cooper, Cary 177-9
corruption 2, 115, 117, 170, 239-41
Craxi, Bettino 34, 117-8
crime 2, 14, 30, 39, 42-3, 45-52,
122, 187, 227, 233, 236-7, 239
Croft Port 95
Crosland, Anthony 1, 31, 143,
191-2
Cruise, Tom 95
Curry, Edwina 88

Dahrendorf, Ralph 38
De Gaulle, General 142
debt 106-7, 116, 118, 179, 187, 196
deforestation 184

de-industrialisation 80-1

Delors, Jacques 54, 69, 229

democracy, challenged by crisis of the 1990s 2; of consumption 85; eastern Europe 146; free market 171; at work 83

Denmark 34-6, 51, 62, 69, 71, 76, 115, 154, 156, 174-5, 204; Progress Party 114; Social Democrats 110, 114; Socialist People's Party 156

dependency culture 39, 45, 108, 163

deregulation 37, 118, 145-6, 158-60, 198, 224, 240

deskilling 75

devaluation 144, 161, 221

Dijon 155-6

disabled people 27, 38

discretionary spending 85-6

distant selling 89

drugs 2, 30, 43, 45, 47-8, 233, 237

Dubet, F. 49

Dukakis, Michael 141, 163

Dunn, Nell 1

economic efficiency 62, 65, 75, 77, 170, 231-2

economic growth, affluence 59; in Asia 20; capital constraint 78; consumption-led 91, 217, 236-7; and crime rate 48; deregulation 158-9; economic integration 155; employment 67, 78-9; environment 183, 194, 217; future of, 188-94, 224, 226, 231, 233-4, 239-40; green growth 193; hidden costs 189; investment 80; liberal capitalism 143-4; limits to 160, 185, 217; managed 31, 147, 149; post-war 4, 13, 15-6, 148, 150; Scandinavia 111; slower 34, 62-3, 218; social justice 10-1, 28; table 58; uneven 47; wages 61

education 13, 39-43, 47-50, 57, 75, 97, 119, 121-3, 127-30, 137, 139-40, 148, 165, 224, 227-8, 232

empowerment 50

Engholm, Bjorn 162

entrepreneurialism 135, 231

environment 3, 4, 22, 122, 143, 160, 183, 185-6, 188-9, 201, 204-9, 215-7, 220, 222, 226, 235, 237

Erhard, Ludwig 142

Ethiopia 42

Europe, advertising 86; anti-tax parties 125; aspirations 134-7; budget deficit 60; capital stock 77-8; cars 183, 194; centre-left coalitions 142; competitive individualism 102, 110; confidence in institutions 128, 130, 224; construction of 107; consumerism 90-1, 93, 212; crime 46-8; decline 3, 5, 225, 230; Eastern 2, 3, 20, 51, 146, 228; Fortress Europe 228; government spending 115; health 139; inflation 59; investment 154; labour market 72; lean production 75, 227; Left parties 125, 162; mall shopping 132; mass production 86; post-war 9, 85; poverty 30, 33; recession 69; right-wing violence 51-2; social attitudes 140, 212; social democracy 146, 149; social welfare 34-8, 44; state intervention 141-2; student revolt 204-5; underclass 43-5, 50; unemployment 55, 64-5, 78; welfare capitalism 11; working hours 177, 181, 221

European Commission 43, 45-6, 48, 49

European Community 2, 33, 40,

41, 55, 63, 69, 114, 152, 159, 175, 222, 229, 240
European Monetary Union 198
exchange rate 59, 152
Exchange Rate Mechanism 2, 152, 154
excluded minority 37-47, 50
exclusion politics of 10, 64
Falklands War 113
family 45, 49, 101, 108, 127, 133-4, 175, 181, 188, 233
single parent 49, 123, 187, 228, 233
famine 1
fashion 17, 102, 104-6, 232
Financial Advisers Promotions 95
Financial Times 197
Finland 69, 71, 118, 154, 156
Food and Agriculture
  Organisation (FAO) 184
Ford 64, 95
Ford, Henry 86
Fordism 92
foreign exchange 154, 232
Fortune magazine 107, 109
France 2, 16, 32, 33, 34, 35, 36, 37, 43, 44, 45, 49, 51, 56, 58, 62, 68-9, 76, 89, 111, 114, 117-8, 127, 132, 138, 140, 142, 144, 146, 152-4, 156, 165, 174-5, 180, 183, 196, 205, 212-3, 227; Freedom Party 51; Socialists 62, 144, 159, 161-2, 239
Franklin, Benjamin 109
Fukuyama, Francis 171, 231
G7 countries 69
Galbraith, John Kenneth 13, 22, 27, 93, 99
General Electric 65
General Motors 65, 75
Germany 2, 3, 5, 16, 30, 34, 35, 36, 40, 44, 51, 52, 56, 58, 60-2, 68-9, 76, 79, 81, 117-8, 130, 137, 140, 145, 153-4, 156, 161, 196,

207, 221, 224, 226; Bundesbank 164; Eastern 64, 68, 126; Christian Democrats 113, 142, 145; SPD 22, 144-5, 160, 162; Western 33, 34, 126-7, 174, 180, 211-3
ghettos 42, 43, 45, 50
Gini 99
Glasgow 45, 155-6
global warming 183-4, 193-4
globalisation 3, 92, 135, 151-6
Glotz, Peter 22
GNP 15
Goffman, Erving 102
Gold Blend 99
Goldberger, Paul 116
Gore, Al 173
Great Depression 85, 142
Greece 35, 183, 227
Green movement 51, 156, 160, 193-4, 204-5, 208-9, 236
greenhouse effect 183
Guinness 117

Habitat 86
Hama, Noriko 195
Hamburg 45, 51
Handy, Charles 223
Harlem 42
Hayek, Friedrich von 163
health 14, 30, 35, 75, 89, 119, 121-3, 127, 134-5, 137-40, 148, 162, 165, 198, 201, 209, 220, 227-8, 233, 235
Henley Centre 43, 52, 88, 102, 121, 123, 194, 201, 207, 212
Heseltine, Michael 54
Hey, Kenneth 201
Hideo, Takayama 97
Hirsch, Fred 13, 17-9, 179
Holstein Lager 95
home ownership 13, 113-4, 196
homelessness 30, 35, 44, 192, 228

Hong Kong 223, 225
Hoover 155
housing 13, 24, 26-7, 35, 39, 44-5, 48-9, 114, 123, 140, 147-8, 212, 218-9
Hume, David 217

IBM 65, 75
ICI 64
Imbert, Sir Peter 48
inclusion 51; politics of 11
incomes, anxiety 27; distribution 23, 33; falling 44; hierarchy 38; inequalities 10, 119; leapfrogging 15; maintenance 34-5; mobility 28; policy 60, 221; in post-war boom 33; relativity 18; rising 13, 31, 74, 80, 88, 175, 181, 221; satisfaction 211-2; segregation 42; taxation 125, 149
Independent, The 133
India 225
individualism 5, 11, 49, 88, 91, 100, 103, 109, 148, 156, 163, 169, 215, 228, 230, 237-8; individualisation of society 127-33
Indonesia 181
industry, banking 66, 75, 116, 164; construction 65; electronics 74, 77-8; financial services 64-5; manufacturing 64-5, 69, 74-5, 77, 80, 81, 93; retailing 65; services 64, 69, 74-5, 77, 80, 231; telecommunications 75
inequality 9, 10, 27, 31, 33-4, 36-7, 40, 46, 48, 83, 108, 129, 139, 145, 148, 158, 163, 169, 186, 192-3, 200, 219, 232, 237, 239-40; table 32
inflation 9, 16, 18, 54-5, 57, 59-63, 70-3, 79, 144, 146, 150-1, 158,

161, 163, 188, 200, 203, 215, 218-9, 230-1, 234-5, 239
information technology 65, 74-5
Inglehart, Ronald 202-4, 216
inner cities 41, 42, 45, 46, 47
Institute of Economic Affairs 119
interest rates 62, 69, 127, 154
International Monetary Fund (IMF) 144
investment 10, 15, 57, 60, 62, 66, 74-5, 77-80, 116, 149, 153-6, 192-3, 219, 226-7, 232, 234-5. 240
Ireland 34, 35, 36, 49, 76, 154, 227
isolation 41-6, 107, 132
Italy 2, 32-6, 40, 43, 45, 51, 56, 58, 68-9, 76, 87-8, 117-8, 125-6, 132, 138, 140, 146, 154, 156, 174-5, 180-1, 183, 196, 212-3, 227, 240-1; Christian Democrats 117; Socialist Party 87, 91, 117

J. Walter Thompson 197
Japan 5, 16, 36, 42, 56, 58, 60-1, 64, 69-71, 75, 77-9, 81, 91, 115, 118, 130, 153-5, 177, 181, 196, 201, 224-5, 227, 241; Liberal Democrats 241
Jefferson, Samuel 109
job creation 63-6, 69, 72, 75, 77, 218, 22
Johnson, Lyndon 59
Joseph, Sir Keith 66, 163
Kennedy, John F. 31
Kennedy, Paul 225-6
Keynesian economics 10, 31, 57, 61-2, 70-1, 73, 143, 145-6, 150-1, 158-9
Keyserling, Leon 31
King, Peter 197
Kohl, Helmut 113, 126, 145, 226
Korea 43

labour market 37-8, 40, 69-71,
80-3, 135, 231-2
Lamont, Norman 54
Lasch, Christopher 105, 195
Latin America 146, 231
lawlessness 46
Lawson, Nigel 63, 65
Le Monde 107
Le Pen, Jean-Marie 51
leap-frogging culture 13-28, 102,
171, 179
Left, the 51, 87, 91, 93, 110, 117,
125, 144-5, 147, 149, 150, 152,
156-7, 162-5, 239
leisure 90, 179-80, 188, 214, 220,
222, 235
Levi jeans 95, 99
Lewis, Michael 107
Limmits 99
Linder, S. 179
Liverpool 45, 187
Louis Vuitton 200
London 107, 152; GLC 113
London Weekend Television 24
Los Angeles 46, 116
Lubbers, Ruud 113, 145
Luxembourg 35
Lyons 44-5
Lyotard, J. F. 103

Maastricht Treaty 161, 232
Macdonald, Ramsay 66
MacDowell, Andie 96
Macmillan, Harold 86, 142
McDonalds 92
McNeal, James 96
Madonna 84-5
mail order catalogues 88
Major, John 137, 240
Malthus, Thomas 226
management 4, 61, 64-5, 82;
economic 9, 11, 31, 54-5, 61, 66,
73, 146, 161, 165, 171, 216, 229,

231, 236; managerial politics
141-66; political 4, 9, 14, 54, 61,
164, 216, 224, 236; social 11, 14,
171
market forces 2, 44, 54, 61, 81, 89,
91, 94-5, 99-100, 117, 121, 137,
141, 146-8, 151, 163-4, 169, 171,
181, 193, 229-33, 238-41
market liberalism 145, 157
market research 94, 197
Marcuse, Herbert 93
Mardle, James 100
Marshall Plan 57, 238
Marxism Today 92
Maserati 96
Maslow, Abraham 20
materialism 84-106, 199-200, 204-5,
216, 220, 235
Maxwell, Robert 117
Maxwell House coffee 99
media 20, 132
Mercedes 197
Mexico 155
Miami 116
migration 1, 20, 30, 51, 70, 114,
162, 226, 228; table 52
Milan 45, 227
Miller, Arthur 88
MIND 179
miners' strike 113
minimum living standard 24, 26,
33, 37
Mitterand, François 144, 146, 152,
161
monetarism 61-2, 73, 145-6
multinationals 154-5
Murray, Charles 39
Murray, Robin 152

Nakano, Koji 201
NALGO 222
Naples 43
National Front 44, 51

nationalisation 152, 158
Nazism 2; neo-Nazis 51
neo-conservatism 36
Nestlé 155
Netherlands 32-6, 52, 58, 62, 68-9, 76, 114, 126, 138-40, 145, 156, 174-5, 180, 207, 211-3; Christian Democrats 113
New Right 61, 66, 88, 110, 112, 150-1, 159
New York 41, 117, 152, 187
New Zealand 36, 146
New York Times 66, 96, 116
Nike 95
Nintendo 181, 186
North American Free Trade Agreement 155
North Sea 70, 185
North-South divide 184-5, 226
Norway 42, 69, 70-1, 81, 89, 115, 118, 154; Labour Party 110; Progress Party 114

OECD 13, 15, 48, 56, 58, 63, 65, 115
oil crisis (1970s) 6, 59, 62
OPEC 59-60, 62
Oslo 114
ozone layer 183-4, 206-7

Pacific Rim 75, 79
Paris 44-5, 227
Parker Pen 98
Pearce, John 97
pensioners 27, 34-5
Perrier 96
Persil 99
Philadelphia 41
pleasure, ideology of 87
pollution 183, 185-6, 189, 192-3
Pope, the 102
population 63, 170, 185, 226
Portugal 40, 45, 154, 227

post-consumerism 234-8
post-Fordism 92
post-industrial society 82-3
poverty 2, 4, 26, 28, 30-1, 33, 37-41, 39, 41-3, 48, 101, 108, 112, 114, 120, 137, 146, 157, 163, 185-7, 191, 193, 217, 233, 236, 240
pragmatism 2
prices 62
privatisation 38, 113, 135, 145, 157, 159-60, 162, 198
productivity 9, 14, 60, 64, 66, 77, 79-80, 86, 155, 159, 170, 176, 218, 220, 222-3, 226, 231
professionals 69, 82-3, 100
prostitution 43
protectionism 155, 230
public spending 30

Quant, Mary 86

Racamier, Henry 200
racism 51, 156, 205, 228
Ratner, Gerald 105
Ratners 105
Ray-Ban Aviators 95
Reagan, Ronald 33, 39, 110, 113, 117, 125, 141, 158, 163, 170
Reaganism 145-6, 240
recession 1, 2, 27, 51, 54-5, 64, 66-7, 69, 72, 85, 87, 105, 110, 117, 141, 144, 152, 154, 158-60, 170-1, 195, 197-8, 208, 215, 218-9, 221-2, 226, 229, 239, 241
recovery 57, 224, 230-1, 234, 238-9
Recruit Research 177
redistribution 11, 36-7, 108, 111-2, 119, 124, 139, 149-50, 162-3, 189, 191, 193, 219, 230, 239-40
Reebok 186
regulation 149, 151, 163
restructuring 75, 227, 231

Right, the 44, 51-3, 91, 114, 117, 142, 145, 147-8, 150, 156-7, 163-5, 240; *see also* New Right
Rio de Janeiro 186
rioting 44, 46-51, 187
Robertson, George 155
Robson, William 149
Rolex 197
Rome 45
Roosevelt, Franklin 110
Rowntrees 155
Royal Family 102-3, 130
Royal Institute of International Affairs 156
Runciman, Gary 19

Saab 98
Sainsbury 132
Sampson, Anthony 115-6
Scarman, Lord 48
Scandinavia 61, 110-1, 142, 149, 203
Schiller, H. L. 96
Schmidt, Helmut 144
Schor, Juliet 177
Scitovsky, Tibor 219
Second World War 57, 85, 142
shopping 17, 88-91
Singapore 225
Singleton, John 46
Sky Television 89
Smith, Adam 217
social corporation 71, 81
social democracy 31, 110, 114, 142, 144, 146-7, 149, 157, 159, 165, 169, 204, *see also by country*
social justice 10, 67, 150
social market 111, 142, 224
social polarisation 10, 30, 33-47, 50, 64, 230
social welfare 34-9, 44-5, 57, 108-12, 114-5, 120-1, 123-4, 127, 135, 145, 158, 161-3, 170, 187, 198, 228-30, 232-3, 240

socialism 2, 34, 118, 142, 152, 157, 159-62, 164, 224, 230, 234, *see also by country*
Somalia 3
South Africa 42
South Korea 225
Soviet bloc, former 225, 231
Spain 35, 45, 52, 68, 88, 132, 138, 146, 156, 162, 165, 180, 183, 213, 227; la Movida movement 87; Socialists 91, 162
speculation 59
sports sponsorship 95
St Louis 41
state, interventionism 57, 60-1, 70-1, 108, 110-2, 121, 123, 141-66, 169, 205, 230, 232, 239; loss of authority 101; weakening of 11
Stisser, Peter 197
Stockholm 186
Stone, Oliver 116
stress 177-9, 235
style, *see* fashion
Sweden 2, 5, 35, 36, 39, 42, 56, 58, 60, 69-72, 81, 115, 117-8, 125, 137, 140, 154, 156, 212, 224, 234; Democratic Party 114; Social Democrats 72, 110, 160, 161
Swissair 155
Switzerland 39, 42, 69, 71

Taiwan 181, 225
takeovers 219
taxation 34, 37, 60, 72, 81, 110, 114-5, 119-27, 141, 146, 148-9, 151, 157-8, 160, 162-3, 169, 194, 210, 215, 219, 223, 230, 232, 239-40; table 36
technological change 37, 40, 65, 73, 83, 85, 93, 95, 132, 154-5, 170-1, 220, 222-3, 226-7, 234
Tesco 66, 97, 132
Texas Homecare 96

Thatcher, Margaret 110, 112-3, 118, 133, 145, 158, 163, 170, 232
Thatcherism 33, 87, 137, 146, 159-60, 231, 240
The Sunday Times 39, 223
third world 30, 42-3, 191
Thorn-EMI 96
Tocqueville, Alexis de 109
Tokyo 97, 152
tourism 182-3
trade unions 61, 64, 70, 82, 87, 91, 101, 112-3, 127-9, 145, 159, 208, 221-2, 231
training 69, 75, 161, 240
transport, public 130, 140, 192-4, 219
travel 13, 20-1
'trickle-down' theory 37, 219, 240
Trinidad 42
Trump, Donald 108
Turkey 154
Tyneside 187

Uhrlau, Ernst 51
underclass 29-53, 72
underdevelopment 42
unemployment 4, 9, 11, 27, 31, 33-4, 37-40, 43-5, 47-9, 51-2, 54-83, 87, 107-8, 112, 114, 123, 127, 139, 144, 146, 151-2, 158, 161-2, 165-6, 170-1, 187, 198, 200, 215, 219-22, 224, 226, 228-9, 233, 235; figure, 75; long-term 37, 41, 44, 55, 73, 75, 82; non-employment 57; tables 35, 56, 68, 69; youth 50
United Nations 3, 42, 155, 173; Earth Summit 185-6
Uruguay 43
US, advertising 86, 89-90, 95; arts sponsorship 96; aspirations 135; capital stock 77-8; cars 155, 183, 194; centre-right governments 62; church attendance 127; cold war ends 3; competitive individualism 110, 115; conspicuous consumption 20; consumerism 11, 16, 59, 85, 90-1, 93; crime 43; debt 196, decline 5, 225, 230; Democratic Party 125, 144, 157, 159-60; distant selling 89; dollar 59; Dow Jones 116; free market 81; government popularity 21, 130; government spending 115, 122; growth 58; industrial bargaining 61; inner cities 30, 41-2; investment 153-4, 156; labour market 72, 82; lean production 75, 227; the Left 145; lifestyles 86, 201; mall shopping 132; materialism 216; New Deal 110, 141, 146; planned obsolescence 94; poverty 31; problems in 1960s 60; recession 65, 197, 218; Republican Party 145, 157, 160; riots 46; social polarisation 33, 37-47; social welfare 11, 72, 142, 146; state employment 71; student revolt 204; taxation 36, 126, 158; trade unions 113-4; underclass 37-47; unemployment 56, 64, 66-7, 69; Wall Street 116; working hours 177, 179, 221

Veblen, Thorstein 20
Vietnam War 59
Vlaams Blok Party 51

W. H. Smith 97
wages 9-10, 37, 41, 60-2, 64, 70, 72, 79, 81, 221-2, 229; wage restraint 70, 72, 81, 222
Wall Street Journal 90, 96-7
waste 84, 93, 125, 173
welfare state 4-5, 9-11, 15, 81, 111,

113-4, 119, 123, 142-3, 148-50, 157, 160, 169, 232, 234
Whitelaw, William 29
Whittle Communications 97
Wilson, Harold 152
Wilson, William J. 41, 47
Wolfe, Tom 116
Woman's Own 133
women 63, 70, 77, 81-2, 143, 160, 204-5
Women's Institute 130-1
workers, low-paid 27-8, 82; part-time 82; skilled 77-8, 81-3, 124, 135; unskilled 40-1, 67, 69, 74, 77, 81-2, 233; white-collar 69, 75, 81
working class 19, 123, 157
working hours 176-7, 179, 201, 219-21
World Bank 3

Yankelovich Clancy Shulman 197
Young, Jock 48
young people 34-5, 46-50, 86-7, 98, 109, 204, 220
yuppies 87, 107, 115-8